Architecture in a Climate of Change

Architecture in a Climate of Change

A guide to sustainable design

Peter F. Smith

ELSEVIER

AMSTERDAM • BOSTON • HEIDELBERG • LONDON • NEW YORK • OXFORD
PARIS • SAN DIEGO • SAN FRANCISCO • SINGAPORE • SYDNEY • TOKYO
Architectural Press is an imprint of Elsevier

Architectural
Press

Architectural Press
An imprint of Elsevier
Linacre House, Jordan Hill, Oxford OX2 8DP
30 Corporate Drive, Burlington, MA 01803

First published 2001
Second edition 2005

British Library Cataloguing in Publication Data
A catalogue record for this book is available from the British Library

ISBN 0 7506 65440

For information on all Architectural Press publication
visit our web site at http://books.elsevier.com

Typeset by Newgen Imaging Systems Pvt Ltd, Chennai, India
Printed and bound in Great Britain

Contents

CONTENTS

CONTENTS

Foreword

This updated book is essential reading especially as it considers the 'why' as well as the 'what' of sustainable architecture. There is now wide agreement that halting global warming and its climatic consequences is likely to be the greatest challenge that we shall face in this century. As populations increase and, at the same time, gravitate to cities, buildings old and new should be a prime target in the battle to reverse the demand for fossil-based energy.

Students and practitioners alike within the construction industry need to be aware of the importance of their role in creating architecture which not only raises the quality of life but also ensures that such quality is sustainable.

Lord Rogers of Riverside

Acknowledgements

I should like to express my thanks to the following practices for their help in providing illustrations and commenting on the text: Bennetts Associates, Bill Dunster Architects, Foster and Partners, Michael Hopkins and Partners, Jestico + Whiles, RMJM, Richard Rogers Partnership, Alan Short Architects, Fielden Clegg Bradley, Studio E Architects, David Hammond Architects, Grimshaw Architects Ove Arup and Partners.

I am also indebted to Dr Randall Thomas for his valuable advice on the text, Dr William Bordass for providing information from his 'Probe' studies, Dr Adrian Pitts of Sheffield University, Nick White of the Hockerton Housing Project, Ray Morgan of Woking Borough Council and finally Rick Wilberforce of Pilkington plc for keeping me up to date with developments in glazing.

Introduction

This book calls for changes in the way we build. For change to be widely accepted there have to be convincing reasons why long-established practices should be replaced. The first part of the book seeks to set out those reasons by arguing that there is convincing evidence that climate changes now under way are primarily due to human activity in releasing carbon dioxide (CO_2) into the atmosphere. Buildings are particularly implicated in this process, being presently responsible for about 47 per cent of carbon dioxide emissions across the 25 nations of the European Union. This being the case it is appropriate that the design and construction of buildings should be a prime factor in the drive to mitigate the effects of climate change.

One of the guiding principles in the production of buildings is that of integrated design, meaning that there is a constructive dialogue between architects and services engineers at the inception of a project. The book is designed to promote a creative partnership between the professions to produce buildings which achieve optimum conditions for their inhabitants whilst making minimum demands on fossil-based energy.

A difficulty encountered by many architects is that of persuading clients of the importance of buildings in the overall strategy to reduce carbon dioxide emissions. The first chapters of the book explain the mechanism of the greenhouse effect and then summarise the present situation *vis-à-vis* global warming and climate change. This is followed by an outline of the international efforts to curb the rise in greenhouse gases. The purpose is to equip designers with persuasive arguments as to why this approach to architecture is a vital element in the battle to avoid the worst excesses of climate change.

At the same time it is important to appreciate that there are absolute limits to the availability of fossil fuels, a problem that will gather momentum as developing countries like China and India maintain their dramatic rates of economic growth.

China may well serve to give a foretaste of the future. By 2005 it had reached 1.3 billion population; at this rate by 2030 it will reach 1.6 billion. The crucial factor is that the great bulk of this population is concentrated in the great valleys of the Yangtze and Yellow Rivers and their tributaries, an area about the size of the USA. China is on the verge of consuming more than it can produce. By 2025 it will be importing 175 million tonnes of grain per year and by 2030 200 million tonnes, which equals present total world exports (US National Intelligence Council). Its appetite for steel and building materials is voracious and already pushing up world prices.

A supply of energy sufficient to match the rate of economic growth is China's prime concern. Between January and April 2004 demand for energy rose 16 per cent. In 2003 it spent £13 billion on hydroelectric, coal fired and nuclear power plants – a rate of expansion that equals Britain's entire electrical output every two years. According to a spokesman for the Academy of Engineering of China, the country will need an additional supply equivalent to four more Three Gorges hydro-electric dams, 26 Yanzhou coal mines, six new oil fields, eight gas pipelines, 20 nuclear power stations and 400 thermal power generators.

Carbon has been slowly locked in the earth over millions of years creating massive fossil reserves. The problem is that these reserves of carbon are being released as carbon dioxide into the atmosphere at a rate unprecedented in the paleoclimatic record. The pre-industrial atmospheric concentration of CO_2 was around 270 parts per million by volume (ppmv). Today it is approximately 380 ppmv and is rising by about 20 ppmv per decade. The aim of the scientific community is that we should stabilise atmospheric CO_2 at under 500 ppmv by 2050 acknowledging that this total will nevertheless cause severe climate damage. However, if the present trend is maintained we could expect concentrations exceeding 800 ppmv by the second half of the century. Given the absence of a political consensus following the refusal of the US to ratify the Kyoto Protocol, the 800 plus figure looks ever more likely unless there are widespread and radical strategies that bypass political agreements, and this is where architects and engineers have a crucial part to play.

The Earth receives annually energy from the sun equivalent to 178 000 terawatt years which is around 15 000 times the present world-wide energy consumption. Of that, 30 per cent is reflected back into space, 50 per cent is absorbed and re-radiated, and 20 per cent powers the hydrological cycle. Only 0.6 per cent powers photosynthesis from which all life derives and which created our reserves of fossil fuel. The security of the planet rests on our ability and willingness to use this free energy without creating unsavoury side effects, like the range of pollutants released by the burning of fossil fuels. The greatest potential for realising this change lies in the sphere of buildings, which, in the UK, account for almost 50 per cent of all CO_2 emissions. The technology exists to cut this by half in both new and existing buildings. Already demonstration projects have proved that reductions can reach 80–90 per cent against the current norm. The opportunity rests with architects and services engineers to bring about this step-change in the way buildings are designed. In the 1960s–1970s buildings were symbols of human hubris, challenging nature at every step. The turn of the millennium saw a new attitude gathering momentum in a synergy between human activity and the forces of nature. Nowhere can this be better demonstrated than in the design of buildings.

In 2000 the Royal Commission on Environmental Pollution produced a report on *Energy – The Changing Climate*. It concludes: 'To limit the damage beyond that which is already in train, large reductions of global emissions will be necessary during this century and the next. Strong and effective action has to start immediately.'

Peter F. Smith
January 2005

Climate change – nature or human nature?

Chapter One

The key question is this: climate change is now widely accepted as being a reality, so, is it a natural process in a sequence of climate changes that have occurred over the paleoclimatic record or is it being driven by humans? If we hold to the former view then all we can hope for is to adapt as best we can to the climate disruption. On the other hand, if we accept that it is largely human induced, then it follows that we ought to be able to do something about it.

There is widespread agreement among climate scientists worldwide that the present clear evidence of climate change is 90 per cent certain to be due to human activity mainly though the burning of fossil-based energy. This should be good enough to persuade us that human action can ultimately put a brake on the progress of global warming and its climate consequences.

Once the issues are understood, a commitment to renewable energy sources and bioclimatic architectural design should become unavoidable. Inspiring that commitment is the purpose of the first part of the book which then goes on to illustrate the kind of architecture that will have to happen as part of a broader campaign to avert the apocalyptic prospect of catastrophic climate change.

The carbon cycle

Carbon is the key element for life on Earth. Compounds of the element form the basis of plants, animals and micro-organisms. Carbon compounds in the atmosphere play a major part in ensuring that the planet is warm enough to support its rich diversity of life.

The mechanism of the carbon cycle operates on the basis that the carbon locked in plants and animals is gradually released into the atmosphere after they die and decompose. This atmospheric carbon is then taken up by plants which convert carbon dioxide (CO_2) into stems, trunks, leaves, etc. through photosynthesis. The carbon then enters the food chain as the plants are eaten by animals.

There is also a geochemical component to the cycle mainly consisting of deep ocean water and rocks. The former is estimated to contain 36 billion tonnes and the latter 75 million billion tonnes of carbon. Volcanic eruptions and the weathering of rocks release this carbon at a relatively slow rate.

Under natural conditions the release of carbon into the atmosphere is balanced by the absorption of CO_2 by plants. The system is in equilibrium, or would be if it were not for human interference.

The main human activity responsible for overturning the balance of the carbon cycle is the burning of fossil fuels which adds a further 6 billion tonnes of carbon to the atmosphere over and above the natural flux each year. In addition, when forests are converted to cropland the carbon in the vegetation is oxidised through burning and decomposition. Soil cultivation and erosion add further carbon dioxide to the atmosphere.

If fossil fuels are burnt and vegetation continues to be destroyed at the present rate, the CO_2 in the atmosphere will treble by 2100. Even if there is decisive action on a global scale to reduce carbon emissions, atmospheric concentrations will still double by this date.

With the present fuel mix, every kilowatt hour of electricity used in the UK releases one kilogram of CO_2. The burning of one hectare of forest gives off between 300 and 700 tonnes of CO_2.

These are some of the factors which account for the serious imbalance within the carbon cycle which is forcing the pace of the greenhouse effect which, in turn, is pushing up global temperatures.

The greenhouse effect

A variety of gases collaborate to form a canopy over the Earth which causes some solar radiation to be reflected back from the atmosphere, thus warming the Earth's surface, hence the greenhouse analogy. The greenhouse effect is caused by long-wave radiation being reflected by the Earth back into the atmosphere and then reflected back by trace gases in the cooler upper atmosphere, thus causing additional warming of the Earth's surface (Figure 1.1).

The main greenhouse gases are water vapour, carbon dioxide, methane, nitrous oxide and tropospheric ozone (the troposphere is the lowest 10–15 kilometres of the atmosphere).

The sun provides the energy which drives weather and climate. Of the solar radiation which reaches the Earth, one third is reflected back into space and the remainder is absorbed by the land, biota, oceans, ice caps and the atmosphere. Under natural conditions the solar energy absorbed by these features is balanced by outgoing radiation from the Earth and atmosphere. This terrestrial radiation in the form of long-wave, infra-red energy is determined by the temperature of the Earth-atmosphere system. The balance between radiation and absorption can change due to natural causes such as the 11-year solar cycle. Without the greenhouse shield the Earth would be 33°C cooler, with obvious consequences for life on the planet.

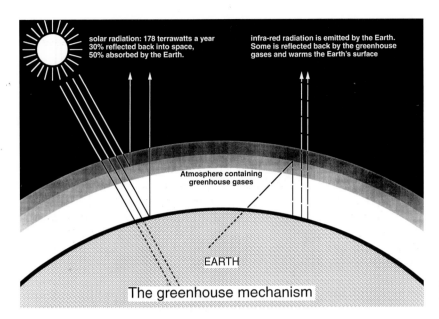

Figure 1.1
The greenhouse 'blanket'

Since the industrial revolution, the combustion of fossil fuels and deforestation has resulted in an increase of 26 per cent in carbon dioxide concentrations in the atmosphere. In addition, rising population in the less developed countries has led to a doubling of methane emissions from rice fields, cattle and the burning of biomass. Methane is a much more powerful greenhouse gas than carbon dioxide. Nitrous oxide emissions have increased by 8 per cent since pre-industrial times (IPCC 1992).

Climate change – the paleoclimate record

In June 1990 scientists were brought up sharp by a graph which appeared in the journal *Nature* (Figure 1.2). It was evidence from ice core samples which showed a remarkably close correlation between temperature and concentrations of CO_2 in the atmosphere from 160 000 years ago until 1989. It also revealed that present concentrations of CO_2 are higher than at any time over that period. Since then the rate of increase has, at the very least, been maintained.

Ice core samples give information in four ways. First, their melt layers provide an indication of the time span covered by the core. Second, a measurement of the extent to which ice melted and refroze after a given summer gives a picture of the relative warmth of that summer. A third indicator is the heavy oxygen isotope ^{18}O in air trapped in the ice. It is more abundant in warm years. Finally, the air trapped in the snow layers gives a measurement of the CO_2 in the atmosphere in a

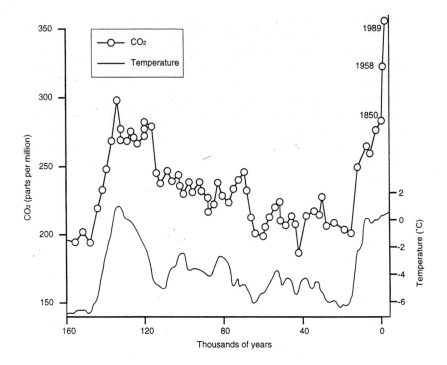

Figure 1.2
Correspondence between historic
temperature and carbon dioxide

given year. Other data from ice cores show that, at the peak of the last
ice age 20 000 years ago, sea level was about 150 m lower than today.

Another source of what is called 'proxy' evidence comes from
analysing tree rings. This can give a snapshot of climate going back 6000
years. Each tree ring records one year of growth and the size of each ring
offers a reliable indication of that year's climate. The thicker the ring, the
more favourable the climate to growth. In northern latitudes warmth is
the decisive factor. Some of the best data come from within the Arctic
Circle where pine logs provide a 6000-year record.

The Climate Research Unit of the University of East Anglia has made
a special study of the evidence for climate changes from different sources
and has concluded that there is a close affinity between ice core evidence and that obtained from tree rings. Also instrumental records going
back to the sixteenth century are consistent with the proxy evidence.

Causes of climate fluctuation

To be able to see the current changes in climate in context, it will be
necessary to consider the causes of dramatic changes in the past.

A major cause of climate fluctuation has been the variation in the
Earth's axial tilt and the path of its orbit round the sun. The Earth is
subject to the influence of neighbouring planets. Their orbits produce
a fluctuating gravitational pull on the Earth, affecting the angle of its

axis. As the Earth wobbles, vast ice sheets wax and wane over a cycle called a Milankovitch cycle. However, thanks to the stabilising pull of the moon, the variation in tilt is contained within limits which preserves the integrity of the seasons. Without the moon, the axis could move to 90 degrees from the vertical meaning that half the planet would have permanent summer and the other endless winter.

It has been calculated that the current orbital configuration is similar to that of the warm interglacial period 400 000 years ago. We may indeed be in the early stages of an interglacial episode and the accompanying natural warming which is being augmented by human induced warming. (For more information on climate fluctuations over the past million years see Houghton J. (2004) *Global Warming*, 3rd edn, Cambridge University Press.)

A second factor forcing climate change is the movement of tectonic plates and the resultant formation of volcanic mountains. In themselves mountains add to the stirring effect on the atmosphere in concert with the rotation of the Earth. They also generate fluctuations in atmospheric pressure, all of which affect climate.

But it is volcanic activity which can cause dramatic changes. The surface of the Earth is constantly shifting. The collision of plates accounts for the formation of mountains. A feature of plate tectonics is that, when plates collide, one plate slides under the other; this is called subduction. In the process rocks are heated and forced through the surface as volcanoes, releasing vast quantities of debris and CO_2 in the process. In the short term this can lead to a cooling as the dust cuts out solar radiation. In the longer term, large injections of CO_2 lead to warming, since CO_2 has a relatively long life in the atmosphere.

A third factor may be a consequence of the second. Paleoclimate data show that there have been periodic surges of ice flows into the north Atlantic which, in turn, affect the deep ocean currents, notably the Gulf Stream. To understand why the ice flows affect the Gulf Stream we need to look at what drives this rather special current.

Particularly salty and warm surface water migrates from the tropics towards the north Atlantic. As it moves north it gradually becomes cold and dense, and, as a consequence, near Greenland it plunges to the ocean floor. This, in turn, draws warmer water from the tropics which is why it is also called the conveyor belt or deep ocean pump. It accounts for 25 per cent of the heat budget of northwest Europe. So, what is the relevance of the icebergs?

As these armadas of icebergs melted as they came south they produced huge amounts of fresh water which lowered the density of surface water undermining its ability to descend to the ocean floor. The effect was to shut down the conveyor belt. As a result northern Europe was periodically plunged into arctic conditions and scientists are concerned that there is now evidence that this process is beginning to happen due to melting ice in the southern tip of Greenland. After the melted iceberg water had dispersed, the conveyor started up again leading to rapid warming. This cycle occurred 20 times in 60 000 years, and the evidence indicates that cooling was relatively slow whilst warming was rapid – 10–12°C in a lifetime. For some reason these forays of icebergs stopped about 8000 years ago, creating relatively stable conditions which facilitated the development of agriculture and ultimately the emergence of urban civilisations.

A fourth factor may seem ironic, because ice ages can be triggered by warm spells leading to the rapid expansion of forests. This, in turn, leads to huge demands for CO_2 which is drawn from the atmosphere. The result of this stripping of atmospheric CO_2 is a weakening of the greenhouse shield, resulting in sharply dropping temperatures.

Changes in energy levels emitted by the sun are also implicated in global fluctuations. In June 1999 the journal *Nature* (vol. 399, p. 437) published research evidence from the Rutherford Appleton Laboratory in Didcot, Oxfordshire which suggests that half the global warming over the last 160 years has been due to the increasing brightness of the sun. However, since 1970 the sun has become less responsible for the warming, yet the rate of warming has been increasing, indicating that increased greenhouse gases are the culprit. Some of the best evidence for the climatic effects of varying levels of radiative output from the sun comes from Africa. Sediment in Lake Naivasha in the Kenya Rift Valley reveals the levels of lake water over the past 1000 years. Periods of high water have higher concentrations of algae on the lake floor which translates to a higher carbon content in the annual layers of sediment. There were long periods of intense drought leading to famine and mass migrations, the worst being from 1000 to 1270 (*Nature*, vol. 403, p. 410).

Finally, we cannot ignore wider cosmic effects. The dinosaurs will testify to the effect on climate of meteor strikes creating perpetual night. New sites of catastrophic impacts are still being discovered on the Earth, but if we want a true picture of the historic record of meteor impact we can see it on Venus. The stability of that planet – no plate movement or vegetation to hide the evidence – ensures that we have a picture of meteor bombardment over hundreds of millennia. The Earth will have been no different.

There is strong historic evidence that life on Earth has a precarious foothold.

The palaeontological record shows that there have been five mass extinctions in the recorded history of the planet. The most widely known on the popular level is the final one which occurred at the end of the Cretacious period 65 million years ago. It is widely attributed to one or more massive meteorites that struck the Earth propelling huge quantities of debris into the atmosphere masking the sun probably for years. Photosynthesising plants were deprived of their energy source and food chains collapsed resulting in the extinction of 75–80 per cent of species, notably the dinosaurs.

However, of all the other mass extinctions, it is the third in the sequence that warrants most attention because it has contemporary relevance. At the end of the Permian period, 251 million years ago, a catastrophic chain of events caused the extinction of 95 per cent of all species on Earth. The prime cause was a massive and prolonged period of volcanic eruptions, not from mountains but from extensive fissures in the ground in the region which ultimately became Siberia. A chain of events caused massive expulsions of CO_2 into the atmosphere which led to rapid warming and plant growth. This had the effect of stripping much of the oxygen from the atmosphere leading to a collapse of much of the biosphere. Plants and animals literally suffocated. For the next 5 million years the remaining 5 per cent of species clung to a precarious existence. It took 50 million years for the planet to return to anything like the previous rate of biodiversity (*New Scientist*, 26 April 2003, 'Wipeout').

The importance of this evidence lies in the fact that this mass extinction occurred because the planet warmed by a mere 6°C over a relatively short period in the paleoclimate timescale. Why this should concern us now is because the world's top climate scientists on the United Nations Inter-Governmental Panel on Climate Change (IPCC 2002) estimated that the Earth could warm to around 6°C by the latter part of the century unless global CO_2 emissions are reduced by 60 per cent by 2050 against the emissions of 1990.

It is the widescale evidence of anomalous climatic events coupled with the rate at which they are occurring that has persuaded the IPCC scientists that much of the blame lies with human activity.

The evidence

- There has been a marked increase in the incidence and severity of storms over recent decades. Over the past 50 years high pressure systems have increased by an average of three millibars whilst low pressure troughs have deepened by the same amount, thereby intensifying the dynamics of weather systems. Greater extremes of the hydrological cycle are leading, on the one hand, to increased area of desert, and, on the other, greater intensity of rain storms which increase run-off and erosion of fertile land. In both cases there is a loss of carbon fixing greenery and food producing land.
- In the first months of 2000 Mozambique experienced catastrophic floods which were repeated in 2001. In 2002 devastating floods occurred across Europe inundating historic cities like Prague and Dresden creating 'one of the worst flood catastrophes since the Middle Ages' (Philippe Busquin, European Union Research Commissioner). The following year saw a similar occurrence with the rivers Elbe and Rhone bursting their banks.
- In July 2004 Southeast Asia experienced catastrophic floods due to exceptional rainfall, rendering 30 million homeless in Bangladesh and the Indian state of Bihar. At the same time central China also

suffered devastating floods whilst Delhi experienced a major draught. The people of Ethiopia are facing starvation in their millions because of the year-by-year failure of the rains.

- Insurance companies are good barometers of change. One of the largest, Munich Re, states that claims due to storms have doubled in every decade since 1960. In that decade there were 16 disasters costing £30 billion. In the last decade of the century there were 70 disasters costing £250 billion. In the first years of this century the pace has quickened. Munich Re has reported that the 700 natural disasters in 2003 claimed 50 000 lives and cost the insurers £33 billion. The Loss Prevention Council has stated that, by the middle of this century, losses will be 'unimaginable'. Yet, these extreme climatic events are only part of the scenario of global warming.

- Besides the effect of increasingly steep pressure gradients another factor contributing to the intensification of storms is the contraction of snow fields. These have in the past created high pressure zones of cold stable air which have kept at bay the Atlantic lows with their attendant storms. This barrier has weakened and shifted further east allowing the storms to reach western Europe. The increased frequency of storms and floods in this area during the last decade of the twentieth century adds weight to this conclusion.

- El Niño has produced unprecedentedly severe effects due to the warming of the Pacific. There is even talk that the El Niño reversal may become a fixture which would have dire consequences for Australia and Southeast Asia.

- Receding polar ice is resulting in the rapid expansion of flora; Antarctic summers have lengthened by up to 50 per cent since the 1970s and new species of plants have appeared as glaciers have retreated. In Iceland Europe's largest glacier is breaking up and is likely to slide into the north Atlantic within the next few years, highlighting the threat to sea levels from land-based ice (*The Observer*, 22 October 2000). The Arctic ice sheet has thinned by 40 per cent due to global warming (report by an international panel of climate scientists, January 2001).

- Sea level has risen 250 mm (10 inches) since 1860. Up to now much of the sea level rise has been due to thermal expansion.

- Sea temperatures in Antarctica are rising at five times the global average, at present a 2.5°C increase since the 1940s. The major threat lies with the potential break-up of land-based ice. The recent breakaway of the 12 000 sq. km of the Larson B ice shelf has serious implications. In itself it will not contribute to rising sea levels. The danger lies in the fact that the ice shelves act as a bulwark supporting the land-based ice. In the May 2003 edition of *Scientific American* it was reported that, following the collapse of the Larson ice shelf 'inland [land based] glaciers have surged dramatically towards the coast in recent years'. Satellite measurements have shown that the two main glaciers have advanced 1.25 and 1.65 km respectively. That represents a rate of 1.8 and 2.4 metres per day. When the West Antarctic ice sheet totally collapses, as it will, this will raise sea level by 5 m (*Scientific American*, op. cit., p. 22). In April 1999 *The Guardian* reported that this ice shelf was breaking up 15 times faster than predicted. Even more disconcerting is the fact that the largest glacier in Antarctica, the Pine Island glacier, is rapidly thinning – 10 metres in eight years – and accelerating towards the sea at a rate of 8 metres a day. This is another indication of the instability of the West Antarctic ice sheet.

- At the same time there has been massive melting of glacier ice on mountains. The Alps have lost 50 per cent of their ice in the past century. The International Commission on Snow and Ice has reported that glaciers in the Himalayas are receding faster than anywhere else on Earth.

- In Alaska there is general thinning and retreating of sea ice, drying tundra, increasing storm intensity, reducing summer rainfall, warmer winters and changes in the distribution, migration patterns and numbers of some wildlife species. Together these pose serious threats to the survival of the subsistence-indigenous Eskimos (*New Scientist*, 14 November 1998).

- From Alaska to Siberia, serious infrastructure problems are occurring due to the melting of the permafrost. Roads are splitting apart, trees keeling over, houses subsiding and world famous ski resorts becoming non-viable. In Alaska and much of the Arctic temperatures are rising ten times faster than the global average – 4.4°C in 30 years. This may, in part, be due to the melting of the snow fields exposing tundra. Whilst snow reflects much of the solar radiation back into space, the bare tundra absorbs heat, at the same time releasing huge amounts of carbon dioxide into the atmosphere – a classic positive feedback situation. The village of Shishmaref on an island on the edge of the Arctic Circle is said to be 'the most extreme example of global warming on the planet' and 'is literally being swallowed by the sea'. Some houses have already fallen into the sea; others are crumbling due to the melting of the permafrost supporting their foundations. The sea is moving inland at the rate of 3 m a year (BBC News, 23 July 2004).

- Global mean surface air temperature has increased between 0.3 and 0.6°C since the later nineteenth century. The average global surface temperature in 1998 set a new record surpassing the previous record in 1995 by 0.2°C – the largest jump ever recorded (Worldwatch Institute in *Scientific American*, March 1999). The warmest year on record was 1999. Global warming is increasing at a faster rate than predicted by the UN IPCC scientists in 1995. They anticipated that temperatures would rise between 1 and 3.5°C in the twenty-first century. According to the Director of the US National Climate Data Center, in only a short time the rate of warming is already equivalent to a 3°C rise per century. This makes it probable that the end of century temperature level will be significantly higher than the IPCC top estimate (*Geophysical Research Letters*, vol. 27, p. 719).

- NASA scientists report satellite evidence of the Greenland land-based ice sheet thinning by 1 m per year. Altogether it has lost 5 m in southwest and east coasts. On the one hand, this threatens the Gulf Stream or deep ocean pump and on the other, it leads directly to a rise in sea level, threatening coastal regions (*Nature*, 5 March 1999). Over the past 20 years the polar ice cap has thinned by 40 per cent.

- Concentrations of CO_2 in the atmosphere are increasing at a steep rate. The pre-industrial level was 590 billion tonnes or 270 parts per million by volume (ppmv); now it is 760 billion tonnes or around 380 ppmv and rising 1.5–2 ppmv per year. Most of the increase has occurred over the last 50 years. According to Sir David King, UK Chief Government Scientist, this is the highest concentration in 55 million years. Then there was no ice on the planet. The previous highest concentration was 300 ppmv 300 000 years ago (*New Scientist*, 29 January 2000, pp. 42–43). At the present rate of emission, concentrations could reach 800–1000 ppmv by 2100. Even if emissions were to be reduced by 60 per cent against 1990 levels by 2050 this will still raise levels to over 500 ppmv with unpredictable consequences due to the fact that CO_2 concentrations survive in the atmosphere for at least 100 years.

- Altogether it would seem that a temperature rise of at least 6°C is very possible with the worst case scenario now rising to 11.5°C. Bearing in mind the observed rate of temperature increase as mentioned above, the aim now should be to prevent the planet crossing the threshold into runaway global warming whereby mutually reinforcing feedback loops become unstoppable.

- Spring in the northern hemisphere is arriving at least one week earlier than 20 years ago; some estimates put it at 11 days. A 40-year survey by Nigel Hepper at the Royal Botanical Gardens at Kew involving 5000 species indicates that spring is arriving 'several weeks earlier'. A study of European gardens found that the growing season has expanded by at least ten days since 1960. Munich scientists studied 70 botanical gardens from Finland to the Balkans (616 spring records and 178 autumn). The conclusion was that spring arrived on average six days earlier and autumn five days later over a 30-year period (*Nature*, February 1999).

- Extreme heat episodes are becoming a feature of hitherto temperate climate zones. The majority of heat-related deaths are due to a lethal assault on the blood's chemistry. Water is lost through sweating and this leads to higher levels of red blood cells, clotting factors and cholesterol. The process starts within 30 minutes of exposure to sun. The summer of 2003 saw heatwaves across Europe that were exceptional, not only in terms of peak temperatures but also their duration. According to the Earth Policy Institute in Washington DC, 35 000 died in August across Europe and 14 800 in France alone from heat-related causes. Other estimates put the figures at 20 000 and 11 000 respectively. According to scientists in Zurich reporting in 'Nature on-line', this kind of sustained summer temperature could normally be expected every 450 years. Towards the latter part of the century they predict such an event every second year. On 4 February 2004 the temperature in central England reached 12.5°C which was the highest early February temperature since records began in 1772 according to the UK Meteorological Office. That month was also the occasion of a severe heatwave in Brisbane, North Australia, where there were 29 sudden deaths in one night.

- One of the predicted results of global warming is that there will be greater extremes of weather, which not only means higher temperatures but also more extensive swings of atmospheric pressure. Research at the University of Lille has indicated that when the pressure falls below 1006 millibars or rises above 1026 millibars the risk of heart attacks increases by 13 per cent. The study also showed that a drop in temperature of 10°C increases the risk of a heart attack by the same percentage (reported at a meeting of the American Heart Association, Dallas, November 1998). According to the UN Environment Protection Agency director, the cost of premature death due to rising numbers of heatwaves is reckoned to be £14 billion a year in the EU and £11 billion in the US. Worldwide the assessment is £50 billion.
- Oceans are the largest carbon sink. As they warm they are becoming less efficient at absorbing CO_2. The latest prediction is that the carbon absorption capacity of oceans will decline by 50 per cent as sea temperatures rise.
- Methane emissions from natural wetlands and rice paddy fields are increasing as temperatures rise. To repeat, methane is a much more potent greenhouse gas than CO_2 and levels are rising rapidly.
- The year 2000 saw an unprecedented catalogue of warnings. The warming that is eroding Europe's largest glacier in Iceland also created clear water across the North West Passage at the top of Canada making navigation possible. This has not happened since prehistoric interglacial warming.

Finally, the assumption generally held by policy makers is that a steady rise in CO_2 concentrations will produce an equally steady rise in temperature. The evidence from ice cores reveals that the planet has sometimes swung dramatically between extremes of climate in a relatively short time due to powerful feedback that tips the system into a dramatically different steady state. Scientists meeting for a workshop in Berlin in 2003 concluded, on the evidence of climate changes to date, that the planet could be on the verge of 'abrupt, nasty and irreversible' change (Bill Clark, Harvard University, quoted in *New Scientist*, 22 November 2003).

Chapter Two   Predictions

There is considerable scientific research effort being targeted on the likely consequences of climate change particularly within the scenario that the industrialised nations will continue indefinitely with 'business as usual' (BaU). This BaU scenario assumes some changes and improvements in efficiency in technology. Here are some of the predictions.

- Historic sea levels are well recorded in the Bahamas and Bermuda because these islands have not been subject to tectonic rise and fall. Ancient shorelines show that, at its extreme, sea level was 20 m (70 ft) above the present level during an interglacial period 400 000 years ago. This would occur if all the world's vast ice sheets disintegrated. There is a serious risk of this happening to the West Antarctic and Greenland ice sheets and their loss would mean a 12 m rise in sea level (*Geology*, vol. 27, p. 375).
- In 2001 Antarctic scientists indicated that sea levels could rise by 6 m (20 ft) within 25 years (*Reuters*). Ultimately, 'when Antarctica melts it [sea level] will be another 110 metres' (Sir David King, *The Guardian*, 14 July 2004).
- Many millions of people live below one metre above sea level. For example, Singapore and its reclaimed territories will be at risk if the sea level rises above 20 cm. The Thames barrage is already deemed to be inadequate. Hamburg is 120 kilometres from the sea but could be inundated. The mean high tidal water level has increased between 40 and 50 cm since the 1970s.
- The condition of the Greenland ice cap is another cause for concern. According to one scenario 'warming of less than 3°C – likely in that part of the Arctic within a couple of decades – could start a runaway melting that will eventually raise sea levels worldwide by seven metres' (*New Scientist*, 'Doomsday Scenario', words attributed to Jonathan Gregory of the Hadley Centre, 22 November 2003). According to a BBC report (28 July 2004) the Greenland ice sheet is melting ten times faster than previously thought. Since May 2004 the ice thickness has reduced by 2–3 m. The same report stated that Alaska is 8°C warmer than 30 years ago.

- In the UK rising sea levels threaten 10 000 hectares of mudflats and salt marshes. But the most serious threat is to 50 per cent of England's grade 1 agricultural land which lies below the 5 m contour (Figure 2.1). Salination following storm surges will render this land sterile. The University of East Anglia Environmental Risk Unit predicts that the 1 in 100 year storm and related floods will show a return rate by 2030 for:

  Milford Haven   3.5 yrs
  Cardiff   5 yrs
  Portland   5 yrs
  Newhaven   3 yrs
  Colchester   4 yrs

- A report from a committee chaired by the UK's Chief Government Scientist, Sir David King, predicts that global warming, coastal erosion and the practice of building on flood plains will increasingly raise the level of risk of loss of life and extensive property damage. The panel of scientists behind the report considered four scenarios. The two worst case scenarios more or less correspond to the IPCC

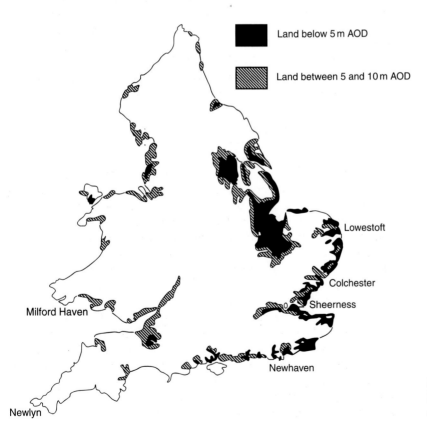

Figure 2.1
Land below 5 metre and 10 metre contours

Business as Usual scenario in which there is unrestricted economic development and hardly any constraints on pollution. The report concludes that the population at risk from coastal erosion and flooding could increase from 1.6 million today to 3.6 million by the 2080s. The cost to the economy could be £27 billion per year (*Future Flooding*, a report from the Flood and Coastal Defence Project of the Foresight Programme, April 2004) (Figure 2.2).

In an interview with *The Guardian* (14 July 2004) Sir David King stated: You might think it is not wise, since we are melting ice so fast, to have built our big cities on the edge of the sea where it is now obvious they cannot remain. On current trends, cities like London, New York and New Orleans will be among the first to go. He went on: 'I am sure that climate change is the biggest problem that civilisation has had to face in 5000 years' which gives added weight to his pronouncement in January 2004 that climate change poses a greater threat than international terrorism.

- It was stated earlier that the geological record over 300 million years shows considerable climate swings every 1–2000 years until 8000 years ago, since which time the swings have been much more moderate. The danger is that increasing atmospheric carbon up to treble the pre-industrial level will trigger a return to this pattern. The IPCC Scientific Committee believes that the absolute limit of

Figure 2.2
Areas in England and Wales at risk of flooding by 2080 under worst case scenario (from the Office of Science and Technology Foresight Report, *Future Flooding*, April 2004)

accumulation of atmospheric carbon should be fixed at double the pre-industrial level at around 500 parts per million by volume (ppmv). Even this will have dramatic climate consequences.

- The paleoclimate record shows that generally cooling occurred at a slow rate, but that warming was rapid as stated earlier, for example 12°C in a lifetime.
- Global warming poses a serious threat to health. Pests and pathogens are migrating to temperate latitudes. It is already widely understood that illnesses like vector borne malaria and Leishmaniasis (affecting the liver and spleen) are predicted to spread to northern Europe. The UK Department of Health predicts that, by 2020, seasonal malaria will have a firm foothold in southern Britain, including the deadly plasmodium falciparum strain which kills around one million children a year in Africa (Figure 2.3). The incidence of the fatal disease West Nile fever has increased in warm temperate zones. New York had an outbreak in 1999. The Department also estimated that there will be around 3000 deaths a year from heatstroke – a prediction seriously understated if the summer of 2003 sets the pace of change. Higher temperatures would also increase the incidence of food poisoning by 10 000 (Department of Health review of the effects of climate change on the nation's health, 9 February 2001).
- A warmer atmosphere means greater evaporation with a consequent increase in cloud cover. IPCC scientists consider that the net

Figure 2.3
Predicted spread of seasonal malaria in Britain by 2020

effect will be to increase global warming. Water vapour is a potent greenhouse gas.

- Historically relatively abrupt changes in climate have been triggered by vegetation. For example, average temperature rose by 5°C in 10 years 14 000 years ago. Earlier it was said that the paleoclimate record shows that in the past the explosive growth of vegetation absorbed massive amounts of atmospheric carbon resulting in a severe weakening of the greenhouse effect and a consequent ice age. Nature could still be the deciding factor. The Hadley Centre forecasts that global warming will cause forests to grow faster over the next 50 years, absorbing more than 100 billion tonnes of carbon. However, from about 2050 the increasing warming will kill many of the forests, thus returning 77 gigatonnes (billion) of carbon to the atmosphere. This will bring a high risk of runaway global warming. Already there is evidence of changes in growth patterns in the Amazon rainforest. Taller, faster growing trees are taking over from the slower growing trees of the understorey of the forest. This is attributed to the higher levels of CO_2 in the atmosphere. In the short term this could mean a net loss in the carbon fixing capacity of the forest since the understorey trees are slower growing and denser in carbon content. Canopy trees are faster growing and lower in carbon content. In the longer term the latter trees are likely to be more susceptible to die-back through heat and drought (*New Scientist*, p. 12, 13 March 2004).
- A report from the Calicut University, Kerala, by British, Indian and Nepalese researchers predicts that the great rivers of northern India and Pakistan will flow strongly for about 40 years causing widespread flooding. After this date most of the glaciers will have disappeared creating dire problems for populations reliant on rivers fed by melt ice like the Indus and Ganges. It is estimated that all the glaciers in the central and eastern Himalayas will disappear by 2035. Melting glaciers in the Andes and Rocky Mountains will cause similar problems in the Americas (*New Scientist*, p. 7, 8 May 2004).
- Another danger is posed by the rapid accumulation of meltwater lakes. Meltwater is held back by the mound of debris marking the earlier extremity of the glacier path. These mounds are unstable and periodically collapse with devastating results. It is predicted that the largest of these lakes in the Sagarmatha National Park in Nepal currently holding 30 million cubic metres of water will break out within five years (*New Scientist*, p. 18, 5 June 1999). The worldwide melting of glaciers and ice caps will contribute 33 per cent of the predicted sea level rise (IPCC).
- The head of research at Munich Re, the world's largest reinsurance group, predicts that claims within the decade 2040–2050 will have totalled £2000 billion based on the IPCC estimates of the rise in atmospheric carbon. He states: 'There is reason to fear that climatic changes in nearly all regions of the Earth will lead to natural catastrophes of hitherto unknown force and frequency. Some regions

will soon become uninsurable' (quoted in *The Guardian*, 3 February 2001).

- We have to add to these natural events the prediction that there will be a substantial increase in world population, mostly in areas which can least accommodate it. At present the greatest concentrations of population are in coastal regions which will be devastated if sea level rise predictions are fulfilled. The UN Population Division estimates that the world figure will reach 8.9 billion by 2050. The US Census Bureau predicted in March 2004 that the present population of 6.2 billion will rise to 9.2 billion by that date. It then believes that the rate of fertility will fall below the replacement level. Even at present 1.3 billion, or one third, of the total world population live in extreme poverty on less than $1 per day.

Recent uncertainties

An article of 10 July 2004 in *New Scientist* was headed 'Peat bogs harbour carbon time bomb'. Research in the University of Wales at Bangor indicates that 'The world's peatland stores of carbon are emptying at an alarming rate' (Chris Freeman). Peat bogs store huge quantities of carbon and the evidence is that this is leaching into rivers in the form of dissolved organic carbon (DOC) at the rate of about 6 per cent per year. Bacteria in rivers rapidly convert DOC into CO_2 that is released into the atmosphere. Recent research shows that DOC in Welsh rivers has increased 90 per cent since 1988. Freeman predicts that, by the middle of the century, DOC from peat bogs could be as great a source of atmospheric CO_2 as the burning of fossil fuels. It appears to be another feedback loop in that an increase in CO_2 in the atmosphere is absorbed by vegetation which in turn releases it into the soil moisture. There it feeds bacteria in the water which, in turn, breaks down the peaty soil allowing it to release stored carbon into rivers. Global warming is causing peat bogs to dissolve.

The uncertainty with perhaps the greatest potential to derail current predictions about global warming is the role of the clouds, described by *New Scientist* as 'the wild card in global warming predictions. Add them to climate models and some frightening possibilities fall out' (Fred Pierce, *New Scientist*, 24 July 2004). The worry is that global warming will either reduce the global level of cloud cover or change the character of the clouds and their influence on solar radiation. Recent modelling conducted by James Murphy of the Met Office Hadley Centre for Climate Prediction has factored in a range of uncertainties in cloud formations such as cloud cover, the lifetime of clouds and their thickness. The model suggested that warming could reach up to 10°C on the basis of a doubling of atmospheric CO_2 which is widely regarded as inevitable. David Stainforth of Oxford University warns of the possibility of a 12°C rise by the end of the century. Cirrus clouds are the most efficient at reflecting heat back to Earth and these are becoming more prevalent. It is expected that the next range of predictions by the IPCC due in 2007 will take account of feedback from cloud cover and produce significantly higher worst case temperature scenarios (from *New Scientist*, 24 July 2004, pp. 45–47).

Another cause for concern stems from research finding from the Universities of Sheffield and Bristol. In the Eocene epoch 50 million years ago there was a catastrophic rise in temperature with seas 12°C warmer than today. The evidence comes from oxygen trapped in the shells of marine fossils. This leaves a distinct isotope pattern which gives an indication of the sea temperature at a given time. Evidence from plant fossils has shown that CO_2 levels were similar to the present day and therefore could not have been responsible for that level of warming. It transpires that this was due to emissions of methane, ozone and nitrous oxide, all more powerful greenhouse gases than CO_2. At the time the Earth was carpeted with wetlands which produced high levels of methane which led to runaway warming. At the present time it is cattle, rice fields and termites which are major sources of the gas. According to Professor Beerling of Sheffield University: 'Methane is being produced in increasing amounts thanks to the spread of agriculture in the tropics. Rice is a particularly intensive source. Car exhaust gases and nitrogen fertilisers are also increasing other gases' (*The Observer*, 11 July 2004). With a predicted steep rise in emissions from transport over the next decades, the latter point is a serious cause of concern.

It is sobering to compare how, according to the UN, different countries are making progress or otherwise in cutting their CO_2 emissions. It should be noted that the improvement in the case of Russia is due to the collapse of its heavy industry since 1990 (Figure 2.4).

Up to now the focus has been on limiting CO_2 emissions almost to the exclusion of other greenhouse gases. It is time to spread the net more widely if there is not to be a rerun of the Eocene catastrophe.

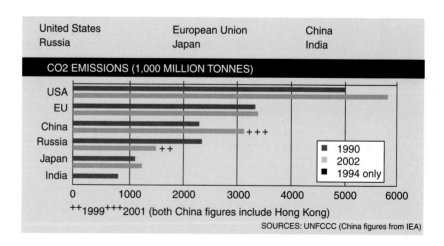

Figure 2.4
CO_2 emissions by principal nations (UNFCCC 2004)

What is being done?

The core of the problem lies in the disparity between the industrial and developing countries in terms of carbon dioxide emission per head. Despite all the international conventions carbon dioxide emissions from developed countries are showing little sign of abating. The USA at twice the European average is still increasing its emissions which currently stand at 23 per cent of the world's total. The average citizen in the North American continent is responsible for around 6 tonnes of carbon per year. In Europe it is about 2.8 tonnes per person. Though starting from a very low base, the most rapidly rising per capita emissions are occurring in Southeast Asia, India and China.

As a first step on the path of serious CO_2 abatement an accord was signed by over 180 countries in 1997 in Kyoto to cut CO_2 emissions by 5.2 per cent globally based on 1990 levels. It has to be remembered that the UN IPCC scientists stated that a 60 per cent cut worldwide would be necessary to halt global warming, later endorsed by the UK Royal Commission on Pollution. The US has refused to ratify Kyoto but Russia has signed up which meant that the Treaty came into force in February 2005. The UK was on track to meet its 12.5 per cent reduction target thanks to the gas power programme and the collapse of heavy industry. However, these benefits have now been offset by the growth in emissions from transport. In 2003 there was a 1–2 per cent increase in CO_2 emissions. Globally the year 2003 witnessed a significant rise in the level of atmospheric carbon to 3 ppm per year – nearly double the average for the past decade. If aircraft emissions were also taken into account the situation would be substantially worse.

One great anomaly is that air travel is excluded from the calculations of CO_2. The Parliamentary Environmental Audit Committee (EAC) forecasts that by 2050 air transport will be responsible for two thirds of all UK greenhouse gas emissions. The Department of Transport expects the numbers flying in and out of the UK to rise from 180 million in 2004 to 500 million in 2030 (reported in *The Observer*, 22 March 2004). Aviation's share of the UK's CO_2 emissions will have increased four-fold by 2030. At the same time it should be noted that CO_2 accounts for only one third of the global warming caused by aircraft (Tom Blundell and Brian Hoskins, members of the Royal Commission on Environmental Pollution, *New Scientist*, 7 August 2004, p. 24).

Even more of a problem faces the USA. Kyoto set its reduction target against the 1990 level at 7 per cent. However, since then it has enjoyed a significant economic boom with a consequent increase in CO_2 emissions. To meet the Kyoto requirement it would now have to make a cut of 30 per cent. The only way it would be prepared to consider this kind if target is by carbon trading, not, in itself, an illegitimate recourse. However, it all depends on the currency of exchange. The US wants to use trees to balance its carbon books. Planting forests may look attractive but it presents three problems.

First, there have been attempts to equate the sequestration capacity of trees with human activities such as driving cars, so, five trees could soak up the carbon from an average car for one year, or 40 trees counteract the carbon emitted by the average home in five years. Unfortunately there is not a reliable method of accounting for the sequestration capacity of a single tree let alone a forest. Another problem recently exposed in the USA is that forests are inclined to burn down. The last point refers back to the Hadley Centre prediction that there will be accelerating forest growth over the next 50 years, then rapid die-back, releasing massive quantities of carbon into the atmosphere. Overall, forests could possibly end up huge net contributors to global warming.

This seems to have been uppermost in the minds of the European delegates to the conference in The Hague in November 2000 when they refused to sign an agreement which allowed the USA to continue with business as usual in return for planting trees.

In the final analysis, if governments and society fail to respond to the imperatives set by climate change, what they cannot escape is the inevitability of dramatic increases in the cost of fossil-based energy as demand increasingly outstrips supply as reserves get ever closer to exhaustion. Market forces are already powering the drive towards renewable energy in some industrialised countries. When you see oil companies investing in renewables then it must be the dawning of the realisation that saving the planet might just be cost effective.

The outlook for energy

A report published in May 2004 from the European Union called 'World Energy, Technology and Climate Change Outlook' offers an insight into a future still dominated by fossil-based energy. It predicts that CO_2 emissions will increase by 2.1 per cent per year for the next 30 years whilst energy use will rise by 1.8 per cent. The reason for the difference is that there will be increasing use of coal as oil and gas prices rise and reserves contract. It also estimates a fall in the share of energy from renewables from 13 per cent today to 8 per cent. This is mainly because growth in renewables will not keep pace with overall energy consumption.

The report expects that energy use in the US will increase by 50 per cent and in the EU by 18 per cent over the same period. Developing countries, especially China and India, will increase their share of global CO_2 emissions from 30 per cent in 1990 to 58 per cent in 2030. China is the world's second biggest emitter of greenhouse gases and the world's biggest producer of coal. To meet its expected energy needs China plans to nearly treble its output from coal fired power stations by

2020. These new power plants are not being constructed to accommodate future CO_2 sequestration equipment and they are likely to be in service for 50 years. Oil consumption has doubled in the last 20 years and now stands at 80 million barrels per day, an all time high. So, for decades to come, with cities like Shanghai growing at an exponential rate, China is virtually ruling out measures to mitigate its CO_2 emissions, which, as a developing country, it is not required to do.

As the economies of the world power ahead on the back of fossil fuels, the spectre of diminishing reserves heightens anxieties within the corridors of government. The oil companies estimate that reserves will be exhausted within about 40 years but that is not so much the prime issue. According to Stephen Lewis, City economic analyst, 'the kind of growth rates to which oil consuming countries are committed appear to be generating the demand for oil well above the underlying growth in the rate of supply . . . the US, the Middle East, the North Sea . . . all appear to be past their production peaks' (*The Guardian*, 9 August 2004).

There are conflicting estimates, but petroconsultants who advise the government claim that only one new barrel of oil is discovered for every four that are used. Their estimate is that we are only two years away from the peak of oil production.

By 2020 the UK will be importing 80 per cent of its energy based on the current rate of consumption. The histogram in Figure 2.5 indicates the rate of decline of UK reserves of both oil and gas. As regards gas, the major reserves are located within countries that do not have a good record of stability. The North Sea reserves are already diminishing with a

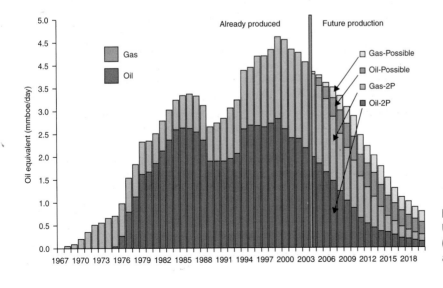

Figure 2.5
UK oil and gas reserves to 2020 (Association for the Study of Peak Oil and Gas 2004)

life expectancy of 15–20 years. The government has acknowledged that, by 2020, 90 per cent of the UK's gas will come from Russia, Iran and Nigeria (Ministry of Defence, 8 February 2001).

For the US the Department of Energy estimates that imports of oil will rise from 54 per cent in 2004 to 70 per cent by 2025 due to its declining reserves and increasing consumption. Add to this the fact that at least half the remaining global reserves will be located in five autocracies in the Middle East who have already demonstrated their ability to manipulate prices causing the oil shocks of the 1970s. These states account for 35 per cent of the market, the point at which it is considered they are able to control prices at a time of rising demand, especially by developing countries on the rapid road to developed status.

According to the environmental policy analyst Dr David Fleming it is 'not possible that we can survive without a dramatic increase in the price of oil' (The Guardian, 2 March 2000). The government was warned that another oil price shock could trigger a stock market crash, or even war. In the oil shocks of the 1970s we were extricated from long-term pain by the discovery of large oil reserves in the North Sea and Alaska. This time there are no escape routes. The Kuwait episode then the Iraq war should remind us of the sensitivity of the situation.

The world is one huge combustion engine which consumes 74 million barrels of oil a day to keep it running for now! At the present time in China one person in 125 has a car. The Chinese economy is growing at 8–10 per cent a year. It has joined the World Trade Organisation and opened its markets to international trade which gives additional impetus to economic growth. In no time there will be one person in 50 then perhaps one in 20 owning a car. Even without including the prospects for China the current demand for oil worldwide is growing at 2 per cent a year. By 2020 it is estimated that there will be one billion cars on the world's roads. At the same time petrol geologists estimate that production of oil will peak in the first decade of 2000 and then output will decline by 3 per cent a year. Oil geologist Colin J. Campbell says we are 'at the beginning of the end of the age of oil'. He predicts that after 2005 there will be serious shortages of supply with steeply rising prices and by 2010 a major oil shock reminiscent of the 1970s except that then there were huge reserves to be tapped. There are still large reserves but they are located in places like the states around the Caspian basin which Russia regards as its sphere of influence – not much comfort to the west, in particular the UK, where it is expected that its North Sea fields will be exhausted by 2016.

An updated 2004 scenario for world peak oil production by Colin Campbell shows, in a graph published on the website of the Association for the Study of Peak Oil (ASPO), that both gas and oil worldwide will peak around 2008 (Figure 2.6).

Beyond 2008, increasing price volatility for both oil and gas seems inevitable.

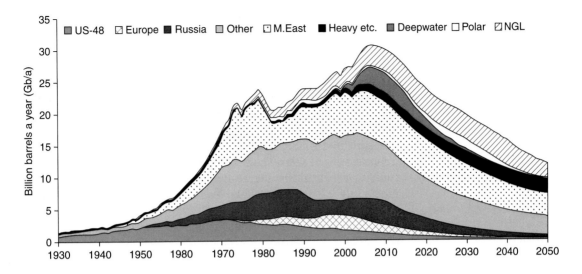

Figure 2.6
World oil and gas production to 2050

The nuclear option

The UK has problems regarding its nuclear capacity. Recently questions have been raised about the government's estimates of future generation capacity within the nuclear industry. Environment Data Services have described them as 'heroically optimistic', a verdict which therefore also applies to the government's target of 20 per cent reduction in CO_2 emissions by 2010 since that target assumes full bore production by its ageing reactors. In fact nuclear output dropped 4 per cent in 1999 and 10 per cent in 2000 and in the latter year coal fired generation was up 13 per cent. All but two of the Magnox stations have closure dates before 2008. The pressurised water and gas cooled reactors have been beset with problems. By 2014 75 per cent of nuclear will have been decommissioned. The DTI's energy predictions assume that, for the next decade, the creaking nuclear industry will operate at full capacity with an unprecedented rate of efficiency. After that, renewables, gas generation and possibly a new batch of nuclear generators will fill the vacuum. As we have noted gas has its uncertainties. The projected fuel mix for the UK in 2010 is:

- Coal 16 per cent
- Nuclear 16 per cent
- Renewables 10 per cent
- Gas 57 per cent.

However, in 2008 the EU will enforce desulphurisation regulations on coal fired plants making them uneconomic. Their only option will be to switch to biofuels such as rapid rotation crops which is already being pioneered at the massive Drax power station in Yorkshire. The use of biofuels may offer a future for coal fired power stations. A plant operated by Biojoule in East Anglia is already producing 15 000 tonnes a year of specially processed wood for partial fuel replacement in coal fired power plants.

The obvious conclusion to draw from all this is that buildings being designed now will, in most cases, still be functioning when the screws on fossil fuels are really tightening. For buildings wholly reliant on fossil-based energy, it will be impossible to make accurate predictions as to running costs in, say, ten years' time. What is certain is that energy prices will rise steeply since there is still only patchy evidence of the will to stave off this crisis by the deployment of renewable energy technologies. The pressure to incorporate the external costs like damage to health, buildings and above all the biosphere into the price of fossil will intensify as the effects of global warming become increasingly threatening. The government undertaking is to meet 10 per cent of electricity demand by 2010 from renewable sources. What tends to be overlooked is that, by then, demand will probably have increased by more than this percentage and, at the same time, many of the nuclear power plants are likely to have been decommissioned. By 2015 the UK could be facing an energy vacuum which emphasises the need to take the plunge into renewable technologies as a matter of urgency, which makes the latest offering from the European Environment Agency (EEA) report of 2004 all the more remarkable and disturbing. It states that within the European Union the share of renewable electricity rose from 12 per cent in 1990 to 14 per cent in 2001. The EU target is 21 per cent

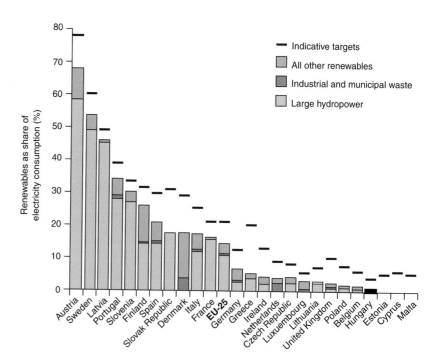

Figure 2.7
Comparison of electricity derived from renewables in 25 EU states
(source: European Environment Agency 2004)

by 2010, suggesting that much more needs to be done. The EEA has produced a histogram which shows the relative performance of member states. The UK is fourth from bottom of the table of all countries which have a contribution from renewables. (Figure 2.7) (EEA 2004; Signals 2004, a European Environment Agency Update on selected issues, Copenhagen, May 2004).

Chapter Three

Renewable technologies – the marine environment

Two quotes set the scene for this chapter:

> A sustainable energy system is probably the single most important milestone in our efforts to create a sustainable future . . . Decarbonisation of the energy system is task number one.
>
> Oystein Dahle, Chairman.
> Worldwatch Institute

and

> Global civilisation can only escape the life-threatening fossil-fuel resource trap if every effort is made to bring about an immediate transition to renewable and environmentally sustainable resources and thereby end the dependence on fossil fuels.
>
> Hermann Scheer, *The Solar Economy*, Earthscan 2002, p. 7

The UK energy picture

In 2002 total inland energy consumption in the UK was 229.6 million tonnes of oil equivalent (mtoe). Nuclear contributed 21.3 mtoe to the total. Renewables and energy from waste accounted for a mere 2.7 mtoe (UK Energy in Brief, DTI, July 2003). Is it fantasy to support that renewable energy sources could equal, even exceed, this capacity without help from nuclear? This is a key question since the Energy White Paper of February 2002 put nuclear on hold pending a demonstration that renewables could fill the void left by the decommissioning of the present cluster of nuclear facilities.

The government has declared a target of 10.4 per cent for renewables by 2010 and an aspiration to achieve 20 per cent by 2020. The 20 per cent figure is significant since it represents the limit at which the present structure of the grid can accommodate small-scale and intermittent suppliers. Beyond this percentage the grid would have to be reconfigured to encompass extensive distributed generation, as recommended by the Royal Commission on Environmental Pollution (ibid., p. xi).

As far as the major power distributors are concerned, the 20 per cent threshold may well be regarded as the 'red line' beyond which they will be forced to run on less than full capacity, at the same time compensating for fluctuations in the supply from renewables. According to Hermann Scheer this would threaten the long-term ambitions of the power industry which sees the prospect of ultimately controlling information transmission as well as energy. 'They hold all the cards they need to construct a comprehensive commodity supply and media empire' (ibid., p. 60).

One of the key factors favouring the big suppliers is the web of direct and indirect subsidies which the industry enjoys such as the fact that its raw material is regarded as being a free gift from nature. Only now is it being widely realised that reserves, apart from coal, will be exhausted sooner rather than later.

At the same time the market pays scant regard to its environmental responsibilities, especially that of driving up global warming. The European Commission's ExternE project has sought to quantify the externalities. For example, it concludes that the real cost of electricity from coal and oil is about double the current economic cost to the producers. For gas generated electricity the shortfall is about 30 per cent. The New Elements for the Assessment of External Costs from Energy (NewExt) is refining the methodology to provide more accurate information and was due to report in 2004. The results should make it possible more accurately to calculate life-cycle environmental costs.

Government claims that energy suppliers operate within the framework of a free market and on a level playing field is based on flawed economics. The anomaly is that the cost–benefit system employed here *ignores the element of risk*. For some reason energy is not subjected to the normal rules of financial risk assessment in determining the market value of the commodity. Never has it been more apparent that oil and gas are high risk commodities that can have a powerful negative impact on the Stock Index due to price volatility.

In contrast, renewables, being relatively high capital cost but low running cost technologies, are not nearly so affected by macroeconomic shifts such as the international price of oil or the Stock Index. Repayment of capital and operating costs are largely fixed and so represent a low risk. The problem is that renewables with their high investment costs violate one of the founding laws of accountancy that investors want a high return on capital in the short term.

This is the market situation in which renewables have to compete and it constitutes a sharply tilted playing field in favour of the fossil fuel industries. We have the bizarre situation that a highly subsidised, highly polluting, high risk energy stream is stifling the almost zero risk renewable systems that draw on solar and lunar energy and are therefore not reliant on a continual input of an extracted fuel. This is clearly an abuse of the term 'free market'. If the contours of the energy playing field really were level, then renewables would offer excellent investment opportunities.

Since it seems inevitable that renewables will have to fight their corner in a free market for an indefinite period, then these anomalies must be corrected if a decarbonised electricity infrastructure is to be a reality.

Energy from rivers and seas

Energy extracted from the marine environment is, on the one hand, the most capital intensive form of energy, but, on the other, offers the longest-term energy certainty coupled with the highest energy density.

Energy can be derived from water according to four basic principles: first, hydroelectricity from the damming of rivers; second, from hydrodynamics or the movement of water by virtue of tidal rise and fall, tidal currents and waves; third, the dynamics of thermal difference; and fourth, the extraction of hydrogen from water via electrolysis. This chapter focuses on the first and second technologies.

Hydroelectric generation

Hydroelectric schemes which exploit height difference in the flow path of water are the oldest method of generation from water. It involves damming a watercourse to create the necessary pressure to drive high speed impulse turbines. The Boulder Dam scheme in the USA was the first large-scale project implemented in the 1930s as a means of driving the country out of recession.

One of the first major projects to be completed after the Second World War was the Aswan Dam scheme initiated by Colonel Nasser, the Egyptian President. Work started in 1960 to create the huge Lake Nasser as the storage facility and as a potential irrigation source for a major part of the country. It cost $1 billion ($10 billion at current prices) and began operations in 1968, delivering 2000 megawatts (MW) of power.

The project has served to illustrate some of the problems which accompany hydroelectric schemes of this massive scale. For example, evaporation from the lake has been much greater than anticipated, and the country is considering reactivating storage schemes beyond its borders. At the same time, the dam has so disrupted the flow of the Nile that it threatens the agriculture of the delta.

A further problem is that, historically, the Nile has conveyed millions of tonnes of silt per year, mostly soil, from the Ethiopian highlands. The silt, part of which used to be deposited in the Nile flood plain, is now trapped behind the dam, a fact which is calculated to have done irreparable damage to the fertility of the Nile valley and delta. To compensate for the loss Egypt is now one of world's heaviest users of agricultural chemicals.

One of the worst drawbacks concerns saline pollution. Salts are dissolved in river water and modern irrigation systems leave salts behind – about one tonne per hectare. Large areas of fertile land are being threatened by the salt which makes the ground toxic to plants and ultimately causes it to revert to desert. There is now a project to remove saline water from two million hectares of land at a cost which exceeds the original price of the dam (*New Scientist*, pp. 28–32, 7 May 1994).

In December 1994 work commenced on the Three Gorges scheme on the Yangtze River. The dam is two kilometres long and some 100 metres high. It has created a lake 600 kilometres long displacing over one million people. In return the country will receive 18 000 MW of power which is 50 per cent more than the world's existing largest dam, the Itaipu Dam in Paraguay. Even so, in the long term this dam will make a relatively small impact on China's dependency on fossil fuel. In addition, in November 1994, plans were revived to generate up to 37 000 MW along the course of Mekong River, again with drastic potential social consequences.

With the exception of projects on the River Danube, Europe gains most of its hydroelectricity from medium to small-scale plants. Most of Norway's supply is from hydro sources; in Sweden it is 50 per cent of the total and Scotland produces 60 per cent of its electricity from non-fossil sources, mostly hydro. According to the Department of Trade and Industry, 'The UK has a considerable untapped small-scale hydro resource' such as the discreet plant at Garnedd in Gwynedd, North Wales. Given the right buying-in rates from the National Grid, such ventures could become a highly commercial proposition.

Small-scale hydro

In small-scale projects water is usually contained at high level by a dam or weir and led down a pipe (penstock) or channel to a generator about 50 m below to create the necessary force to drive the generator. An intermediate technology version has been designed for developing countries in which a standard pump is converted to a turbine and an electric motor to a generator (*New Scientist*, p. 29, 29 June 1991) (further information in Smith, P.F. (2002) 'Small-scale hydro,' in *Sustainability at the Cutting Edge*, Ch. 10, Architectural Press).

'Run of river' systems

Many rivers have a flow rate in excess of 0.75 m per second which makes them eligible to power so-called run of river generators. The conventional method is to create a dedicated channel which

Figure 3.1
WPI turbine (courtesy of CADDET, issue 1/04)

accommodates a cross-flow generator which is a modern version of a water wheel or a 'Kaplan' turbine which has variable blades.

A Norwegian company, Water Power Industries (WPI), has developed a water turbine on floats that has a vertical axis rotor fitted with blades shaped like an aircraft wing. The 'waterfoils' are vertical and the flow of a river creates negative pressure which causes the wheel to rotate (Figure 3.1). The wings are continuously adjusted by computer monitoring to keep them at their most efficient angle. It is claimed that the water turbine converts 50 per cent of the energy in the water to electricity with a theoretical maximum of 59 per cent.

Assuming a steady flow of water with a velocity of 3 m/s and a regularity of 96 per cent a 15 m diameter 500 kW turbine would produce 4 million kWh/year. Not only could this system capture the energy of many rivers, it could also be situated in channels with a high tidal flow which are too shallow for other types of tidal turbine.

Tidal energy

Tidal energy is predictable to the minute for at least the rest of the century. Tide levels can be affected by storm surges as experienced dramatically in the UK in 1953. The British Isles benefit from some of the greatest tidal ranges in Europe. In summary, there are at least four technologies that can exploit the action of the tides, offering reliable electricity in the multi-gigawatt range. They are:

- The tidal barrage
- The tidal fence or bridge
- Tidal mills or rotors
- Impoundment.

The tidal barrage

Trapping water at high tide and releasing it when there is an adequate head is an ancient technology. A medieval tide mill is still in working order in Woodbridge, Suffolk. In the first quarter of the twentieth century this principle was applied to electricity generation in the feasibility studies for a barrage across the River Severn.

Tidal power works on the principle that water is held back on the ebb tide to provide a sufficient head of water to rotate a turbine. Dual generation is possible if the flow tide is also exploited.

A Royal Commission was formed in 1925 to report on the potential of the River Severn to produce energy at a competitive price. It reported in 1933 that the scheme was viable. Since then the technology has improved including a doubling of the size of generators. This increases the volume of water passing through the barrage by the square. A further study was completed in 1945 and the latest in-depth investigation was concluded in 1981. In all cases the verdict was positive, though the last report was cautious about the cost/benefit profile of the scheme in the context of nuclear energy. Despite this supporting evidence the UK still shows reluctance to exploit this source of power. Recently a discussion document produced by the Institution of Civil Engineers stated in respect of tidal energy:

> it appears illogical that so potentially abundant an option will be deferred perpetually when the unit power costings involved are estimated to be reasonably competitive with all alternatives except combined cycle gas turbines.

Power generation is obviously intermittent but the spread of tide times around the coasts helps to even out the contribution to the grid.

The only operational barrage in Europe is at La Rance, Normandy. It is a bidirectional scheme, that is, it generates on both the flow and ebb tides. Two-way operation is only beneficial where there is a considerable tidal range and even then only during spring tides. Annual production at La Rance is about 610 gigawatt hours (GWh). Despite its success as a demonstration project, the French government elected to concentrate its generation policy on nuclear power which accounts for about 75 per cent of its capacity.

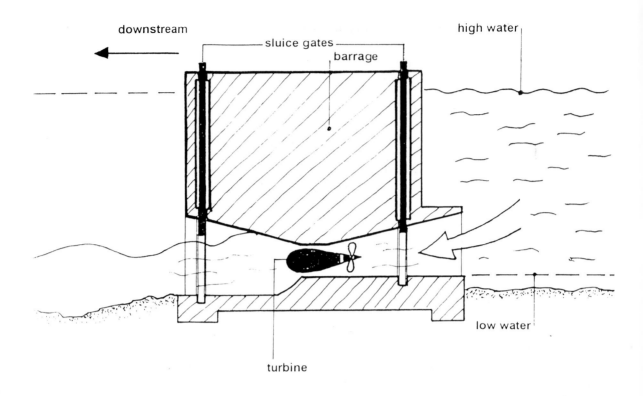

Figure 3.2
Basic tidal barrage

Up to now, schemes proposed in the UK have been one directional, generating only on the ebb tide. The principle is that water is held upstream at high tide until the downstream level has fallen by at least 2.0 metres. The upstream volume of water is supplemented by pumping additional water from downstream on the flood tide. This is reckoned to be more cost effective than bidirectional generation in most situations (Figure 3.2).

The technology of barrages was transformed by the caisson techniques employed in the construction of the Mulberry Harbour floated into place after D-Day in the Second World War. It is a modular technique with turbine caissons constructed on slipways or temporary sand islands. According to the Department of Trade and Industry's Energy Paper Number 60, November 1992: 'The UK has probably the most favourable conditions in Europe for generating electricity from the tides.' In fact, it has about half of all the European Union's tidal generating potential of approximately 105 terawatt hours per year (TWh/y) (ETSU). The DTI report concludes:

> There are several advantages arising from the construction of tidal barrages in addition to providing a clean, non-polluting source of energy. Tidal barrages can assist with the local infrastructure of the region, create regional development

opportunities and provide protection against local flooding within the basin during storm surge.

Around the world numerous opportunities exist to exploit tidal energy, notably in the Bay of Fundy in Canada where there is a proposal to generate 6400 MW. China has 500 possible sites with a total capacity of 110 000 MW.

Professor Eric Wilson, a leading tidal expert in the UK, sums up the situation by saying that a tidal power scheme may be expensive to build, but it is cheap to run. 'After a time, it is a gold mine.'

In 1994 the government decided to abandon further research into tidal barrages for a variety of reasons ranging from the ecological to the economic. In market terms a normal market discount rate heavily penalises a high capital cost, long life, low running cost technology. The economic argument could be countered if the market corrections stated earlier were to be implemented. However, another concern has grown in stature, namely, the threat from rising sea level amplified by an accelerating rate of storm surges.

Following the 1953 floods, it was decided that London should be protected by a barrage. It was designed in the 1970s to last until 2030. However, the threat from rising sea level was hardly a factor in the 1970s; now it is a major cause of concern that the barrage will be overwhelmed by a combination of rising sea level, storm surges and increased rainfall and river rundown well before that date. In the year 1986/87 the barrage was not closed once against tidal and river flooding; in 2001 it closed 24 times. A further complication is the Thames Gateway project which includes 120 000 new homes *below sea level*. If one flood breaks through the Thames Barrier it will cost about £30 billion or roughly 2 per cent of GDP (Sir David King, Government Chief Scientist, *The Guardian*, 9 January 2004). All this combines to make a strong case for an estuary barrage that will protect both the Thames and the Medway and, at the same time, generate multi-gigawatt power for the capital (Figure 3.3).

One of the arguments against tidal barrages is that they would trap pollution upstream. Since rivers are now appreciably cleaner than in the 1970s, thanks largely to EU Directives, this should not now be a factor. The Thames is claimed to be the cleanest river in Europe, playing host to salmon and other desirable fish species. A group of engineering companies has renewed the argument in favour of the River Severn barrage, indicating that it would meet 6 per cent of Britain's electricity needs whilst protecting the estuary's coastline from flooding (*New Scientist*, 25 January 2003).

The tidal fence

There is, however, an alternative to a barrage which can also deliver massive amounts of energy at less cost/kWh, namely, the tidal fence or

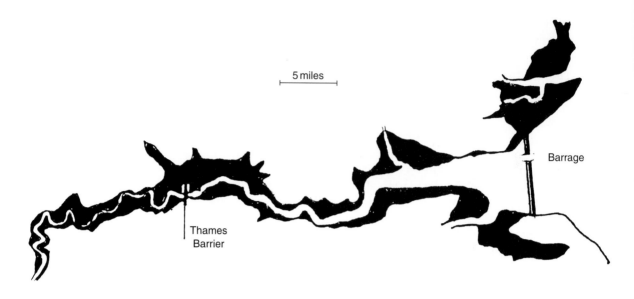

5 miles

Barrage

Thames
Barrier

Figure 3.3
River Thames flood risk zones below
5m contour and suggested barrage

bridge which has only recently come into prominence. The tidal fence system, for example as designed by Blue Energy Canada Inc., consists of modular shell concrete marine caissons linked to form a bridge. Vertical axis Davis Hydro Turbines are housed between the concrete fins. Multiple Darrieus rotors capture energy at different levels of the tide. The rotors are 10.5 m in diameter and rotate at 25 rpm, each turbine having a peak output of up to 14 MW. They can function within a tidal regime of at least 1.75 m. The generators are housed in the box structure bridge element which can also serve as a highway or platform for wind turbines (Figure 3.4).

From the ecological point of view the system has the advantage over the barrage option of preserving the integrity of the intertidal zones. Wading birds have nothing to fear. The slow rotation of the turbines poses minimum risk to marine life, with large marine mammals protected by a fence with a backup of an automatic braking system operated by sonar sensors. At the same time the system allows for the free passage of silt.

In terms of energy density, the tidal fence outstrips other renewable technologies:

Wind   1000 kWh/m²
Solar (PV)   1051 kWh/m²
Wave   35–70 000 kWh/m²
Tidal fence   192 720 kWh/m²

(Source: Blue Energy Canada Inc.)

Blue Energy has designed a major installation at Dalupiri in the Philippines. It is a four-phase project with the first phase comprising a 4 kilometre tidal fence between the islands of Dalupiri and Samar in the

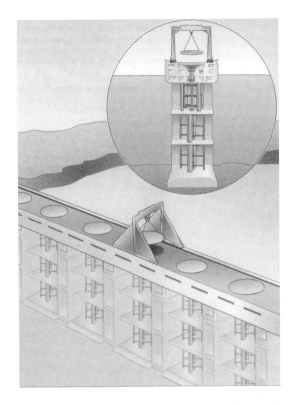

Figure 3.4
Blue Energy tidal fence concept

San Bernardino Strait. The estimated maximum capacity of the 274 turbines housed in the tidal fence is 2.2 GW guaranteeing a base daily average of 1.1 GW. The structure is designed to withstand typhoons of 150 mph and tsunami waves of 7 m.

The potential for the UK

Many speculations have been offered regarding the ultimate generating potential of various renewable technologies. The data which are used here have been extracted from a paper from the Tyndall Centre in the University of Sussex, *UK 'Electricity Scenarios for 2050'* Working paper 41, 2004, by Jim Watson which, in turn, cites data from the DTI 1999 and the RCEP 2000. The Tyndall paper suggests that the optimum output from renewables is 136.5 GW as defined in the first of four scenarios Many of these are intermittent and unpredictable. An exception is tidal energy which is predictable and this is where the tidal fence comes into its own.

The British Isles offer considerable opportunities for the application of this technology. Blue Energy has already identified the Severn estuary as a suitable site. The Open University Renewable Energy Team has selected 17 estuary sites suitable for medium to large-scale barrage systems (Boyle, G. (ed.) (1996) *Renewable Energy – Power for a Sustainable Future*, Oxford University Press). On the assumption that these sites would be equally suitable for tidal fences, they add up to a linear capacity of 208 km. If only half of the full estuary width were available to house turbines in each case, this would produce a peak output of about 60 GW and a daily average of 30 GW. This is based on an extrapolation from the Dalupiri scheme and is therefore only a rough estimation. However, it should be enough to cause a reappraisal of the tidal potential of the UK, especially as the cost is highly competitive. The installed cost at present is estimated to be US$1400 per kW.

Since the output from the tidal fence is predictable and peak output may not coincide with peak demand from the grid, it is an appropriate system to combine with pumped storage to even out the sinusoidal curves.

Tidal currents

The European Union has identified 42 sites around the coasts of the UK which have sufficient tidal velocity to accommodate tidal turbines. It is estimated that tidal stream energy has the potential to meet one quarter of the electricity needs of the UK which amounts to about 18 GW. With a load factor of 0.50, this technology would deliver 9 GW. A 1993 DTI report claimed that the Pentland Firth alone could provide 10 per cent, or about 7 GW, of the UK's electricity demand. However, the greatest potential source of tidal currents is located off the islands of Guernsey. According to Blue Energy they have the potential to generate 26 GW or more than one third of the UK's generating capacity.

There are several technologies being researched, including the Stingray project which exploits the tidal currents to operate hydroplanes which oscillate with the tide to drive hydraulic motors that generate electricity. The hydroplanes are profiled like an aircraft wing to create 'lift'. It is still at the development stage and its final manifestation will operate in streams in both directions.

However, the most likely technology to succeed in the gigawatt range are the vertical or horizontal turbines. The tidal fence vertical turbine is claimed to be ideal for tidal streams since it has multiple rotors which can capture tidal energy at different depths. The minimum velocity of tidal flow to operate a tidal fence is 1.75 m/s or 3.5 knots. The strength of the current tends to be strongest near the surface so a vertical series of rotors could accommodate the different speeds at various depths. An ideal site could be the Pentland Firth.

The tidal mill

Horizontal axis turbines are similar to wind turbines but water has an energy density four times greater than air, which means that a rotor 15 m in diameter will generate as much power as a wind turbine of 60 m diameter. They operate at a minimum velocity of about 2 m/s. Since the tidal flow is constant, underwater turbines are subject to much less buffeting than their wind counterparts.

Figure 3.5
Tidal stream turbines or tidal mills,
serviced above water

According to Peter Fraenkel, Director of Marine Current Turbines, the best tidal stream sites could generate 10 MW per square kilometre. His company has built a 300 kW demonstration turbine off the Devon coast and has a project for a turbine farm in the megawatt range (Figure 3.5). This company is presently investigating the opportunities around Guernsey and Alderney.

Offshore impoundment

An alternative to estuary tidal generation is the concept of the tidal pound. The idea is not new as mentioned earlier. The system is ideal for situations in which there is a significant tidal range and shallow tidal flats encountered in many coasts of the UK. The system consists of a circular barrage built from locally sourced loose rock, sand and gravel similar in appearance to standard coastal defences. It is divided into three or more segments to allow for the phasing of supply to match demand. According to Tidal Electricity Ltd, computer simulations show that a load factor of 62 per cent can be achieved with generation possible 81 per cent of the time. Tidal pounds would be fitted with low-head tidal generating equipment which is a reliable and mature technology.

In its Memorandum submitted to the House of Commons Select Committee on Science and Technology this company claimed that 'The UK has very large tidal ranges and many suitable for sites . . . that could conceivably generate thousands of megawatts.' It has been estimated that impoundment electricity could meet up to 20 per cent of UK demand at around 15 GW. With a load factor of 0.62 this amounts to 9.3 GW.

Besides having the potential to generate substantial amounts of electricity, tidal pounds can also provide coastal flood protection which was an important factor in determining the viability of the first large-scale project in the UK off the North Wales coast. In 1990 Towyn near Rhyl experienced devastating floods. The pound will be about 9 miles wide and 2 miles deep and located a mile offshore. It should generate 432 MW. The life expectancy of the structure is 100 years.

This is a popular holiday coast and it is expected that the project will become an important visitor attraction. There is talk of added attractions like a sea-life musuem and an education centre. The tidal barrage at La Rance in Normandy attracts 600 000 visitors a year.

This is perceived as a cost-effective technology thanks in part to the extra revenue from the Renewables Obligation Certification. Because it is located in shallow water construction costs are much less than for barrage systems. It is relatively unobtrusive and much kinder to marine life than a tidal barrage. It offers predictable power with a load factor which is significantly better than, for example, wind power.

In total the potential capacity of the various technologies that exploit the tides around Britain is in the region of 65 GW. The variation in high water times around the coasts coupled with pumped storage help to even out the peaks and troughs of generation before any account is taken of the range of other technologies.

Wave power

Wave power is regarded as a reliable power source and has been estimated as being capable of meeting 25 per cent or 18 GW of total UK demand with a load factor of 0.50, giving a reliable output of about 9 GW, and is already contributing 500 kW to the grid.

The World Energy Council estimates that wave power could meet 10 per cent of world electricity demand.

The most favoured system uses the motion of the waves to create an oscillating column of water in a closed chamber which compresses air which, in turn, drives a turbine. There are both inshore and offshore versions either in operation or projected. The first inshore version in the UK was positioned on an inlet in the Scottish Isle of Islay (Figure 3.6).

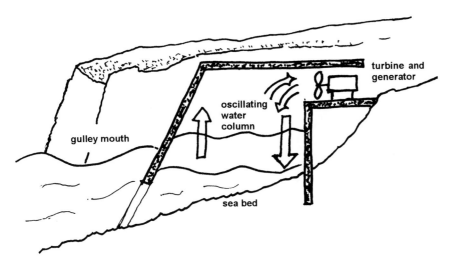

Figure 3.6
Principle of the Isle of Islay OWC wave generator

It was designed by Queen's University, Belfast, and has an output of 75 kW which is fed directly to the grid. The success of this pilot project justified the construction of a full-scale version which is now in operation.

A 25 metre slit has been cut into the cliffs facing the north Atlantic at Portnahaven to accommodate a wave chamber inclined at 45 degrees to the water. Two turbines are driven by positive pressure as air is compressed by incoming waves, and negative pressure as the receding waves pull air into the chamber. The rather clever Wells turbine rotates in one direction in either situation. It is rated at 500 kW which is enough to power 200 island homes.

Currently under test in the Orkneys is a snake-like device called Pelamis which consists of five flexibly linked floating cylinders, each of 3.5 m diameter. The joints between the cylinders contain pumps which force oil through hydraulic electricity generators in response to the rise and fall of the waves. It is estimated to produce 750 kW of electricity. The manufacturer, Ocean Power Devices (OPD), claims that a 30 MW wave farm covering a square kilometre of sea would provide power for 20 000 homes. Twenty such farms would provide enough electricity for a city the size of Edinburgh.

Like Scotland, Norway enjoys an enormous potential for extracting energy from waves. As far back as 1986 a demonstration ocean wave power plant was built based on the 'Tapchan' concept (Figure 3.7). This consists of a 60 m long tapering channel built within an inlet to the sea. The narrowing channel has the effect of amplifying the wave height. This lifts the sea water about 4 m depositing it into a 7500 m² reservoir. The head of water is sufficient to operate a conventional hydroelectric power plant with a capacity of 370 kW.

A large-scale version of this concept is under construction on the south coast of Java in association with the Norwegians. The plant

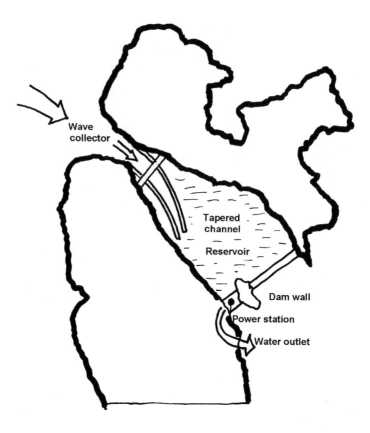

Figure 3.7
Wave elevator system, the 'Tapchan'

will have a capacity of 1.1 MW. As a system this has numerous advantages:

- The conversion device is passive with no moving parts in the open sea.
- The Tapchan plant is able to cope with extremes of weather.
- The main mechanical components are standard products of proven reliability.
- Maintenance costs are very low.
- The plant is totally pollution free.
- It is unobtrusive.
- It will produce cheap electricity for remote islands.

The total for the three tide and wave technologies, taking account of load factors, could come to about 74 GW.

If we substitute these figures for the quantities indicated in Jim Watson's paper (op. cit.) for wave, tidal stream and tidal barrage of around 16 GW, and add the remaining renewable technologies from this source amounting to 119 GW taking account of load factors, the total comes to about 193 GW. This amounts to more than twice the present electricity generating capacity of the UK.

The other part of the equation is the demand side and Watson's scenarios include a reduction in electricity demand of up to one third. Assuming significant gains in energy efficiency, even if half the natural assets of the UK are exploited to produce carbon-free electricity, this leaves an appreciable margin of supply over demand. The logical use for this surplus capacity is to maximise pumped storage and to create hydrogen from electrolysis. This could provide further backup capacity from megawatt grid connected fuel cells in addition to fuelling the growing population of hydrogen powered road vehicles expected over the next decade.

It has been estimated that converting transport to hydrogen would require 143 GW of electrical power to extract hydrogen from water via electrolysis.

There is no doubt that the UK has the natural assets to enable it to be fossil fuel free in meeting its electricity needs by 2030. However, this would require an immediate policy decision by the government to make a quantum leap in its investment in renewable technologies, especially the range of opportunities offered by the tides. Tidal energy could more than fill the void in supply left by the demise of nuclear. What is needed is cross-party political support so that the subject of renewable energy is removed from the cut and thrust of politics.

In his 'green speech' in March 2003 Prime Minister Blair stated that he wanted Britain 'to be a leading player in this green industrial revolution . . . We have many strengths to draw on. Some of the best marine renewable resources in the world – offshore wind, wave energy and tidal power.' This chapter suggests a 'road map' that would enable actions to be matched to words.

Chapter Four Renewable technologies – the wider spectrum

Whilst Chapter 3 has focused on marine renewable technologies with special emphasis on the UK, this chapter scans more widely to include the opportunities that occur in different climates.

The sun is the primary source of renewable energy. Besides offering a direct source of energy, it drives the Earth's climate creating opportunities to draw energy from wind, waves, tides (together with the moon) and a host of biological sources. It is particularly appropriate as an energy source for buildings. The following paragraphs are by way of an introduction. More detailed explanations will appear later.

Passive solar energy

Advocates of passive solar design have been around for many decades and the prize-winning schemes in a European competition for passive solar housing mounted in 1980 show that the technology has not advanced significantly since that time. However, the intensification of the global warming debate has led to increasing pressure to design buildings which make maximum use of free solar gains for heating, cooling and lighting. This will be considered in detail in later chapters.

Because it displaces the use of fossil fuel it is estimated that passive solar design could lead to a reduction in carbon dioxide (CO_2) amounting to 3.5 million tonnes per year in the UK alone by the year 2025 (*DOE Energy Paper 60*).

Active solar

This term refers to the conversion of solar energy into some form of usable heat. In temperate climates the most practical application of solar radiation is to exploit the heat of the sun to supplement a conventional heating system.

Communities in a situation where there are high levels of insolation can benefit from technologies not viable in temperate climes.

Solar thermal electricity

In areas where there is substantial sunshine, solar energy can be used to generate electricity in a number of ways. One method which has been successfully demonstrated is the **solar chimney**.

Designed primarily for desert locations it consists of a tall column surrounded by a glass solar collector. In effect it is a chimney surrounded by a huge solar collector or greenhouse. The air is heated by the circular greenhouse and drawn through the chimney which acts as a thermal accelerator. Within the chimney are one or more vertical axis turbines. A prototype has been built in Manzanares, Spain, with a 195 metre tower served by a greenhouse collector 240 metres in diameter. The collector warms the air by around 17°C creating an updraught of 12 metres per second giving an output of 50 kilowatts (Figure 4.1).

The project has demonstrated the viability of the principle and plans are being drawn up for a giant version in Mildura, Australia. The economics suggest that the tower would produce about 650 gigawatt hours per year or enough to serve a population of 70 000. The tower will be 1000 metres high with a solar collector of glass and plastic 7 kilometres across. The updraught would be about 15 metres per second or 54 km/hr and will drive 32 turbines at the base. The outer areas of the collector, where the temperature would be near the ambient level, would be used to grow food. The plant would operate over night by using daytime heat to warm underground water pipes connected to an insulated chamber, returning heat to the surface of the collector during the night. The scheme would carry low maintenance costs and would have a life expectancy of 100 years. Construction of the tower will consume an estimated 700 000 m³ of high strength concrete. A lookout gallery at the top of the tower promises to be a not-to-be-missed tourist attraction (see *New Scientist*, 31 July 2004, pp. 42–45).

The Almeria region of Spain is the sunniest location in Europe, achieving about 3000 hours of sun a year. This is why the area has been chosen to demonstrate another technology for producing electricity called the SolAir project. In essence it produces superheated steam to drive a turbine.

The idea has been made possible by the development of ceramics that can tolerate high temperatures. At ground level 300 large mirrors or heliostats each 70 m² track the passage of the sun and focus its rays on a silicon carbide ceramic heat absorber. The surface of the absorber reaches 1000°C. Air blown through its honeycomb structure reaches 680°C. The hot air travels down the absorber tower to a heat exchanger where it generates steam to drive a conventional turbine. The system produces up to 1 megawatt of electricity. The ceramic is also able to store heat to compensate for cloudy conditions.

According to the Spanish Ministry of Science: 'In five to ten years' time there should be several plants across Europe, each 15 to 20 times larger than the demonstration plant and together generating hundreds

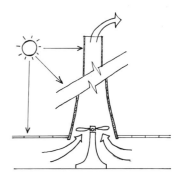

Figure 4.1
Solar chimney generator

of megawatts' (*New Scientist*, 'Power of the midday sun', 10 April 2004). At current prices it is expected to produce electricity at one third the price of photovoltaics. Plans are already in place to locate these plants along the Algerian coast to export electricity to Europe. Egypt is also warming to the possibility of this new export opportunity.

The parabolic solar thermal concentrator

This is another option for sun-drenched locations which focuses the radiation to produce intense heat – up to 800°C. A version in the United States links this to a unique helium-based Stirling engine. The concentrator mirrors produce about 30 kW of reflective power to the heat pipe receiver which is linked to the engine. The engine operates on the basis that the heat vaporises liquid sodium in its receiver at the focal point of the dish. Condensation of the sodium on the heater tubes raises the temperature of an internal helium circuit. The expanding helium drives pistons which in turn drive an alternator to produce electricity (Figure 4.2).

An alternative solar concentrator built by the Australian National University uses a computer to enable it to track the sun with extreme accuracy. This system produces superheated steam in a solar boiler at the focal point. The steam is piped to a four cylinder expansion engine that drives a 65 kVA generator.

One spin-off from this technology is a demonstration scheme which has attached 18 solar thermal power dishes to an existing coal fired steam turbine power station producing the equivalent of 2.6 MW for the grid which saves some 4500 tonnes/year of CO_2. The development

Figure 4.2
Solar concentrator, Abilene, Texas
(courtesy of CADDET)

potential is to use the waste heat from the system for co-generation. In hot dry climates an ideal application for this system is in desalination.

A variation of this principle is the SunDish Tower System of STM Power in the USA, which uses a unique type of Stirling engine with integral electricity generation within the sealed chamber (see p. 91).

Photovoltaics

The amount of energy supplied to the Earth by the sun is five orders of magnitude larger than the energy needed to sustain modern civilisation. One of the most promising systems for converting this solar radiation into usable energy is the photovoltaic (PV) cell. PV materials generate direct electrical current (DC) when exposed to light. The uniqueness of PV generation is that it is based on the 'photoelectric quantum effect in semi-conductors' which means it has no moving parts and requires minimum maintenance. Silicon is, at present, the dominant PV material which is deposited on a suitable substrate such as glass. Its disadvantages are that it is expensive; it is, as yet, capable of only a relatively low output per unit of area, and, of course, only operates during daylight hours and is therefore subject to fluctuation in output due to diurnal, climate and seasonal variation. As it produces DC current, for most purposes this has to be changed to alternating current (AC) by means of an inverter.

Growth in the manufacture of PVs has been accelerating at an extraordinary pace. In 2002 it was 56 per cent in Europe and 46 per cent in Japan, greater than in 2001. We are now seeing the emergence of large plants producing PVs on an industrial scale, that is, over 200 MW per year. The result is that unit costs have almost halved between 1996 and 2002. Significant further cost reductions are confidently predicted coupled with steady improvements in efficiency.

One application of PVs is its potential radically to improve the quality of life in the rural regions of developing countries. This is certainly one area on which the industrialised countries should focus capital and technology transfer to less and least developed countries. Already rural medical facilities are being served by PV arrays, for example the rural hospital at Dire' in Mali. On a smaller scale, compact and mobile PV arrays can operate refrigerators and water pumps.

PV technology will be considered further in Chapter 7.

Wind power

Wind is a by-product of solar power and, as with the tides, wind power has been exploited as an energy source for over 2000 years. Whilst it is an intermittent source of power, in certain countries such as the UK and Denmark, wind is a major resource. The UK has the best wind regime in

Europe but still has a considerable distance to go to meet its target of 8 per cent of total demand for wind generation by 2010.

There are two basic types of wind generator: horizontal and vertical axis. The great majority of generators in operation are of the horizontal axis type with either two or three blades. Vertical axis machines such as the helical turbine are particularly appropriate for siting on buildings.

Whilst the technology is well developed and robust, there are drawbacks to this form of power. The most frequently cited are:

- Often the most advantageous onshore sites are also places of particular natural beauty.
- Such sites are often some distance from the grid and centres of population.
- At full revolutions the noise they create can be intrusive.
- They have been implicated in interfering with television reception.
- They are a particular hazard to birds and have attracted severe criticism from the Royal Society for the Protection of Birds (RSPB).
- They are said to interfere with radar signals and have raised concerns in the Ministry of Defence.
- The output is unpredictable.

On the other hand, they are relatively cheap and in the UK can generate electricity at a cost of 7 p/kWh assuming a 20-year life and a 15 per cent rate of return (*Energy Paper 60*). Of course the required rate of return is a contentious issue, as mentioned earlier, since it takes no account of the avoided cost to both the lower and upper atmosphere with all its global warming implications.

Several of the negative factors can be overcome by locating the generators offshore. The conventional method is to fix the machine to the sea bed. The UK government announced in 2003 that it is planning a 6000 MW expansion of offshore wind generation by 2010. At that time the existing installed capacity was 570 MW. The target is, to say the least, ambitious but necessary if wind is to supply its overall share of 8 GW towards the declared 10 GW target for renewables by 2010. Two major offshore wind farms have already been installed off the coast of North Wales near Rhyl and Scroby Sands off the Norfolk coast.

Expert opinion has it that, with the best wind regime in Europe, Britain has the capacity to generate three times as much electricity by windpower as it consumes. It is estimated that it would be feasible to produce 55 TWh/y by wind generation, the majority of which would be located in Scotland. However, in practice there is a limit to the amount of unpredictable power the grid can accept and the realistic limit is said to be 32 TWh/y.

In addition to offshore sites, as sea levels rise and storm intensities increase, some exposed estuaries will need hard barrages which could serve as tidal generators as well as affording ideal sites for wind turbines.

Harbour walls also have a highly favourable wind regime and therefore offer excellent sites, as demonstrated by Blyth in Northumberland.

There is a growing market for domestic scale wind power and several firms are producing small-scale generators with an output ranging from 3.5 to 22 kW which could be installed on buildings. These turbines will be considered in more detail in Chapter 9.

Biomass and waste utilisation

The term 'biomass' refers to the concept either of growing plants as a source of energy or using plant waste such as that obtained from managed woodlands or saw mills. It is estimated that the amount of fixed carbon in land plants is roughly equivalent to that which is contained in recoverable fossil fuels (*The World Directory of Renewable Energy* (2003), p. 42, James and James, London). Whilst the economics of converting biomass and waste to energy are still somewhat uncompetitive compared with fossil fuels, the pressure to reduce CO_2 emissions combined with 'polluter pays' principles and landfill taxes for waste will change the economic balance in the medium term. Within the European Union the 'set-aside' land regulations have created an opportunity to put the land to use to create bio-fuels.

Increasing environmental pressures are stimulating the growth of waste to energy schemes. An ever increasing body of regulations is limiting the scope to dispose of waste in traditional ways. Sorted municipal solid waste (MSW) represents the greatest untapped energy resource for which conversion technology already exists.

There are three ways in which biomass and waste can be converted into energy:

- Direct combustion
- Conversion to biogas
- Conversion to liquid fuel.

Direct combustion

Direct combustion represents the greatest use of biomass for fuel worldwide. Sweden and Austria generate a significant proportion of their electricity by burning the residue from timber processing. The direct burning of municipal waste is becoming increasingly popular. However, the presence of heavy metals in such waste poses a danger from toxic emissions including, it is claimed, dioxins. In the UK there is a major plant in Lewisham in southeast London, capable of generating 30 MW of electricity (DTI Renewable Energy Case Study: 'Energy from Municipal Solid Waste', SELCHP, Lewisham). Sheffield has one of the most extensive systems using Finnish technology and providing the city centre with heat and supplying power to the grid.

The direct burning of rapid rotation crops is a technology which is said to be CO_2 efficient since the carbon emissions balance the carbon fixed during growth. However, a paper published in 1980 by Michael Allaby and James Lovelock drew attention to the risks to health associated with wood burning ('Wood stoves: the trendy pollutant', *New Scientist*, 13 November 1980). The authors identified nine compounds found in wood smoke that are known or suspected carcinogens.

The first UK commercial biomass electricity generating plant fuelled by poultry litter (a mixture of straw, wood and poultry droppings) was built at Eye, Suffolk. It has a capacity of 12.5 MW and uses about half the total of litter from broiler farms in the county. It is claimed to reduce greenhouse gas emissions by 70 per cent compared with coal-fired plants. It also eliminates the production of the powerful greenhouse gas methane and nitrates which enter the water supply. A much larger biomass plant is in operation in Thetford which consumes 450 000 tonnes per year of poultry litter to deliver 38.5 MW of power. Its environmental benefit is that it reduces net CO_2 emission by recycling carbon rather than producing new CO_2. It also eliminates methane emissions from stored poultry litter.

In the UK about 1.8 million tonnes of poultry waste and 12 million tonnes of livestock slurry are produced annually. This offers substantial biomass-to-energy conversion opportunities either as direct combustion or by using anaerobic digestion technologies.

Biogas

The most straightforward exploitation of biogas involves the tapping of methane produced by decaying waste material in landfill sites. This has a considerable environmental benefit since it burns the methane which would otherwise add more intensively to the greenhouse problem. Gas is collected using a series of vertical collection wells connected to a blower which draws gas from the waste. Foreign matter is extracted and the gas then fed to a conventional engine which drives a generator. The engine would use 'lean-burn' technology to minimise emissions of nitrogen oxides and carbon monoxide (Power generation from landfill gas; Cuxton, UK, DTI Renewable Energy Case Study 2).

Anaerobic digestion uses wet waste products to produce energy in the form of methane-rich biogas. The process, which involves a fermentation stage, takes place in large heated tanks at either 30–35°C or 55°C during which 60 per cent of the organic material is converted to biogas. The liquids and solids which remain after digestion are used as fertilisers and soil conditioners.

The methane-rich gas is most effectively employed to fuel combined heat and power (CHP) schemes which is how the technology has been employed on an ambitious scale in Denmark. Here co-operative ventures receiving waste from all the farms in a viable collection area are combined with non-toxic industrial and food waste to fuel extensive CHP networks.

The next logical step is to employ the technology to exploit the energy potential of human sewage on a national scale, thus alleviating two problems simultaneously.

One of the most promising technologies to have developed in recent years involves the gasification of municipal waste. Non-solid waste is superheated to produce methane which then fuels a steam turbine. The process involves heat recovery so that there is a commercial net energy gain in the process. The unit price of electricity generated by this process can be offset by the avoided costs of landfill disposal together with the taxes this incurs.

Liquid fuels

The advantage of converting crops to liquid fuel is that it is portable and therefore suitable for vehicles. The damage to health from low-level pollution is becoming increasingly a matter of concern and overtaking the greenhouse factor as the driving force behind the development of minimum polluting vehicles.

The world's largest experiment in alternative fuel has been taking place in Brazil since 1975. Ethanol produced from sugar cane powers about 4 million cars in that country. It produces fewer pollutants than petrol and is a net zero carbon fuel. A problem for Brazil was that world energy prices had fallen to such an extent as to make ethanol uneconomic without government subsidy. There was a danger that the ethanol programme would collapse under the weight of market forces. However, improvements in the rate of growth per hectare combined with greater use in the generation of power for the grid together with steeply rising oil prices could save the situation.

Another use for ethanol is in the creation of hydrogen for fuel cells. A mixture of ethanol, water and air is fed to a reactor which is a compact fuel cell hydrogen generator. The mixture is heated and passed through two catalysts. About half the gas emerging from the process is hydrogen. It has the potential to produce electricity for the grid using biowaste from agriculture and dedicated energy crops.

Geothermal energy

Natural hot water has been used since at least the nineteenth century for industrial purposes. The first geothermal power station was built in Italy in 1913 and produced 250 kW. Now 22 countries generate electricity using geothermal energy. However, its conversion efficiency is low, ranging from 5 to 20 per cent. Much greater efficiency is realised with the direct use of this energy for space or district heating. Then it rises to between 50 and 70 per cent.

Alternatively, hot dry rocks can supply energy by means of boreholes through which water is pumped and returned to the surface to provide space heating. This is known as the borehole heat exchanger system (BHE). In Switzerland, for example, it is a major source of energy with one borehole for every 300 persons.

If much more heat is required from the BHE in winter than can flow back in summer, a means must be found to regenerate the ground by artificial means. This opens the way for the dual use of BHEs – heat collection in winter and heat rejection in summer. With buildings they can therefore be used for both heating and cooling.

The UK was one of the leaders in the field of hot dry rocks geothermal research. However, efforts to achieve a commercial return on this energy route have proved unsuccessful and further work has been abandoned.

Hydrogen

This is widely seen as the fuel of the future and will come in for further consideration in Chapter 13. It is non-polluting, has a reasonable calorific value, and can be safely stored. Off-peak or PV electricity can be used to split water via an electrolyser to make hydrogen. This can be used as a direct fuel or to make electricity through the chemical reaction in a fuel cell (see p. 90).

Nuclear power

There are some who would place nuclear generation in the renewables category. Whilst there may be as yet no known limit to the availability of fuel for fission nuclear power stations, the problems of security, decommissioning and waste disposal remain largely unsolved. The UK's radioactive waste tally currently stands at 10 000 tonnes. For these reasons, in this context, nuclear power will remain an unsustainable energy source until its problems are solved in a way that will not impose a burden on future generations. Those opposed to nuclear generation have been encouraged by the decision of the UK government to abandon plans to construct two further pressurised water plants. The Energy White Paper of 2002 deferred a decision on nuclear expansion until 2005 on the grounds that it would then review the potential of renewable technologies to fill the impending energy gap. At the present rate of progress it would seem that this is a forlorn hope even though studies have shown that renewables can generate at least twice the capacity needed for the UK as stated earlier.

Events of 2002 have illustrated how international terrorism has reached new heights of sophistication. Some consider that it would be folly to construct a new generation of tempting targets.

There has been progress on the development of nuclear fusion – the power source that replicates the energy of the sun. The principle is that a mix of hydrogen isotopes is heated to 100 million degrees which causes their nuclei to fuse producing helium and massive amounts of energy. Powerful elecromagnetic rings called tokamaks (like a doughnut) are able to store the superheated plasmas. So far the problem has been that it has taken more energy to heat the gas to fusion temperature than is produced by the reaction. There has also been a problem of maintaining the high temperatures. However, the UK's fusion laboratory at Culham has achieved breakeven between energy input and output. A Japanese facility has achieved the same result.

Designs have been produced for the next generation of reactor by a consortium of the European Union, Japan and Russia – the International Tokamak Experimental Reactor (ITER). It is predicted to produce ten times as much power as it consumes. According to Sir David King, UK Chief Government Scientist, we could have commercial fusion electricity within 30 years. 'If successful, it could be the world's most important energy source over the next millennium' (*New Scientist*, 10 April 2004, p. 20). Unlike the present day nuclear fission reactor, fusion reactors will not produce masses of highly radioactive waste staying a hazard for 250 000 years.

Those concerned about a new generation of nuclear fission reactors should note the prediction in a Royal Commission report of 2000 that, if current trends continue, including the present rate of installing renewable technologies, then by 2050 the country will need the equivalent of 46 of the latest Sizewell B type nuclear reactors to meet demand (*Energy – The Changing Climate*, Royal Commission on Environmental Pollution Report, 2000).

Chapter Five Low energy techniques for housing

It would appear that, for the industrialised countries, the best chance of rescue lies with the built environment because buildings in use or in the course of erection are the biggest single indirect source of carbon emissions generated by burning fossil fuels, accounting for over 50 per cent of total emissions. If you add the transport costs generated by buildings the UK government estimate is 75 per cent. It is the built environment which is the sector that can most easily accommodate fairly rapid change without pain. In fact, upgrading buildings, especially the lower end of the housing stock, creates a cluster of interlocking virtuous circles.

Construction systems

Having considered the challenge presented by global warming and the opportunities to generate fossil-free energy, it is now time to consider how the demand side of the energy equation can respond to that challenge. The built environment is the greatest sectoral consumer of energy and, within that sector, housing is in pole position accounting for 28 per cent of all UK carbon dioxide (CO_2) emissions.

In the UK housing has traditionally been of masonry and since the early 1920s this has largely been of cavity construction. The purpose was to ensure that a saturated external leaf would have no physical contact with the inner leaf apart from wall ties and that water would be discharged through weep holes at the damp-proof course level. Since the introduction of thermal regulations, initially deemed necessary to conserve energy rather than the planet, it has been common practice to introduce insulation into the cavity. For a long time it was mandatory to preserve a space within the cavity and a long rearguard battle was fought by the traditionalists to preserve this 'sacred space'. Defeat was finally conceded when some extensive research by the Building Research Establishment found that there was no greater risk of damp penetration with filled cavities and in fact damp through condensation was reduced.

Solid masonry walls with external insulation are common practice in continental Europe and are beginning to make an appearance in the UK.

In Cornwall the Penwith Housing Association has built apartments of this construction on the sea front, perhaps the most challenging of situations.

The advantages of masonry construction are:

- It is a tried and tested technology familiar to house building companies of all sizes.
- It is durable and generally risk free as regards catastrophic failure – though not entirely. A few years ago the entire outer leaf of a university building in Plymouth collapsed due to the fact that the wall ties had corroded.
- Exposed brickwork is a low maintenance system; maintenance demands rise considerably if it receives a rendered finish.
- From the energy efficiency point of view, masonry homes have a relatively high thermal mass which is considerably improved if there are high density masonry internal walls and concrete floors.

Framed construction

Volume house builders are increasingly resorting to timber-framed construction with a brick outer skin, making them appear identical to full masonry construction. The attraction is the speed of erection especially when elements are fabricated off site. However, there is an unfortunate history behind this system due to shortcomings in quality control. This can apply to timber which has not been adequately cured or seasoned. Framed buildings need to have a vapour barrier to walls as well as roofs. With timber framing it is difficult to avoid piercing the barrier. There can also be problems achieving internal fixings. For the purist, the ultimate criticism is that it is illogical to have a framed building clad in masonry when it cries out for a panel, boarded, slate or tile hung external finish.

Pressed steel frames for homes are now being vigorously promoted by the steel industry. The selling point is again speed of erection but with the added benefit of a guaranteed quality in terms of strength and durability of the material.

From the energy point of view, framed buildings can accommodate high levels of insulation but have relatively poor thermal mass unless this is provided by floors and internal walls.

Innovative techniques

Permanent Insulation Formwork Systems (PIFS) are beginning to make an appearance in Britain. The principle behind PIFS is the use of precision moulded interlocking hollow blocks made from an insulation material, usually expanded polystyrene. They can be rapidly assembled on site and then filled with pump grade concrete. When the concrete has set the result is a highly insulated wall ready for the installation of services and internal and exterior finishes. They can achieve a U-value as low as 0.11 W/m²K. Above three storeys the addition of steel reinforcement is necessary.

The advantages of this system are:

- Design flexibility; almost any plan shape is possible.
- Ease and speed of erection; skill requirements are modest which is why it has proved popular with the self-build sector. Experienced erectors can achieve 5 m² per man hour for erection and placement of concrete.
- The finished product has high structural strength together with considerable thermal mass and high insulation value.

Solar design

Passive solar design

Since the sun drives every aspect of the climate it is logical to describe the techniques adopted in buildings to take advantage of this fact as 'solar design'. The most basic response is referred to as 'passive solar design'. In this case buildings are designed to take full advantage of solar gain without any intermediate operations.

Access to solar radiation is determined by a number of conditions:

- the sun's position relative to the principal facades of the building (solar altitude and azimuth);
- site orientation and slope;
- existing obstructions on the site;
- potential for overshadowing from obstructions outside the site boundary.

One of the methods by which solar access can be evaluated is the use of some form of sun chart. Most often used is the stereographic sun chart (Figure 5.1) in which a series of radiating lines and concentric circles allow the position of nearby obstructions to insolation, such as other buildings, to be plotted. On the same chart a series of sun path trajectories are also drawn (usually one arc for the 21st day of each month); also marked are the times of the day. The intersection of the obstructions' outlines and the solar trajectories indicate times of transition between sunlight and shade. Normally a different chart is constructed for use at different latitudes (at about two degree intervals).

Sunlight and shade patterns cast by the proposed building itself should also be considered. Graphical and computer prediction techniques may be employed as well as techniques such as the testing of physical models with a heliodon.

Computer modelling of shadows cast by the sun from any position is offered by Integrated Environmental Solutions (IES) with its 'Suncast'

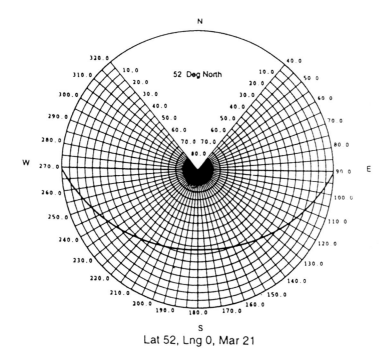

S
Lat 52, Lng 0, Mar 21

Figure 5.1
Stereographic sun chart for 21 March

program. This is a user-friendly program which should be well within normal undergraduate competence (www.ies4d.com).

The spacing between buildings is important if overshading is to be avoided during winter months when the benefit of solar heat gain reaches its peak. On sloping sites there is a critical relationship between the angle of slope and the level of overshading. For example, if over-shading is to be avoided at a latitude of 50°N, rows of houses on a 10° north-facing slope must be more than twice as far apart than on 10° south-facing slope.

Trees can obviously obstruct sunlight. However, if they are deciduous, they perform the dual function of permitting solar penetration during the winter whilst providing a degree of shading in the summer. Again spacing between trees and buildings is critical.

Passive solar design can be divided into three broad categories:

- direct gain;
- indirect gain;
- attached sunspace or conservatory.

Each of the three categories relies in a different way on the 'greenhouse effect' as a means of absorbing and retaining heat. The greenhouse effect in buildings is that process which is mimicked by global environmental warming. In buildings, the incident solar radiation is transmitted by facade glazing to the interior where it is absorbed by the internal surfaces causing warming. However, re-emission of heat back through the glazing is blocked by the fact that the radiation is of a much longer wavelength than the incoming radiation. This is because the re-emission is from surfaces at a much lower temperature and the glazing reflects back such radiation to the interior.

Direct gain

Direct gain is the design technique in which one attempts to concentrate the majority of the building's glazing on the sun-facing facade. Solar radiation is admitted *directly* into the space concerned. Two examples 30 years apart are the author's house in Sheffield, designed in 1967 (Figure 5.2) and the Hockerton Project of 1998 by Robert and Brenda Vale (Figure 5.3). The main design characteristics are:

- Apertures through which sunlight is admitted should be on the solar side of the building, within about ±30° of south for the northern hemisphere.
- Windows facing west may pose a summer overheating risk.
- Windows should be at least double glazed with low emissivity glass (Low E) as now required by the UK Building Regulations.
- The main occupied living spaces should be located on the solar side of the building.
- The floor should be of a high thermal mass to absorb the heat and provide thermal inertia, which reduces temperature fluctuations inside the building.
- As regards the benefits of thermal mass, for the normal daily cycle of heat absorption and emission, it is only about the first 100 mm of thickness which is involved in the storage process. Thickness greater than this provides marginal improvements in performance but can be useful in some longer-term storage options.
- In the case of solid floors, insulation should be beneath the slab.
- A vapour barrier should always be on the warm side of any insulation.
- Thick carpets should be avoided over the main sunlit and heat-absorbing portion of the floor if it serves as a thermal store. However, with suspended timber floors a carpet is an advantage in excluding draughts from a ventilated underfloor zone.

During the day and into the evening the warmed floor should slowly release its heat, and the time period over which it happens makes it a very suitable match to domestic circumstances when the main demand for heat is in the early evening.

As far as the glazing is concerned, the following features are recommended:

- Use of external shutters and/or internal insulating panels might be considered to reduce night-time heat loss.
- To reduce the potential of overheating in the summer, shading may be provided by designing deep eaves or external louvres. Internal

blinds are the most common technique but have the disadvantage of absorbing radiant heat thus adding to the internal temperature.
- Heat reflecting or absorbing glass may be used to limit overheating. The downside is that it also reduces heat gain at times of the year when it is beneficial.
- Light shelves can help reduce summer overheating whilst improving daylight distribution (see Chapter 14).

Figure 5.2
Passive solar house, Sheffield 1960s

Figure 5.3
Passive solar houses, Hockerton
Self-Sufficient Housing Project 1998

Figure 5.4
Hockerton individual house unit solar space

Direct gain is also possible through the glazing located between the building interior and attached sunspace or conservatory; it also takes place through upper level windows of clerestory designs. In each of these cases some consideration is required concerning the nature and position of the absorbing surfaces.

In the UK climate and latitude as a general rule of thumb room depth should not be more than two and a half times the window head height and the glazing area should be between about 25 and 35 per cent of the floor area.

Indirect gain

In this form of design a heat absorbing element is inserted between the incident solar radiation and the space to be heated; thus the heat is transferred in an indirect way. This often consists of a wall placed behind glazing facing towards the sun, and this thermal storage wall controls the flow of heat into the building. The main elements contributing to the functioning of the design are:

- High thermal mass element positioned between sun and internal spaces, the heat absorbed slowly conducts across the wall and is liberated to the interior some time later.
- Materials and thickness of the wall are chosen to modify the heat flow. In homes the flow can be delayed so that it arrives in the evening matched to occupancy periods. Typical thicknesses of the thermal wall are 20–30 cm.
- Glazing on the outer side of the thermal wall is used to provide some insulation against heat loss and help retain the solar gain by making use of the greenhouse effect.
- The area of the thermal storage wall element should be about 15–20 per cent of the floor area of the space into which it emits heat.
- In order to derive more immediate heat benefit, air can be circulated from the building through the air gap between wall and glazing and back into the room. In this modified form this element is usually referred to as a Trombe wall. Heat reflecting blinds should be inserted between the glazing and the thermal wall to limit heat build-up in summer (Figures 5.5 and 5.6).

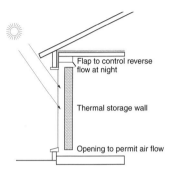

Figure 5.5
Indirect solar – Trombe wall

In countries which receive inconsistent levels of solar radiation throughout the day because of climatic factors (such as in the UK), the option to circulate air is likely to be of greater benefit than awaiting its arrival after passage through the thermal storage wall.

At times of excess heat gain the system can provide alternative benefits with the air circulation vented directly to the exterior carrying

Figure 5.6
Freiburg Solar House showing Trombe walls with blinds in operation. Note the hydrogen storage tank on the right

away its heat, at the same time drawing in outside air to the building from cooler external spaces.

Indirect gain options are often viewed as being the least aesthetically pleasing of the passive solar options, partly because of the restrictions on position and view out from remaining windows, and partly as a result of the implied dark surface finishes of the absorbing surfaces. As a result, this category of the three prime solar design technologies is not as widely used as its efficiency and effectiveness would suggest.

Attached sunspace/conservatory

This has become a popular feature in both new housing and as an addition to existing homes. It can function as an extension of living space, a solar heat store, a preheater for ventilation air or simply an adjunct greenhouse for plants (Figure 5.7). On balance it is considered that conservatories are a net *contributor* to global warming since they are often heated. Ideally the sunspace should be capable of being isolated from the main building to reduce heat loss in winter and excessive gain in summer. The area of glazing in the sunspace should be 20–30 per cent of the area of the room to which it is attached. The most adventurous sunspace so far encountered is in the Hockerton housing development which will feature later (Chapter 8 and see Figure 5.4).

Ideally the summer heat gain should be used to charge a seasonal thermal storage element to provide background warmth in winter. At the very least, air flow paths between the conservatory and the main building should be carefully controlled.

Active solar thermal systems

A distinction must be drawn between passive means of utilising the thermal heat of the sun, discussed earlier, and those of a more 'active' nature.

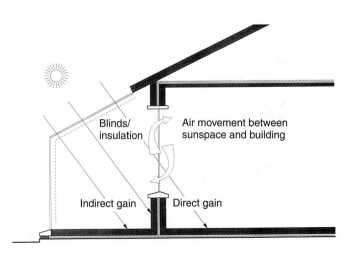

Figure 5.7
Attached sunspace

Blinds/insulation

Air movement between sunspace and building

Indirect gain   Direct gain

Active systems take solar gain a step further than passive solar. They convert direct solar radiation into another form of energy. Solar collectors preheat water using a closed circuit calorifier. The emergence of Legionella has highlighted the need to store hot water at a temperature above 60°C which means that for most of the year in temperate climes active solar heating must be supplemented by some form of heating.

Active systems are able to deliver high quality energy. However, a penalty is incurred since energy is required to control and operate the system known as the 'parasitic energy requirement'. A further distinction is the difference between systems using the thermal heat of the sun, and systems, such as photovoltaic cells, which convert solar energy directly into electrical power.

For solar energy to realise its full potential it needs to be installed on a district basis and coupled with seasonal storage. One of the largest projects is at Friedrichshafen (Figure 5.8). The heat from 5600 m²

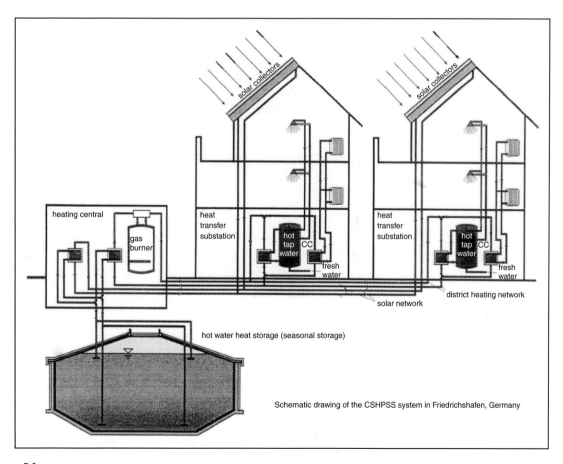

Figure 5.8
Diagram of CSHPSS system, Friedrichshafen (courtesy of Renewable Energy World (REW))

Figure 5.9
Seasonal storage tank under construction, Friedrichshafen (courtesy of REW)

of solar collectors on the roofs of eight housing blocks containing 570 apartments is transported to a central heating unit or substation. It is then distributed to the apartments as required. The heated living area amounts to 39 500 m².

Surplus summer heat is directed to the seasonal heat store which, in this case, is of the hot water variety capable of storing 12 000 m³. The scale of this storage facility is indicated by Figure 5.9.

The heat delivery of the system amounts to 1915 MWh/year and the solar fraction is 47 per cent. The month by month ratio between solar and fossil-based energy indicates that from April to November inclusive, solar energy accounts for almost total demand, being principally domestic hot water.

In places with high average temperatures and generous sunlight, active solar has considerable potential not just for heating water but also for electricity generation. This has particular relevance to less and least developed countries.

Types of solar thermal collector
The flat plate collector

These units are, as the name indicates, flat plates tilted to receive maximum solar radiation. Behind the plate are pipes which carry the heat extraction medium. There are two types of heat absorbing medium, air and water. Water containing an anti-freeze solution is the most common and is circulated behind an absorber plate to extract and transfer its heat. In the UK they are usually limited to providing domestic hot water, mainly in the summer months. To exploit their efficiency to the full there should be a heat storage facility which accepts excess heat during the summer to top up heating needs the rest of the year. However, the size of both the collectors and storage tanks makes this an uneconomic proposition in most cases.

There are four main components to the design:

- transparent cover plate;
- heat absorber plate;
- a pipe circuit to absorb and transport the heat;
- insulation behind the plate and pipes (Figures 5.10 and 5.12).

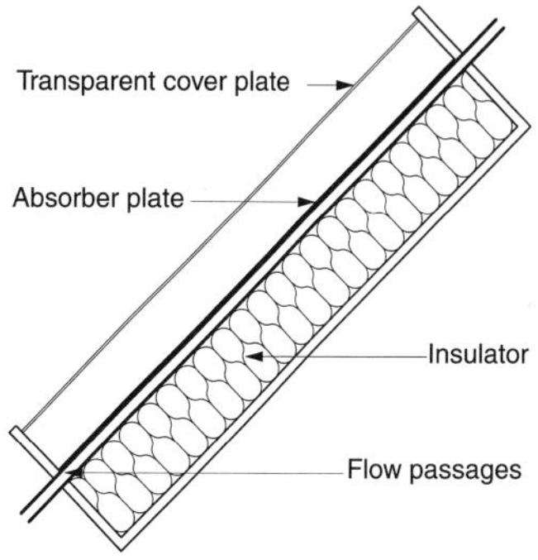

A more sophisticated version was devised for the Freiburg Solar House. The collector is placed within a semi-circular reflector. The reflected radiation means that the collector receives heat on both sides, nearly doubling its efficiency. Coupled with insulated water storage this system was able to supply all the domestic hot water for the whole year (Figure 5.11).

Evacuated tube collectors

The most recent form of collector is the evacuated tube or vacuum tube system. It works by exploiting a vacuum around the collector which reduces heat loss from the system, making it especially suitable for more temperate climes. These units heat water from 60 to 80°C which is

Figure 5.10
Flat plate collector

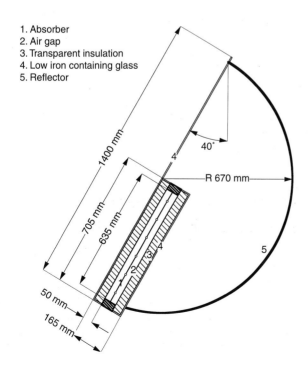

1. Absorber
2. Air gap
3. Transparent insulation
4. Low iron containing glass
5. Reflector

Figure 5.11
Double-sided solar collector, Freiburg Solar House

Figure 5.12
Flat bed solar thermal collectors, Osney Island, Oxford (courtesy of David Hammond, Architect)

sufficient for providing domestic hot water. They can continue to operate under cloudy conditions and should be linked to an insulated storage facility for continuity of supply. However, the installation cost is significantly higher than for flat bed collectors. (For more information see Smith, P.F. (2002) *Sustainability at the Cutting Edge*, Ch. 2, Architectural Press.)

Windows and glazing

In recent years there has been rapid development in the technology of the building envelope, especially in the sphere of glass. Glazing systems are now possible which react to environmental conditions such as light and heat, yet these are merely a foretaste of things to come. Also there have been considerable advances in the thermal efficiency of glazing, with U-values now commercially better than 1.0 W/m^{2}K. Table 5.1 shows the heat transfer characteristics of seven glazing systems.

Table 5.2 illustrates the impact of solar gain according to orientation by giving the net U-values.

Windows have many benefits, aside from the obvious. Nevertheless, they are the main weak thermal link when incorrectly specified. Discomfort arises in summer, not just from the rise in air temperature due to heat gains, but also due to the rise in radiant temperature from the glass surface itself. Radiant effects are further increased if the

Glazing	U-value (W/m^{2}K)
Single glazing	5.6
Double glazing	3.0
Triple glazing	2.4
Double with Low E	2.4
Double with Low E and Argon	2.2
Triple with 2 Low E and 2 Argon	1.0
Double with Aerogel	0.5–1.0

Table 5.1
Comparison of typical heat transfer through different glazing options

Glazing	U-value (W/m^{2}K) with solar gain		
	South	East/west	North
Single glazing	2.8–3.7	3.7–4.6	4.6–5.6
Double glazing	0.7–1.4	1.4–2.2	2.2–3.0
Triple glazing	0.0–0.6	0.6–1.1	1.1–2.4
Double with Low E	0.1–0.8	0.8–1.2	1.2–2.4
Triple with Low E	−0.5–0.3	0.3–0.9	0.9–1.6

Table 5.2
Effective net U-value taking account of solar heat gain

occupant experiences unshaded sunlight. In winter, cold window surfaces cool the adjacent internal air, which then falls under the buoyancy effect leading to a cold downdraught. This would also be accompanied by a cool radiant temperature. Along with the change in temperature, there may well be an asymmetric temperature field leading to greater discomfort.

As pressure has increased to improve the thermal efficiency of buildings this has forced the pace of developments in glass technology. The following are some examples.

Heat reflecting and heat absorbing glazing

These products are usually considered for application in situations where overheating poses a risk. Visible light and solar heat gain are both parts of the electromagnetic spectrum of energy emitted by the sun. The interaction of glazing with light and solar heat has three components: reflection, absorption and transmission.

Modifications in the proportions of reflected, absorbed and transmitted radiation could be engineered by changing the glazing system properties. There are several ways of achieving this:

- using 'body tinted' glass, which increases absorption;
- using reflective coatings, which increase the reflected component and, usually, the absorbed component;
- using combinations of body tinted and reflective coatings.

It must be remembered that a reduction in solar heat gain can only be achieved at the cost of reducing daylight transmission, though some tinting and reflective products are more selective than others. The reflected component can be increased by changing the angle of incidence – the more acute the angle, the greater the reflection.

Body tinted glass is normally available in a range of colours including grey, green, bronze and blue. The tinting is produced by the addition of small amounts of metal oxides during production, and it is present throughout the thickness of the glass. The effect is to increase the absorption of the radiation within the glazing, reducing the directly transmitted component. However, the heat absorbed must be dissipated as the glass temperature increases. The warmth of the glass transmits heat inwards as well as outwards. Because of this the body tinted layer would normally be installed as the outer pane of a multi-pane unit. Though body tinted glass has an effect on heat transmission it also has aesthetic implications.

For improved solar heat gain attenuation, reflective coated glass has a better performance. The coating is applied to the surface of the glass which must be installed on the side facing in towards the cavity of a sealed unit, or by applying a second laminating layer.

Reflective coatings are available in a wide range of colours and with a wide range of performance specifications. It is easier to specify and produce a glass with specific properties for a specific application than with body tinted varieties. In hot climates, glazing is specified to reduce heat gain, both by direct solar transmission, which can be as low as 10 per cent in some cases, and by conduction. To achieve this second aim, a double glazed unit with a reflective outer layer is combined with a low emissivity coated inner layer to reflect outwards the heat which is transmitted. Avoidance of glare and the provision of some natural light and view, are also considerations. In temperate climates a balance must be struck between control of summer heat gain and the benefits of winter sun, plus the fact that higher levels of natural daylight are required. No two situations are quite the same and it is important to consider the full range of options before choosing a particular product or glazing system.

Photochromic, thermochromic and electrochromic glass

Each of these terms describes a variety of glazing in which the transmission properties are variable. Extensive opportunities exist for the development of some of these technologies to allow dynamic control of light and heat gain to match building and occupant requirements. Photochromic devices change transmission in response to prevailing radiation levels. Small examples have been in everyday use for some years in the form of sunglasses and spectacles. These react automatically to light levels. There are considerable technical problems to scaling up photochromic glass to normal window size.

Thermochromic glass has changing optical properties in response to temperature variations. It has a laminated structure incorporating a chemical which turns opaque at around 30°C, reducing insolation by about 70 per cent. For this reason an ideal application is as external solar shading. As it reacts to heat it may not be so suitable for windows since it could react to the internal temperature and again cannot be independently controlled.

The most refined and controllable of the three options is electrochromic glass, the properties of which can be changed by the application of a small electrical current. Their construction consists of complex multi-layered transparent coatings. The electrical signal reduces the transmission capacity of the electrochromic layer between two sheets of glass affecting not only daylight but also solar heat.

The latest version from Pilkington is EControl glass which can, at the flick of a switch, cut out over 80 per cent of solar radiation. It can also achieve an airborne sound insulation level of 42 dB using thicker internal glass and a special sound insulating gas between the panes. Pilkington is also developing a solid state electrochromic glass, in other words, without any applied coatings.

Capital cost savings in terms of reduced cooling requirements and the exclusion of blinds plus revenue savings in respect of lower energy costs make electrochromic glass an attractive option, especially since it can be controlled by the occupants – a major factor in workplace satisfaction.

Pilkington has recently marketed a self-cleaning or 'hydrophilic' glass known commercially as 'Pilkington Activ'. Rainwater forms an overall film on the glass rather than collecting in drops that deposit dirt which remains after drying. This should offer significant revenue cost savings in maintenance, especially for commercial buildings.

Romag, a company specialising in laminated glass, has joined with BP Solar to produce a composite glass which incorporates PV cells. It will be marketed as PowerGlaz and should be available towards the end of 2004. It will be available in a range of sizes up to 3.3 × 2.2 metres.

Chapter Six   Insulation

Warmth is a valuable commodity and it will seek every possible means of escape from walls, roofs, windows and floors. Most UK buildings make escape easy.

Heat flow through building components can be modified by the choice of materials. The main heat transfer process for solid, opaque building elements is by conduction. Thermal insulation, which provides a restriction to heat flow, is used to reduce the magnitude of heat flow in a 'resistive' manner. Since air provides good resistance to heat flow, many insulation products are based upon materials that have numerous layers or pockets of air trapped within them. Such materials are thus low density and lightweight, and, in most cases, not capable of giving structural strength. Generally, the higher the density, the greater the heat flow. Since structural components are often, of necessity, rather high in density, they are unable to provide the same level of resistive insulation. Warmth is a valuable commodity and it will seek every possible means to escape from a building. Walls, roofs, floors, chimneys, windows are all escape routes.

It may be necessary to provide additional layers of insulation around them to prevent such elements acting as weak links or 'cold bridges' in the thermal design.

Increased levels of insulation are a cost-effective way of reducing heating energy consumption. In several domestic and other small buildings, it has already been demonstrated that the additional costs of insulation can be offset against a much reduced cost for the heating system involving a whole building radiator and central boiler option.

When specifying insulation materials it is important avoid those which are harmful to the environment such as materials involving chlorofluorocarbons (CFCs) in the production process and to select materials with zero ozone depletion potential (ZODP). Insulation materials fall into three main categories:

- Inorganic/mineral – these include products based on silicon and calcium (glass and rock) and are usually evident in fibre boards, e.g. glass fibre and 'Rockwool'.

- Synthetic organic – materials derived from organic feedstocks based on polymers.
- Natural organic – vegetation-based materials like hemp and lamb's wool which must be treated to avoid rot or vermin infestation.

For fibrous materials such as glass and mineral fibres there is a theoretical risk of cancer and non-malignant diseases like bronchitis. This is a matter that is still under review (Thomas, R. (ed.) (1996) *Environmental Design*, E & FN Spon).

The range of insulation options

There are numerous alternatives when it comes to choosing insulation materials. They differ in thermal efficiency and in offering certain important properties like resistance to fire and avoidance of ozone depleting chemicals. Some also lose much their insulating efficiency if affected by moisture. So, at the outset it is advisable to understand something about the most readily available insulants. The thermal efficiency of an insulant is denoted by its thermal conductivity, termed lambda value, measured in W/mK. The thermal conductivity of a material 'is the amount of heat transfer per unit of thickness for a given temperature difference' (Thomas, R. (ed.) (1996) *Environmental Design*, E & FN Spon, p. 10). Technically it is a measure of the rate of heat conduction through 1 cubic metre of a material with a 1°C temperature difference across the two opposite faces. The lower the value the more efficient the material.

Inorganic/mineral-based insulants

Inorganic/mineral-based insulants come in two forms, fibre or cellular structure.

Fibre

Rock wool
Rock wool is produced by melting a base substance at high temperature and spinning it into fibres with a binder added to provide rigidity. It is vapour and air permeable due to its structure. Moisture can build up in the insulant reducing its insulating value. May degrade over time. Lambda value 0.033–0.040 W/mK.

Glass wool
As for rock wool.

Health and safety

There is a health issue with fibrous materials. Some cause skin irritation and it is advisable to wear protective gear during installation. Loose fill fibre insulants should not be ventilated to internal habitable spaces. There has been the suggestion that fibrous materials constitute a cancer risk. However, they are currently listed as 'not classifiable as to carcinogenicity in humans'.

Cellular

Cellular glass
Manufactured from natural materials and over 40 per cent recycled glass. It is impervious to water vapour and is waterproof, dimensionally stable, non-combustible, vermin-proof and has high compressive strength as well as being CFC and HCFC free.

Lambda value 0.037–0.047 depending on particular application. Typical proprietary brand: Foamglas by Pittsburgh Corning (UK) Ltd.

Vermiculite
Vermiculite is the name given to a group of geological materials that resemble mica. When subject to high temperature the flakes of vermiculite expand due to their water content to many times their original size to become 'exfoliated vermiculite'. It has a high insulation value, is resistant to decay, odourless, and non-irritant.

Organic/synthetic insulants

Organic/synthetic insulants are confined to cellular structure:

EPS (expanded polystyrene)
Rigid, flame retardant cellular, non-toxic, vapour resistant plastic insulation, CFC and HCFC free.

Lambda value 0.032–0.040 W/mK.

XPS (extruded polystyrene)
Closed cell insulant water and vapour tight, free from CFCs and HCFCs.

Lambda value 0.027–0.036 W/mK.

PIR (polyisocyanurate)
Cellular plastic foam, vapour tight, available CFC and HCFC free.

Lambda value 0.025–0.028 W/mK.

Phenolic
Rigid cellular foam very low lambda value, vapour tight, good fire resistance, available CFC and HCFC free.

Lambda value 0.018–0.019 W/mK.

In general, cellular materials do not pose a health risk and there are no special installation requirements.

Natural/organic insulants

Fibre structure

Cellulose   Mainly manufactured from recycled newspapers. Manufactured into fibres, batts or boards. Treated with fire retardant and pesticides.
Lambda value 0.038–0.040 W/mK.

Sheep's wool   Must be treated with a boron and a fire retardant. Disposal may have to be at specified sites.
Lambda value 0.040 W/mK.

Flax   Treated with polyester and boron.
Lambda value 0.037 W/mK.

Straw   Heat treated and compressed into fibre boards. Treated with fire retardant and pesticide. It can be used as a wall material with a high thermal efficiency. In its present day form it should be much more reliable than the strawboard of the 1960s which had a tendency to germinate.
Lambda value 0.037 W/mK.

Hemp   Under development as a compressed insulation board. A highly eco-friendly material, grows without needing pesticides and produces no toxins. Initial tests have used hemp as a building material mixed with lime and placed like concrete. Test houses have proved as thermally efficient as identical well-insulated brick built houses built alongside the hemp examples.

Main points

Insulation materials should be free from HFCs and HCFCs:

- The choice of insulation material is governed primarily by two factors: thermal conductivity and location in the home.
- The ecological preference is for materials derived from organic or recycled sources and which do not use high levels of energy during production. However, there are certain overriding factors which will be described below.

Embodied energy, that is, energy involved in the extraction and manufacturing process, is also a factor to consider. Insulation materials derived from mineral fibres tend to be among the lowest in embodied energy and also CO_2 emissions. However, overall the use of insulation saves many times the embodied energy of even the worst cases, for example 200 times for expanded polystyrene and 1000 times for glass fibre.

Table 6.1
Summary of comparative performance
of insulation materials

	Thermal conductivity (W/mK)
Expanded polystyrene slab	0.035
Extruded polystyrene	0.030
Glass fibre quilt	0.040
Glass fibre slab	0.035
Mineral fibre slab	0.035
Phenolic foam	0.020
Polyurethane board	0.025
Cellulose fibre	0.035

Table 6.1 shows the thermal conductivity of the main insulants.

Finally, there is the factor of internal strength or friability. Rockwool products are among the most stable in this respect. Extruded polystyrene foams are attractive to house builders because they have good water resistance and a stiffness that enables them to be used in cavities.

High and superinsulation

In recent years attention has been focused towards the use of very thick layers of insulation within the building fabric in order to minimise heat flow. This technique has become known as superinsulation. The use of superinsulation has so far been best demonstrated at the domestic scale. This may be partly due to the problems of overheating experienced in many larger, deeper plan commercial buildings, problems which override the benefits of reduced winter heating requirements. In the future, however, buildings which exhibit less tendency to overheat due to better environmental design may modify the priorities and make superinsulation attractive in all circumstances where buildings experience cold seasons.

Superinsulation is associated with several design features:

- To qualify as superinsulated the building fabric should have U-values that are less than 0.2 W/m²K for all major non-transparent elements and often below 0.1 W/m²K.
- Insulation thickness is often constrained by accepted construction techniques, for instance by allowable cavity widths in cavity wall construction.
- A broader definition of superinsulation is one which specifies a maximum overall building heat loss which permits 'trade-offs' within certain limits, rather than individual component values, for example by an allowance for solar gain.

- In the case of *low-energy* housing, the typical thickness of insulation material is likely to be of the order of 150 mm in walls and 300 mm in roofs (Figure 6.1); *superinsulated* walls may have 200–300 mm with 400 mm in the roof (Figure 6.2).
- Achieving a superinsulation standard also requires a high level of air tightness of the building envelope which means that there will need to be trickle ventilation or even mechanical ventilation with heat recovery to reinforce the 'stack effect' in order to provide one to two air changes per hour.

With cavities of 200–300 mm width it is essential to have rigid wall ties of either stainless steel or tough rigid plastic.

The Jaywick Sands development is a social housing project which is designed on sustainability principles. Its 'breathing' walls consist of

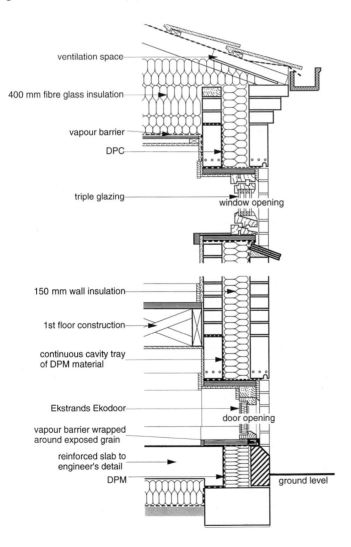

ventilation space

400 mm fibre glass insulation

vapour barrier

DPC

triple glazing
window opening

150 mm wall insulation

1st floor construction

continuous cavity tray of DPM material

Ekstrands Ekodoor
door opening

vapour barrier wrapped around exposed grain

reinforced slab to engineer's detail

DPM
ground level

Figure 6.1
Section, typical low energy construction

Figure 6.2
Superinsulation in the Autonomous
House, Southwell (courtesy of Robert
and Brenda Vale)

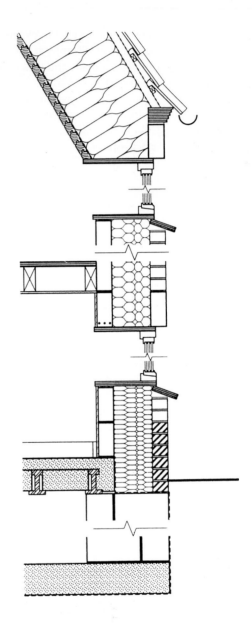

partially prefabricated storey height structural panels (Figure 6.3). They
are filled with 170 mm Warmcell insulation and clad with 9 mm sheathing board faced with a breather membrane. The exterior finish is western red cedar boards on battens. The floor is a pot and beam precast
concrete slab with 60 mm rigid insulation on the upper surface. It can
be argued that the insulation would have been better on the underside
of the concrete to allow the slab to provide a degree of thermal
mass (the scheme is described in detail in *The Architects Journal*,
23 November 2000).

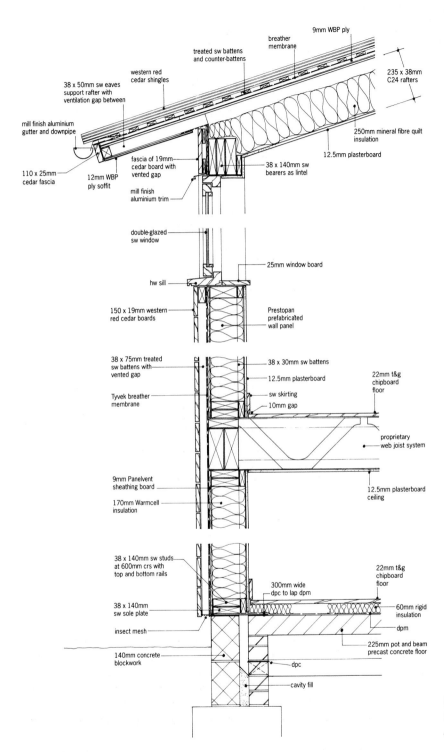

9mm WBP ply

breather membrane

treated sw battens and counter-battens

western red cedar shingles

235 x 38mm C24 rafters

38 x 50mm sw eaves support rafter with ventilation gap between

mill finish aluminium gutter and downpipe

250mm mineral fibre quilt insulation

12.5mm plasterboard

fascia of 19mm cedar board with vented gap

38 x 140mm sw bearers as lintel

110 x 25mm cedar fascia

12mm WBP ply soffit

mill finish aluminium trim

double-glazed sw window

25mm window board

hw sill

150 x 19mm western red cedar boards

Prestopan prefabricated wall panel

38 x 75mm treated sw battens with vented gap

38 x 30mm sw battens

12.5mm plasterboard

22mm t&g chipboard floor

Tyvek breather membrane

sw skirting

10mm gap

proprietary web joist system

9mm Panelvent sheathing board

170mm Warmcell insulation

12.5mm plasterboard ceiling

38 x 140mm sw studs at 600mm crs with top and bottom rails

22mm t&g chipboard floor

300mm wide dpc to lap dpm

38 x 140mm sw sole plate

60mm rigid insulation

insect mesh

dpm

140mm concrete blockwork

225mm pot and beam precast concrete floor

dpc

cavity fill

Figure 6.3
Low energy timber panel housing,
Jaywick Sands, Essex

75

On mainland Europe solid wall construction is much more common than in the UK. An example is the Zero-energy House at Wadenswil, Switzerland. The structural wall consists of 150 mm dense concrete blocks. These are faced with 180 mm of extruded polystyrene insulation protected by external cladding. The walls have a U-value of 0.15 W/m²K. The roof has 180 mm of mineral fibre insulation giving it a U-value of 0.13 W/m²K.

Timber framed windows are triple glazed with Low-E coatings and an argon gas filled cavity achieving a U-value of 1.2 W/m²K. North facing windows are quadruple glazed achieving a U-value of 0.85 W/m²K.

Air tightness is a prime consideration at this level of energy efficiency. Pressure tested to 50 pascals (Pa) the rate of air change was 0.4 per hour. Polycarbonate honeycomb collectors absorb solar radiation to heat domestic water to 25°C even on cloudy days. Space heating is also supplied by solar collectors and delivered in pipes embedded in the concrete floors. This is supplemented by a heat storage facility and backup liquid petroleum gas (LPG) heater unit. The annual energy consumption is around 14 kWh/m² excluding solar energy (Figure 6.4).

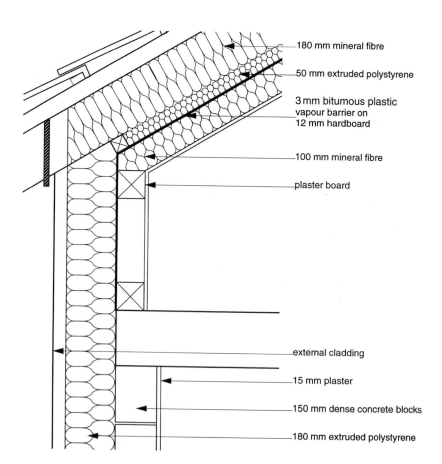

180 mm mineral fibre

50 mm extruded polystyrene

3 mm bitumous plastic vapour barrier on 12 mm hardboard

100 mm mineral fibre

plaster board

external cladding

15 mm plaster

150 mm dense concrete blocks

180 mm extruded polystyrene

Figure 6.4
Section of the Wadenswil House

Transparent insulation materials

Transparent insulation materials (usually abbreviated to TIMs) are a class of product which make use of particular materials to enhance the solar heat gain whilst simultaneously reducing the heat loss by conduction and radiation. The technology has similarities to the passive solar thermal mass wall designs already described, except the gap between glazed outer skin and the surface of the wall which faces into it contains insulation which is transparent rather than just air. The insulation allows transmission of the incoming solar radiation but acts as a barrier to conductive and radiative heat loss, retaining absorbed heat very effectively. Aerogels are a form of translucent insulation material which is located within a glazing sandwich.

Aerogels

Aerogels are materials that are mostly air – usually around 99 per cent by volume – and can be fabricated from silica, metals even rubber. They are extremely light. For example, a cubic metre of silica glass would weigh about 2000 kilograms. A silica aerogel block of the same dimensions would weigh 20 kilograms. Despite this aerogels are relatively strong. They are sometimes called 'frozen smoke' due to their translucent appearance. In the case of the silica aerogel it consists of tiny dense silica particles about 1 nanometre across which link up to form a gel.

Aerogels are excellent insulators, having about one hundredth the thermal conductivity of glass. Double glazing which replaced the gap with an aerogel would improve the insulation value by a factor of three as against the very best current multiple glazing. It would be possible to achieve a 99 per cent vacuum between the panes since they are supported by a solid. However, even with a thin aerogel sandwich the window would have a slightly frosted appearance.

The thermal properties of aerogels also make them ideal for harvesting solar heat. Flat plate solar panels collect heat then radiate it back into space. An aerogel glass sandwich would provide a one-way barrier to the re-radiation of heat from the absorbing surface. This would have an obvious application in active solar panels and also in solar walls. The outer surface of the wall would be coated black to maximise absorption. Faced with a glass aerogel screen the heat would be retained and radiated into the interior of the building. A blind behind a glazed rain screen would minimise an excessive build-up of heat in summer (Figure 6.5). The Freiburg Solar House shows Trombe walls with some blinds lowered (Figure 5.6).

Insulation – the technical risks

The use of high levels of insulation brings with it some risks. Some problems relate to the presence of moisture within the building

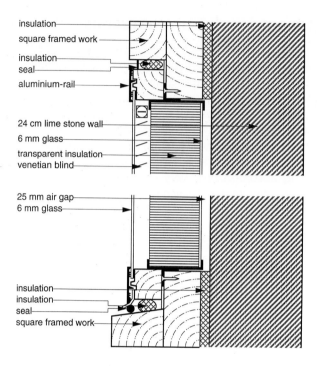

insulation
square framed work
insulation
seal
aluminium-rail

24 cm lime stone wall
6 mm glass
transparent insulation
venetian blind

25 mm air gap
6 mm glass

insulation
insulation
seal
square framed work

Figure 6.5
Transparent/translucent insulation wall

construction which, because the temperature gradient has been changed by the presence of insulation, condenses into water. This can lead to several difficulties such as rotting, rusting or other degradation of components, and in addition can pose a safety risk if it comes into contact with electrical circuitry. Some insulation materials absorb moisture, and when wet, their insulating effect is very much reduced. Cavity insulation should be treated with a water repellent.

If substantial variations exist between the insulation levels of different parts of the building fabric, this creates weak links, which then become the main cold bridges or 'thermal bridges'. It is on the inner surfaces of such cold bridges that condensation will occur. The answer is to ensure continuity of insulation. The problem mainly occurs at the junction between main structural components, for example:

- at the junction of roof and wall;
- or wall and floor;
- around windows and doors, particularly frames and lintels;
- around apertures for building services – electrical, water, drainage, etc.;
- at positions where structural framing elements connect with roofs, walls and floors.

When considering floors, the majority of the heat loss occurs at its exposed edges. Particular attention must therefore be paid to ensuring adequate and correctly designed insulation details at floor edges.

The use of vapour barriers becomes more important as insulation levels rise, since it is the appropriate construction and positioning of such layers that reduces condensation risk. It is advisable to carry out a technical assessment of the condensation risk if this is suspected of being a problem. It is even more important to design components correctly and ensure that the construction is carried out according to the specification. A large proportion of the reported faults associated with condensation are attributable to poor workmanship. As stated earlier, as a general principle, vapour barriers should always be on the warm side of the insulation, otherwise they will actually cause condensation.

Chapter Seven   Domestic energy

Electricity produced by a stand-alone system within, or linked to, a building is called 'embedded' energy generation. By far the most convenient form of renewable energy system which can be linked to housing is photovoltaic cells. As unit costs fall PV arrays attached to individual houses will become increasingly evident. In several countries there are substantial state subsidies to kick-start the PV industry so that costs can quickly fall due to the economy of scale. One of the pioneer examples of a domestic application in the UK is the Autonomous House by Robert and Brenda Vale in Southwell, Nottinghamshire (Figure 7.1).

Photovoltaic systems

As stated earlier PV cells have no moving parts, create no noise in operation, and seem attractive from both aesthetic and scientific perspectives.

Figure 7.1
Remote PV array, Autonomous House, Southwell, also with an indication of the sunspace

Power output is constrained by the availability of light falling on the cell, though significant output is still possible with overcast skies.

The development of PV cells is gathering pace as indicated by the fact that the manufacturing capacity for PVs increased by 56 per cent in Europe and 46 per cent in Japan alone between 2001 and 2002. The greatest potential growth area is with building integrated PVs within facade and roof components. Examples of PV integrated cladding include the adaptation of rain screens, roof tiles and windows.

The advantages of building integrated systems are:

- clean generation of electricity;
- generation at its point of use within the urban environment thus avoiding infrastructure costs and line losses;
- no additional land requirements.

As a result a number of national and international development programmes now exist to help exploit the opportunities offered.

Germany has been one of the frontrunners in promoting the application of PVs to buildings. Its Renewable Energy Law offered significant added value to the production of electricity from domestic PV roofs. Its initial target of 100 000 PV roofs has been surpassed. This law has recently been re-enacted and a further 100 000 PV roofs target has been instigated.

The principle of photovoltaic cells (PVs)

PVs are devices which convert light directly into electricity. At present most PVs consist of two thin layers of a semi-conducting material, each layer having different electrical characteristics. In most common PV cells both layers are made from silicon but with different, finely calculated amounts of impurities: p-type and n-type. The introduction of impurities is known as 'doping'. As a result of the doping one layer of silicon is negatively charged (n-type) and has a surplus of electrons. The other layer is given a positive charge (p-type) and an electron deficit. These two neighbouring regions generate an electrical field. When light falls on a PV cell electrons are liberated by the radiative energy from the sun and able to migrate from one side to the other. Some of the electrons are captured as useful energy and directed to an external circuit (Figure 7.2).

Cells with different characteristics and efficiencies can be created by using different base and doping materials. The output is direct current (DC) which must be changed to alternating current (AC) by means of an inverter if it is to be fed to the grid. Converting to AC current involves a power loss.

The capacity of cells to convert light into electricity is defined by watts peak (Wp). This is based on a bench test and is the power generated by a PV under light intensity of 1000 watts per square metre, equivalent to bright sun. The efficiency of a cell is a function of both peak output and area. This is a laboratory measurement and does not necessarily give a true indication of energy yield.

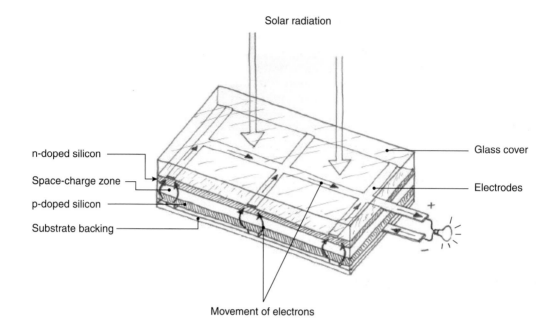

Solar radiation

n-doped silicon

Space-charge zone

p-doped silicon

Substrate backing

Glass cover

Electrodes

Movement of electrons

Figure 7.2
Photovoltaic cell structure and function

At the time of writing the most efficient PVs are monocrystalline silicon consisting of wafers of a pure crystal of silicon. They achieve a peak output of about 15 per cent. That means that 15 per cent of daylight is converted to electricity when daylight is at its maximum intensity. Due to the production processes involved these cells are expensive.

The solar cell size of around 10 cm × 10 cm has a peak output of about 1.5 watts. To realise a usable amount of electricity cells are wired into modules which, in turn, are electrically connected to form a string. One or more strings form an array of modules.

The cells are sandwiched between an upper layer of toughened glass and a bottom layer of various materials including glass, Tedlar or aluminium. It must be remembered that a number of linked cells produces a significant amount of current, therefore during installation solar cells should be covered whilst all the electrical connections are made.

Polycrystalline silicon

In the production process of this cell, molten silicon is cast in blocks containing random crystals of silicon. In appearance cells are blue and square. It is cheaper than a monocrystalline cell but has a lower efficiency ranging between 8 and 12 per cent.

A variation of silicon technology has been developed by Spheral Solar of Cambridge, Ontario. It consists of 1 mm diameter silicon balls made from waste silicon from the chip making industry. The core of each sphere is doped to make it a p-type semi-conductor and the outer surface to make it an n-type semi-conductor. Each sphere is therefore a miniature

PV cell. The spheres are contained within a flexible aluminium and plastic matrix producing an effect similar to blue denim. The system has a claimed efficiency of 11 per cent and can be formed to almost any profile, which should make it attractive to architects. It is planned to market it during 2005.

Amorphous silicon

This cell does not have a crystalline structure but is stretched into thin layers which can be deposited on a backing material which can be rigid or flexible. It is the first of a new breed of PVs based on thin film technology. By building up layers tuned to different parts of the solar spectrum known as a double or triple junction cell, a peak efficiency of 6 per cent is achievable. Unlike the crystalline cells it is capable of bulk production and is therefore potentially much cheaper.

Cadmium telluride (CdTe) and copper indium diselenide (CIS)

These cells are a further development of thin film technology, having efficiencies of about 7 per cent and 9 per cent respectively. At present prices are comparatively high but will reduce as volume of sales increases.

In summary, costs range between £2 and £4 per Wp. However, unit cost is not necessarily the only criterion. Different cells have varying optimum conditions which has been highlighted by a research programme recently completed by the Oxford University Environmental Change Institute. This showed that the amount of electricity generated by a PV array rated at 1 kWp in one year varies considerably between different technologies. For example, CIS (Seimens ST 40) gave the best returns at over 1000 kWh per kWp per year in the UK. Double junction amorphous silicon cells were close behind. This is because these cells are more effective in the cloudy conditions so prevalent in the UK. Single junction amorphous silicon cells were the poorest performers. The best performing modules produced nearly twice as much power as the lowest yielding cells, so it is very much a case of 'buyer beware'.

A sloping roof facing a southerly direction is the ideal situation, provided it is not overshadowed by trees or other buildings. However, east and west orientations can produce significant amounts of electricity. The optimum angle of tilt depends on latitude. In London it is 35°. As a rough guide, in London 1 square metre of monocrystalline PVs could produce 111 kWh of electricity per year. On low pitch or flat roofs it is advisable to mount the cells on tilt structures at the correct orientation. However, in the UK climate, a flat roof can still deliver 90 per cent of the optimum output.

Standard PV modules can easily be fixed to an existing roof. However, if a roof covering needs to be replaced, it then could become a cost-effective option to use solar slates, tiles or shingles to maintain a traditional appearance.

A housing project which integrates PVs into its elevations and roofs is the Beddington Zero Energy Development (BedZED) in the London Borough of Sutton, designed by Bill Dunster with Arup as the services engineers. Originally the intention was to use their power to meet the needs of the buildings. The problem was the extent of the expected payback time at current low energy prices. Their purpose is now to provide battery charging for a pool of electric vehicles for the residents which has the advantage of avoiding conversion to AC current (Figure 7.4).

It is important to ventilate PV cells since their efficiency falls as temperature increases. This requirement has been put to good use in a restaurant

Figure 7.4
Southern elevation, BedZED housing development, South London

in North Carolina, USA. Its integrated roof system has 32 amorphous PV modules serving a 20 kWh battery facility. This supplements demand at peak times and also bridges interruptions in the grid supply.

What makes this system special is the fact that warmth that builds up under the cells is harnessed to heat water which supplements space heating. A fan circulates air through a series of passages beneath the modules. As solar heat builds up, the fan cuts in automatically to circulate heat away from the PVs and direct it in a closed loop to a heat exchanger. This technology will save the restaurant about $3000 per year in utility and hot water costs, at the same time avoiding 22 680 kg of CO_2 emissions (Figure 7.5). See also Figure 18.16, p. 234.

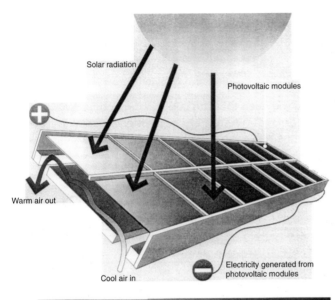

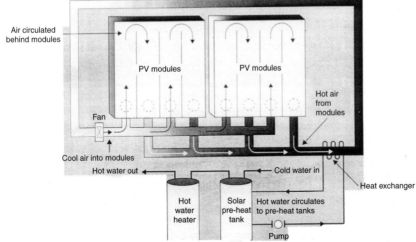

Figure 7.5
Diagrams of PV heat recovery system (courtesy of CADDET)

Energy output

The energy output from a monocrystalline cell varies with insolation level in an almost linear fashion across its operating range. Output is adversely affected by high operating temperature with a drop in efficiency from about 12 per cent at 20°C to about 10 per cent at 50°C.

Photovoltaic panels would need active cooling in many building situations to maintain maximum output during summer months. Clearly this is impractical and costly and at present the drop in efficiency has to be accepted. An alternative is to encourage ventilation of the panels by suitable design of their location and position in order to permit air flow and natural ventilation cooling to front and, if possible, rear of the array.

Since most uses of electricity require alternating current (AC), as stated earlier, an inverter must be employed. However, in the US PVs are now available from the Applied Power Corporation which deliver AC electricity which means they can be connected directly to the grid. An AC inverter is integrated with the cells (CADDET Renewable Energy Newsletter, March 2000).

It is often the case that the supply of electrical energy is not concurrent with demand, perhaps because of occupancy and use patterns. In such situations two alternatives exist: either the excess power can be stored in some form of battery or used to heat water to be stored in an insulated tank to provide space heating. Alternatively it can simply be offloaded to the electricity grid. The former of these options causes an energy loss in the conversion process and additionally requires the provision of a suitable and substantial battery store. The preferred option in most urban situations at the present time is the grid-connected system, though a sophisticated control system is required to ensure the output matches the grid phase. This also provides a backup supply when PV generation is insufficient. A major drawback at present is the price at which the utility companies purchase the excess PV production.

Pressure is mounting for the adoption of reversible meters that accumulate credit units from a renewable on-site installation but this is being resisted by some energy companies. The UK has some of the worst buy-back rates in Europe, currently about 5 p per unit as against the utility price of approximately 15 p. A combination of high capital cost and miserly buy-in rates is seriously undermining the adoption of this technology by householders in the UK in contrast to Germany where subsidised demand is outstripping manufacturing capacity.

It may be easier to justify the cost of PV cladding materials for commercial buildings where occupancy patterns coincide with peak production levels.

PV cladding materials can now be obtained in different patterns and colours depending upon the nature of the cells and the backing material to which they are applied. This offers an increasing range of facade options which might be exploited by architects to create particular aesthetic effects. Thin film photovoltaic systems, which basically have a layer of a coating layer applied to glass, look particularly promising.

In the Netherlands PV cells are being mounted on motorway sound barriers. The UK Highways Agency gave approval in 2004 for PVs to be mounted in panels alongside motorways. A pilot project array has been installed on the M27 in Hampshire to feed directly into the national grid.

Micro-combined heat and power (CHP)

It is interesting how two nineteenth century technologies, the Stirling engine and the fuel cell, are only now coming into their own. Invented by Robert Stirling in 1816, the engine that bears his name is described as an 'external combustion engine'. This is because heat is applied to the outside of the unit to heat up a gas within a sealed cylinder. The heat source is at one end of the cylinder whilst the cooling takes place at the opposite end. The internal piston is driven by the successive heating and cooling of the gas. When the gas is heated it expands, pushing down the piston. In the process the gas is cooled and then pushed to the heated top of the cylinder by the returning piston, once again to expand and repeat the process. Because of advances in piston technology and in materials like ceramics from the space industry and high temperature steels allowing temperatures to rise to 1200°C, it is now considered a firm contender for the micro-heat-and-power market.

Heat can be drawn off the engine to provide space heating for a warm air or wet system. Alternatively it can supply domestic hot water. In one system on the market, 'Whispergen', the vertical motion of the piston is converted to circular motion to power a separate generator.

MicroGen is currently conducting trials of a Stirling CHP system in which the generator is contained within the cylinder. At the heart of the system is a unique technology developed by Sunpower in the US. This consists of a sealed chamber containing a single piston integrated with an alternator. At the top of the piston there is a magnate which interacts with the alternator coil to produce electricity at 240 volts single phase. (Figure 7.6)

The top of the chamber is heated to a temperature of 500°C whilst the lower part is water cooled to 45°C creating the necessary pressure difference in the captive gas. The MicroGen unit is designed to produce 1.1 kW of electricity which is considered to be adequate for base load for most domestic requirements. Any further load will be drawn from the grid in the normal way.

Because the system is strictly controlled to 240 volts and 50 Hz it is compatible with mains electricity and therefore it is claimed that it can be linked directly to the domestic ring main. It will be possible to feed

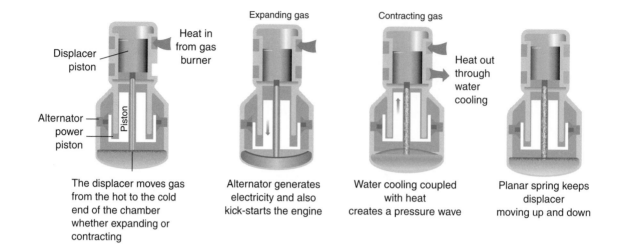

Expanding gas

Contracting gas

Displacer piston

Heat in from gas burner

Heat out through water cooling

Alternator power piston

Piston

The displacer moves gas from the hot to the cold end of the chamber whether expanding or contracting

Alternator generates electricity and also kick-starts the engine

Water cooling coupled with heat creates a pressure wave

Planar spring keeps displacer moving up and down

Figure 7.6
Four phases of the Stirling engine cycle

excess electricity to the grid. The four phases of the Stirling cycle are explained in Figure 7.6.

As regards the warming function, the heat which is drawn off by the water coolant is reinforced by heat from the flue gases extracted by a heat exchanger. There is a supplementary heating element in the system for occasions when demand exceeds the output from the engine. The heat is transmitted either to a condensing or combi-boiler. There are three heat output options ranging from 15 kW (51 000 btu/h) to 36 kW (122 000 btu/h). All models will be able to reduce their heating output to 5 kW when necessary. It is expected that future models will be adapted to serve warm air heating systems. There is also the possibility of creating a multiple unit system to provide increased power and heat at a commercial scale.

Because there is only one moving part within the closed chamber the Stirling engine requires no maintenance. The boiler element needs the same level of maintenance as a conventional boiler.

The cost estimate is that the system will pay back the additional cost over and above a conventional boiler in 4–5 years.

The unit is compact, can fit between modular kitchen units and creates a noise level comparable to an average refrigerator (Figure 7.7).

Despite some current regulatory problems in the UK the Department of Environment, Transport and the Regions is optimistic about the prospects for micro-CHP or 'micro-cogeneration', estimating the potential domestic market to be up to 10 million units. With the opening up of the energy markets, micro-CHP is likely to become a major player in the energy stakes, accounting for some 25–30 GW of electricity (GWe). One of the factors favouring this technology is that it can be up to 90 per cent efficient and result in a reduction in total carbon dioxide emissions of up to 50 per cent when compared with the separate production of heat and energy. Large power stations are about 30 per cent

Figure 7.7
MicroGen kitchen wall-mounted unit

efficient. Add to this line losses of 5–7 per cent and it is obvious there is no contest.

In summary, the advantages of micro-CHP or micro-cogeneration are:

- It is a robust technology with few moving parts.
- Maintenance is simple, consisting of little more than cleaning the evaporator every 2000–3000 hours (on average once a year).
- Since there is no explosive combustion the engine produces a noise level equivalent to a refrigerator.
- It is compact with a domestic unit being no larger than an average refrigerator.
- It operates on natural gas, diesel or domestic fuel oil. In the not distant future machines will be fuelled by biogas from the anaerobic digestion of waste.
- The efficiency is up to 90 per cent compared with 60 per cent for a standard non-condensing boiler.
- Unlike a boiler it produces both heat and electricity, reducing energy use by about 20 per cent and saving perhaps £200–£300 on the average annual electricity bill.
- It can be adapted to provide cooling as well as heat.

The UK government is keen to promote this technology and it is always worth checking if grants are available. The best source of advice is the Energy Saving Trust (www.est.org.uk).

Fuel cells

Looking towards the next decade, the source of heat and power for many homes could well be the fuel cell. This is an electrochemical device which feeds on hydrogen to produce electricity, heat and water (see Chapter 13 'Energy options'). In January 2004 the first UK domestic-scale fuel cell began operation at West Beacon Farm in Leicestershire.

The most common fuel cell at the moment is the proton exchange membrane type (PEMFC) which feeds on pure hydrogen. It has an operating temperature of 80°C and at the moment is 30 per cent efficient. This is expected to improve to 40 per cent.

The farm is owned by the energy innovator Professor Tony Marmont. Rupert Gammon of Loughborough University is the project leader as part of the Hydrogen and Renewables Integration Project (HARI). It is designed to provide entirely clean energy.

The hydrogen is extracted from water by means of an electrolyser which splits water into oxygen and hydrogen by means of an electric current (Figure 7.8).

The electricity for the electrolyser is provided by wind, PV and micro-hydro generation. An alternative is to extract H_2 from natural gas by means of a reformer but then it is no longer zero carbon.

The fuel cell installation is compact and can fit into a cupboard. It has no moving parts and is therefore almost silent. At the moment it is producing 2 kW electricity and 2 kW heat. A second 5 kW fuel cell from Plugpower is in the process of being commisioned (Figure 7.9).

Figure 7.8
Electrolyser at West Beacon Farm

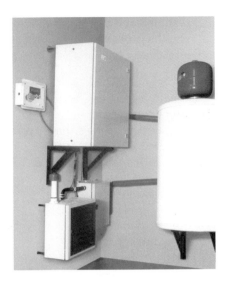

Figure 7.9
Fuel cell installation, West Beacon
Farm (courtesy of Intelligent Energy
2004)

The production and storage of hydrogen as the energy carrier are the problems still to be solved satisfactorily. Cracking water into hydrogen and oxygen by electricity is analogous to the sledge hammer and the nut. An alternative method of producing hydrogen is to extract it from ethanol derived from biowaste as has recently been demonstrated at the University of Minnesota.

The reactor is, in effect, a compact fuel cell hydrogen generator which would be ideal for vehicle application. It can be scaled up to provide the hydrogen for grid-connected fuel cells using ethanol fermented from both biowaste and energy crops.

Sanyo plans to launch a domestic fuel cell using natural gas or propane in 2005. It will be used to power TVs, air conditioners, refrigerators and PCs as well as catering for domestic hot water requirements. It plans to export the system to the US and Europe. Other companies like Mitsubishi Heavy Industries Ltd and Matsushita Electrical Industrial Co. are developing a similar system also due on the market in 2005.

Currently under development is a microbial fuel cell which avoids the need for hydrogen. It converts sewage to electricity. Bacterial enzymes break down the sewage liberating protons and electrons. The system then behaves like a proton exchange membrane fuel cell with protons passing through the membrane and electrons diverted to an external circuit to provide useful electricity (see pp. 255–256).

Embodied energy and materials

It is not just the energy consumed during the life of a building which has to be considered. Energy is involved in the extraction, manufacture and transportation of building materials and this is known as the 'embodied energy' and directly relates to the gross carbon intensity of a material.

The overall environmental credentials of a building are affected by a number of factors:

- energy used over its estimated lifetime;
- energy used in the construction process;
- the extent to which recycled materials have been used (see Chapter 18);
- the presence of pollutants in a material such as volatile organic compounds (VOCs);
- toxic substances used in the production process;
- energy used in demolition;
- level of recyclable materials at demolition;
- materials used in refurbishment.

At the moment the consensus is that a building consumes much more energy during its lifetime than is involved in extraction, manufacture and transportation. However, it will increasingly be the case that the embodied energy will be a significant fraction of the total as buildings become more energy efficient. It can still be difficult to assess the full impact at present because of the scarcity of detailed information. This arises from a natural reluctance on the part of manufacturers to disclose too much information about their commercial processes and also because of natural variations in techniques, which can lead to a wide band of values for similar products.

It is clear, however, that the area of materials energy and environmental effect is one which can only grow in coming years. It is also a sphere where much more information is required in order to exploit opportunities associated with carbon taxes and other fiscal measures to improve design. A number of assessment tools and techniques are becoming available.

Advanced and ultra-low energy houses

Chapter Eight

Besides designing the Autonomous House in Southwell, the Vales designed a group of ultra-low energy houses at Hockerton in Nottinghamshire. This is a narrow plan single aspect group of houses fully earth sheltered on the north side with the earth carried over the roof. The south elevation is completely occupied by a generous sun-space across all the units.

This is designed to be a partially autonomous scheme using recycled grey water and with waste products being aerobically treated by reed beds. A wind generator supplements its electricity needs. It is described as a *net zero energy* scheme which is defined as a development which is connected to the grid and there is at least a balance between the exported and imported electricity. There is an imbalance in cost for reasons stated earlier. A development that meets all its electricity needs on site and therefore is not connected to the grid is an *autonomous* development.

Hockerton is a project designed for a special kind of lifestyle which will only ever have minority appeal. For example, it plans to be self-sufficient in vegetables, fruit and dairy products employing organic-permaculture principles. One fossil fuel car is allowed per household and 8 hours' support activity per week is required from each resident. This would not be to everyone's taste, but it is important to demonstrate just how far things can be taken in creating architecture that harmonises with nature (Figures 8.1 and 8.2, 5.3 and 5.4).

It has a number of key features:

- ninety per cent energy saving compared with conventional housing;
- self-sufficient in water with domestic water collected from the conservatory roof and reed bed-treated effluent for purposes that require the EU bathing water standard;
- considerable thermal storage due to earth sheltering;
- seventy per cent heat recovery from extracted warm air;
- triple glazed internal windows and double glazed conservatory;
- 300 mm of insulation in walls;
- a wind generator will reduce reliance on the grid;
- roof-mounted photovoltaics.

Figure 8.1
Earth sheltered south and solar west elevations

The Beddington Zero Energy Development – BedZED

The Innovative Peabody Trust commissioned this development as an ultra-low energy mixed use scheme in the London Borough of Sutton. It consists of 82 homes, 1600 m² of work space, a sports club, nursery, organic shop and health centre, all constructed on the site of a former sewage works – the ultimate brownfield site. Peabody was able to countenance the additional costs of the environmental provisions on the basis of the income from the offices as well as the homes. Though the Trust is extremely sympathetic to the aims of the scheme, it had to stack up in financial terms. It is described in detail in Chapter 18 'State of the art case studies'.

The David Wilson Millennium Eco-House

A demonstration Eco-House has been built in the grounds of the School of the Built Environment, University of Nottingham (Figure 8.3). It is designed as a research facility and a flexible platform for the range of systems appropriate to housing. Its features are:

*   PV tiles integrated into conventional slates providing 1250 kWh/year;
*   solar collectors of the vacuum tube type on the south elevation to meet the demand for domestic hot water;
*   light pipe illuminating an internal bathroom and providing natural ventilation;

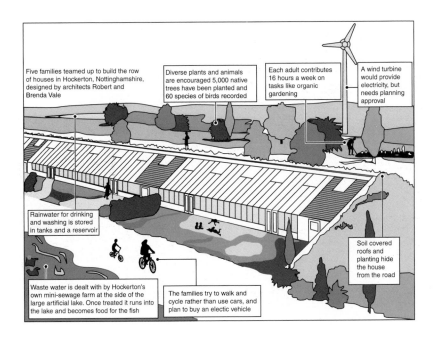

Five families teamed up to build the row of houses in Hockerton, Nottinghamshire, designed by architects Robert and Brenda Vale

Diverse plants and animals are encouraged 5,000 native trees have been planted and 60 species of birds recorded

Each adult contributes 16 hours a week on tasks like organic gardening

A wind turbine would provide electricity, but needs planning approval

Rainwater for drinking and washing is stored in tanks and a reservoir

Soil covered roofs and planting hide the house from the road

Waste water is dealt with by Hockerton's own mini-sewage farm at the side of the large artificial lake. Once treated it runs into the lake and becomes food for the fish

The families try to walk and cycle rather than use cars, and plan to buy an electic vehicle

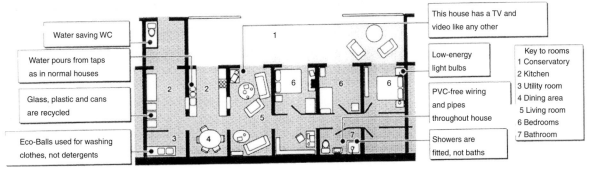

Water saving WC

Water pours from taps as in normal houses

Glass, plastic and cans are recycled

Eco-Balls used for washing clothes, not detergents

This house has a TV and video like any other

Low-energy light bulbs

PVC-free wiring and pipes throughout house

Showers are fitted, not baths

Key to rooms
1 Conservatory
2 Kitchen
3 Utility room
4 Dining area
5 Living room
6 Bedrooms
7 Bathroom

- solar chimney to provide buoyancy ventilation in summer and passive warmth in winter;
- helical wind turbine;
- ground source heat pump to supplement space heating.

The output from the energy systems is constantly monitored.

Associated with the Eco-House are several free-standing sun-tracking PV panels tilted to the optimum angle.

Figure 8.2
Hockerton overall life-style specification

Demonstration House for the Future, South Wales

A competition winning 'House for the Future' has been designed by Jestico Wiles within the grounds of the Musuem of Welsh Life in

Figure 8.3
David Wilson Millennium Eco-House,
Nottingham University

South Wales. Its two key attributes are sustainability and flexibility. It is capable of occupying a variety of situations: a rural location, a greenfield suburban site or high density urban sites in terrace form.

The structure of the house consists of a post and beam timber frame prefabricated from locally grown oak. A superinsulated timber stud wall faced with oak boarding and lime render occupies three sides of the building. The void between the timbers is filled with 200 mm of sheep's wool, specially treated, giving a U-value of 0.16 W/m²K. Internally much of the space is defined by non-load bearing stud partitions, allowing total flexibility and adaptability. There are some earth block partitions on the ground floor using clay found on the site. These provide thermal mass, supplementing the thermal storage properties of the concrete floor slab. All materials were selected with a view to minimising embodied energy (Figures 8.4 to 8.6).

The north facing roof is covered with sedum plants laid on a recycled aluminium roof. Cellulose fibre provides 200 mm of insulation between the deep rafters giving the roof a U-value of 0.17 W/m²K. This insulation is manufactured from recycled paper and treated with borax as a flame and insect retardant.

Considerable south facing glazing provides substantial amounts of passive solar energy. Windows on the south elevation are designed to change according to the seasons of the year.

As regards the plan, living space is fluid to accommodate the needs of different occupants. Open living and daytime spaces face south whilst more private cellular spaces are on the north side. The

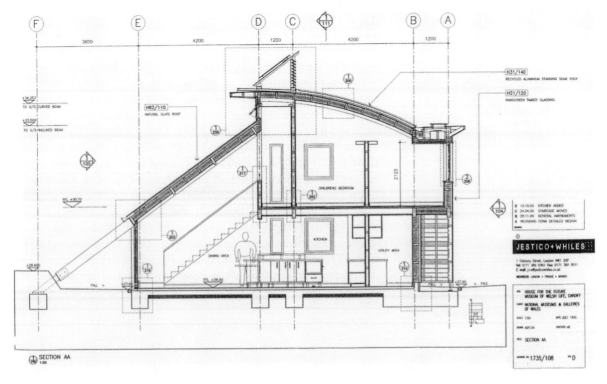

Figure 8.4
House for the Future – cross-section

Figure 8.5
Internal views obtained by
Architectural Press

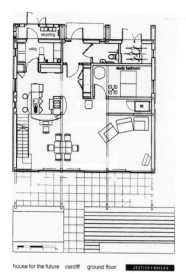

house for the future   cardiff   ground floor   JESTICO + WHILES

house for the future   cardiff   first floor   JESTICO + WHILES

Figure 8.6
Ground and first floor

number of bedrooms can vary from one to five according to family needs. The house can contract as well as expand.

The energy regime makes maximum use of both passive and active solar systems. Space heating can be supplemented by a ground source heat pump fed by a 35 m bore hole. A heat pump is driven by electricity but one unit of electricity produces 3.15 units of heat. A pellet burning wood stove rounds off the space heating. Gas is not available on the site.

Roof-mounted solar collectors provide water heating for most of the year and a ridge-mounted wind generator and a PV array producing 800 W go some way to meeting the electricity demand. When renewable energy technologies become more affordable the house will become self-sufficient in energy.

Finally, water conservation measures are an important component of its ecological credentials. Rainwater is collected in a specially enlarged gutter which can store 3 m³. It is mechanically filtered and gravity fed to toilets and washing machine. This should meet about 25 per cent of an average family's demand.

The prospects for wood

The House of the Future raises the question of the structural use of timber in buildings. Timber scores well on the sustainability scale, provided it is obtained from an accredited source such as the Forestry Stewardship Council. The Weald and Downland Open Air Museum 7 miles north of Chichester is a national centre for the conservation and study of traditional timber-framed buildings. The Conservation Centre explores new techniques in greenwood timber construction. Edward Cullinan Architects in association with Buro Happold Engineers have produced an undulating structure which rhymes with the South Downs landscape. The timber structure comprises a clear span gridshell formed out of a weave of oak laths. The high moisture content of the timber allows it to be formed into the necessary curves and then locked into shape. Once the laths are in place natural drying strengthens the structure. Oak is twice as strong as an equivalent size of other timbers which means that the cross-section of members can be reduced. The longest laths are 37 metres. Unique to the structure is the green jointing of the gridshell laths from freshly sawn oak. It is developments in glue technology which have made this possible.

The structure is set on an earth sheltered masonry ground floor. The lower storey is temperature controlled to safeguard archival material. A central row of glue-laminated columns supports the floor of the workshop.

This is the first timber gridshell structure in Britain and should become an icon of sustainable construction (Figure 8.7).

An even more ambitious gridshell structure is taking shape in Savill Garden in Windsor Great Park. Architects Glenn Howells won a competition for a visitor centre with a wave form grid structure that

Figure 8.7
Interior of the Weald and Downland
Conservation Centre (Edward Cullinan
and Partners)

differs from the Weald and Downland building in that it is raised above ground, allowing panoramic views of the park. It will be the largest grid-shell structure in the UK at 90 m long and 25 m wide. The structure has been designed by Buro Happold, the engineers involved at Weald and Downland, using 80 by 50 mm larch timbers harvested from the Park with oak forming the outer rainscreen.

As a research exercise in multi-storey timber buildings, the Building Research Establishment Centre for Timber Technology and Construction has built a six-storey timber-framed apartment block as a test facility in its vast airship hangar at Cardington (Figure 8.8). The results of the tests may well have a profound impact on the house building industry. The building comprises:

- four flats per floor;
- a plan-aspect ratio of c.2:1;
- platform timber frame;
- timber protected shaft;
- single timber stair and lift shaft;
- brick cladding.

The report on the project concludes:

This high profile project has provided a unique opportunity to demonstrate the safety, benefits and performance of timber frame construction technologies. This project has brought all aspects of construction together, including Regulations,

Figure 8.8
Building Research Establishment experimental timber-framed apartments

Research, Design, Construction and Whole Building Evaluation. Many Building Regulations, codes and standards are being updated as a result of this project. It has been the most challenging and exciting opportunity to obtain technical backup data for promotion of timber frame in the last 20 years and it has been recognised as one of the most valued projects (Enjily, V. (2003) *Performance Assessment of Six-Storey Timber Frame Buildings against the UK Building Regulations*, BRE Garston)

A *tour de force* of timber construction is the recently completed Sibelius Hall at Lahti in Finland. This concert hall epitomises how timber used both as a structural and sheeting material can produce a building great elegance and beauty. It is a testimony to the mastery of timber developed by the Finns over the centuries and serves to exemplify the versatility of this material as the ultimate renewable resource for construction. The architects are Hanna Tikka and Kimmo Lintula.

As well as being a renewable resource, timber also has a good strength to weight ratio, which is why it was used to construct one of the most famous aircraft of the Second World War, the Mosquito. The designers of this aircraft pioneered timber monocoque construction in which the skin and framework as a unified whole coping with both compression and tension. The advantage is this system is that it can accommodate curved and flowing shapes combining lightness with strength. The main structural element is laminated veneered lumber (LVL) typically

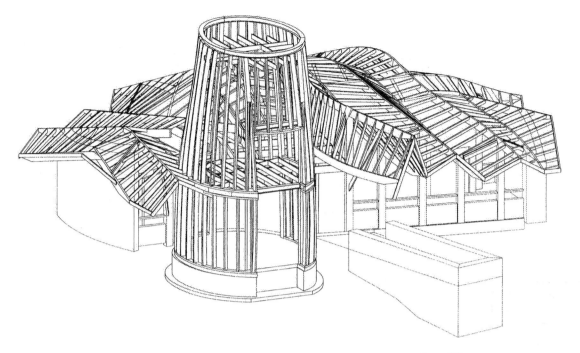

Figure 8.9
Roof formation, the Maggie Centre,
Dundee (courtesy of RIBA Journal)

Figure 8.10
Maggie Centre, Dundee. RIBA Building
of the Year for 2004

made from Norwegian spruce. It can be produced in sheets up 26 m long by using staggered and scarf jointing.

Timber can even accommodate the fluid imagination of Frank Gehry. LVL was chosen for the roof of the Maggie Centre in Dundee. It is finished in stainless steel (Figures 8.9 and 8.10).

The Winter Gardens form a spectacular element of the 'heart of the city' project for Sheffield (Figure 8.11). It is conceived partly as a glazed street in the spirit of the *galleria* connecting with the wider urban structure. It opens at right angles to the Millennium Galleries that also integrate a pedestrian route with gallery and restaurant provision. The contrasting space and architectural expression of the two buildings achieve the height of the poetic in urban terms. The most striking feature is the laminated larch parabolic arches which support the glass skin forming a counterpoint to the trees within. Larch was chosen for its

Figure 8.11
Winter Gardens, Sheffield 2002
(architects: Pringle Richards Sharratt)

durability and minimal maintenance characteristics. In time it will turn a silvery grey.

The space is 65.5 m long and 22 m wide and designed to accommodate a wide variety of exotic plants, many of which are under threat, in a frost-free environment. Underfloor heating in winter is provided by the city centre district low grade heating scheme. In summer surrounding buildings will provide solar shading. Vents in the roof and at both ends of the building encourage stack effect ventilation. Trees such as Norfolk Island Pine and New Zealand Flax occupy the highest central zone of the space which rises to 22 m. For the citizens of Sheffield it has been a spectacular success.

A useful guide to designing in timber is provided by Willis, A.-M. and Toukin, C. (1998) *Timber in Context – A Guide to Sustainable Use*, NATSPEC 3 Guide.

The external environment

- Wind
- Rain
- Solar shading
- Evaporative cooling.

The orientation of a property can have a significant impact on the extent to which it is adversely affected by wind. This can create a pressure difference between the faces of a building: positive on the windward side and negative on the lee face. This means that cold air tends to be forced into the windward elevation and warmth sucked out of the lee side (Figure 8.12).

The UK has one of the most turbulent climates in Europe. In the UK the average wind speed for 10 per cent of the time ranges from 8 to about 12.5 metres per second, the higher figures being in Scotland.

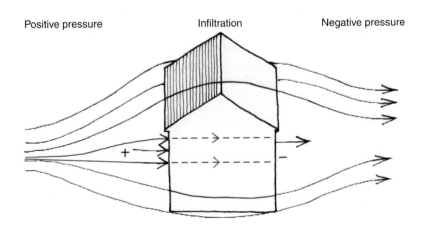

Figure 8.12
Wind pressure and infiltration

At the same time, average wind speeds increase by 7 per cent for every 100 m increase in altitude.

Wind speeds can be considerably reduced by the introduction of natural or artificial dampeners. A solid wind break can greatly reduce wind speed in its immediate vicinity but beyond that zone will cause turbulence. On the other hand, an openwork fence with only 50 per cent solid resistance to wind will moderate wind speed over a much greater area. At the same time a timber fence of this nature will be less likely to become a casualty of gale force winds.

Natural features can be effective wind breaks. Even low level planting creates drag, thereby slowing the wind force. Trees are the best option, remembering that deciduous trees are much less effective in winter. As a rule of thumb, the distance from a house to a tree break should be 4–5 times the height of the trees to optimise the dampening effect.

Climatologists predict that global warming will result in wetter winters and much drier summers with droughts a regular occurrence. This gives shrubs and trees a further benefit in the degree to which they protect from the drying or desiccating effect of wind. According to the TV gardening personality Monty Don 'In the British climate, wind is far more of a problem than sunshine and can be drought-inducing in the middle of winter when there is not a ray of sunshine to be seen for days' (*Observer Magazine*, 19 January 2003).

Wind plus driving rain can affect the thermal efficiency of a property. When brickwork becomes saturated the thermal conductivity of brickwork or blockwork increases since moist masonry transmits heat more effectively than in a dry condition. This problem would be cured with a polymer-based render.

Summary checklist for the energy efficient design of dwellings

With the predicted growth in the house building sector over the next decade it is important that architects exert maximum pressure to ensure that new homes realise the highest standards of bioclimatic design. The following are recommendations for minimising the use of energy and exploiting natural assets.

Building features

- In considering the plan a compact building shape reduces heat loss.
- Some situations may allow for the protection afforded by earth-berming and buffer spaces.
- Heated areas within the dwelling should be isolated from unheated spaces by providing insulation in the partitions between such spaces.

- Glazing must be low emissivity (Low E) double glazing, preferably in a timber frame. If metal frames are necessary there should be a thermal break between the frame and the glass.
- Areas of non-beneficial windows should be minimised.
- The detailing of joints in the building fabric can have a significant impact on energy efficiency.
- Potential cold bridges should be eliminated.
- Fabric insulation which is significantly better than the minimum required by regulation is strongly recommended.
- Air tightness should achieve a level of at most three air changes per hour at 50 pascals pressure in association with heat recovery ventilation.
- Care should be taken in the design of conservatories which should be able to be isolated from the main occupied area; at the same time account should be taken of probable air flow patterns. The heating of conservatories usually results in a net energy deficit.

Passive solar heat gain

External considerations:

- The main facade of a dwelling should face close to south (±30° approximately).
- The spacing between dwellings should be sufficient to avoid overshading.
- Where possible contours should be exploited either to maximise solar gain or minimise adverse effects.
- Areas with particular overheating risk should be considered when planning building layout and form.
- The provision of deciduous trees and shrubs will offer summer shade whilst allowing penetration by winter sun.

The built form

- The internal layout should place rooms on appropriate sides of the building either to benefit from solar heat gain or to avoid it where necessary.
- Shading (externally if possible) should be installed for windows posing overheating risk.
- The effect on heat gain of window frames and glazing bars can be significant.
- In the design and positioning of windows the effect of solar gain must be considered in conjunction with daylight design.
- As a general rule it is desirable to maximise south facing windows and minimise north facing windows.
- High thermal mass construction levels out the peaks and troughs of temperature.
- Internal surfaces should maximise solar heat absorption.

- A conservatory or other buffer space can be used to preheat incoming ventilation air.

Climate change is predicted to increase the risk of flooding from a combination of rising sea level, increased storm surges, greater precipitation and river run-down. In areas where there is the probability of flood risk special measures should be adopted, for example:

- Most living accommodation should, if possible, be on the first and upper floors.
- Floor and wall surfaces on the ground floor should be capable of recovery from flooding, e.g. tiled finishes.
- Power sockets should be at least at bench height.
- Door openings should be water tight for at least 1 m about ground;
- Windows sills should be at least 1 m above ground.
- Ventilation grilles and air bricks should be capable of being sealed.
- Bathrooms should be on the first floor; where they are on the ground floor non-return valves should be fitted to WCs.
- The electrical circuit on the ground floor should be able to be isolated, allowing power to be available on upper floors in times of flooding.

Systems

- Environmental considerations should be a priority when making the choice of fuel.
- High efficiency heating systems should be installed, for example condensing boilers, and space heating and hot water systems should be appropriately sized.
- In wet central heating systems thermostatic radiator valves are essential.
- Controls, programmers, and thermostats should be appropriate to the task and correctly positioned and their operation easily understood by occupants.
- The heating system should be geared to the thermal response of the building fabric and occupancy pattern of the dwelling.
- Hot water storage cisterns and the distribution system should be effectively insulated.
- Where there is a high standard of air tightness a heat recovery ventilation system is essential.
- Ventilation of utility areas, bathrooms and kitchens is especially desirable to prevent condensation.
- The venting of hot air in summer should be considered.
- The environmental benefits of conservatories are cancelled out if they are centrally heated.

Also linked to evolving climate change will be the need to take account of increased wind speeds, extremes of climate, heat episodes leading to the drying out of ground at normal foundation level. A guide to revised building practices has been published as part of the government's advice as to how business can respond to climate change. It includes such points as:

- deeper foundations to cope with ground shrinkage;
- more robust walls and roofs to withstand intense storms;
- orientation to present shorter elevation to prevailing winds;
- Consider more aerodynamic forms (e.g. Swiss Re, p. 158–159).

(DEFRA 2004.)

To conclude this chapter it is worth summarising points from an Arup report of Autumn 2004 on the likely impact of climate change on UK buildings.

Report by Arup Research and Development for the DTI's Partners in Innovation Programme 2004

Points raised in the report relevant to housing

Housing built to 2002 Building Regulations will be uncomfortably warm to live in by 2020. By 2080 internal temperatures could reach 40°C. It suggests that air conditioning and mechanical ventilation will be necessary, adding that the air conditioning should be driven by PVs or other renewable energy sources. Natural ventilation will be counterproductive when outside temperature exceeds internal temperature.

It recommends masonry buildings with high thermal mass over timber frame lightweight construction. Smaller windows with shutters are recommended. On south facing elevations solar blinds will be essential. Where buildings are deficient in thermal mass a possible solution is to apply a phase change material to internal surfaces. These are now becoming available in plaster form (see p. 137).

There is a conflict here with the principle of optimising passive solar energy. The answer could be removable or sliding heat reflective panels which reduce the glazed area in summer. Fitting louvres or external shutters to windows or internal blinds is recommended.

Arup concludes that by 2080 London will have the climate of the Mediterranean coast and we should consider adopting similar building techniques to that region.

Chapter Nine   Harvesting wind and water

This chapter is concerned with wind generation which can operate as embedded generation in buildings down to the scale of the individual house and the conservation of water as the pressure on this resource increases.

Small wind turbines

In this context 'small' means wind machines that are scaled from a few watts to 20 kW. Machines between 1 and 5 kW may be used to provide either direct current (DC) or alternating current (AC). They are mainly confined to the domestic level and are often used to charge batteries. The larger machines are suitable for commercial/industrial buildings and groups of houses.

Small-scale electricity production on site has economic disadvantages in the UK given the present buy-in rates for small operators. Currently the government is considering how to redress this inequity and thereby give a substantial boost to the market for small-scale renewables. Wind generation will do well if this happens since it is much less expensive in terms of installed cost per kilowatt than PV which makes it an attractive proposition as a building integrated power source.

Wind patterns in the built environment are complex as the air passes over, around and between buildings. Accordingly a wind generator introduced into this environment must be able to cope with high turbulence caused by buildings. Such conditions tend to favour vertical axis machines as opposed to the horizontal versions which have proliferated in wind farms. This is because the vertical versions may be able to operate at lower wind speeds and they are less stressed mechanically by turbulence. In addition, horizontal axis machines mounted on roofs tend to transmit vibrations through the structure of the buildings. Because of the bending moment produced by the tower under wind load, measures must be taken to provide adequate strength in the building structure. This may not easily be achieved in retrofit situations.

By their very nature the vertical axis machines are not affected by changes in wind direction or turbulence. They can be sited on roofs or walls. They have been particularly successful mounted on the sides of oil platforms in the North Sea (Figure 9.1).

The machines are well balanced, transmitting minimum vibration and bending stress to walls or roofs. They also have a high output power to weight ratio. A further advantage is that the electricity generator can be located beneath the rotors and therefore can be located within the envelope of the building.

Wind generation can be complemented by PVs as illustrated below (p. 114) by the system patented by Altechnica. The wind generators continue operating at night when PVs are in retirement (see Figure 9.9).

A prediction in 'WIND Directions', March 2001, estimates that the global market for small turbines by 2005 will be around Euros 173 million and several hundreds of million by 2010. For example, in the Netherlands alone there is the potential for 20 000 urban turbines to be installed on industrial and commercial buildings by 2011.

The increasing deregulation of the energy market creates an increasingly attractive proposition for independent off-grid small-scale generation insulating the operator from price fluctuations and reliability uncertainties, with the proviso that there is a level playing field.

Currently there are several versions of vertical axis machines on the market. However, they are still undergoing development. When it is fully appreciated that these machines are reliable, silent, low maintenance, easy to install and competitive on price, it is likely the market will expand rapidly. At present the regulatory regime for small turbines is much less onerous than for >20 kW machines. It is to be hoped that the bureaucrats fail to spot this red tape opportunity.

Research conducted by Delft University of Technology and Ecofys identified five building conditions to determine their effectiveness for wind turbines. They are described as 'wind catchers', 'wind collectors', 'wind sharers' and 'wind gatherers', terms which define their effect on wind speed. The wind catcher is well suited to small turbines being usually high and benefiting from a relatively free wind flow. Small horizontal axis machines could be satisfactory in this situation.

The wind collector type of building has a lower profile and can be subject to turbulence. This is where the vertical axis machine comes into its own. The third type, wind sharers, are found in industrial areas and business parks. Their relatively even roof height and spaced out siting makes such buildings subject to high winds and turbulence. Ecofys has produced a diagram which depicts how four urban situations cope with varying wind conditions. There is a fifth category, the 'winddreamer' which relates to low rise developments (Figure 9.2).

Development work is continuing on designs for turbines which are suitable for the difficult wind conditions found in urban situations. This is appropriate since climate change predictions indicate that wind speeds will increase as the atmosphere heats up and so becomes more dynamic. There is growing confidence that there will be a large market

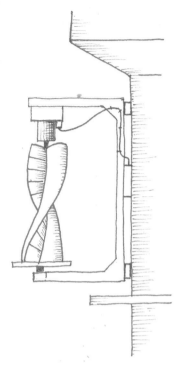

Figure 9.1
Helical side mounted turbine on oil platform

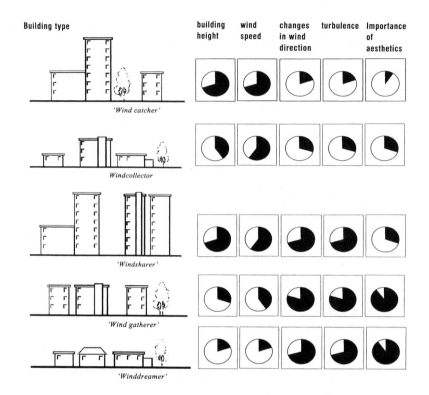

Figure 9.2
Categories of building cluster and their effectiveness for wind generation (courtesy of Ecofys and REW)

for mini-turbines in various configurations on offices, housing blocks and individual dwelling.

Types of small-scale wind turbine

Most small systems have a direct drive permanent magnet generator which limits mechanical transmission losses. Systems under 2 kW usually have a 24–48 volt capacity aimed at battery charging or a DC circuit rather than having grid compatibility.

Up to the present, horizontal axis machines are much more in evidence that the vertical axis type even at this scale. These machines have efficient braking systems for when wind speed is excessive. Some even tip backwards in high winds adopting the so-called 'helicopter position'. There are advantages to horizontal axis machines such as:

• the cost benefit due to economy of scale of production;
• it is a robust and tested technology;
• automatic start-up;
• high output.

The disadvantages are:

• the necessity of a high mast;
• mounted on buildings they require substantial foundation support;

- in urban situations where there can be large variations in wind direction and speed, this necessitates frequent changes of orientation and blade speed. This not only undermines power output, it also increases the dynamic loading on the machine with consequent wear and tear;
- there are noise problems with this kind of machine especially associated with braking in high winds;
- they can be visually intrusive.

As stated earlier, vertical axis turbines are particularly suited to urban situations and to being integrated into buildings. They are discrete and virtually silent and much less likely to trigger the wrath of planning officials.

The most common vertical axis machine is the helical turbine as seen at Earth Centre, Doncaster (Figure 9.3). In that instance it is mounted on a tower but it can also be side-hung on a building.

Another variety is the S-Rotor which has an S-shaped blade (Figure 9.4).

The Darrieus-Rotor employs three slender elliptical blades which can be assisted by a wind deflector. This is an elegant machine which nevertheless needs start-up assistance (Figure 9.4).

A variation of the genre is the H-Darrieus-Rotor with triple vertical blades extending from the central axis (Figure 9.4).

Yet another configuration is the Lange turbine which has three sail-like wind scoops (Figure 9.4).

Last in this group is the 'Spiral Flugel' turbine in which twin blades create, as the name indicates, a spiral profile (Figure 9.5).

Produced by Renewable Devices Ltd, the Swift wind turbine claims to be the world's first silent rooftop mounted wind turbine (35 dB) by incorporating silent aerodynamic rotor technology coupled with a revolutionary electronic control system. Care has been taken to provide a secure mounting system which will not transfer vibrations. Its peak output is 1.5 kW and it is estimated that avoided fossil fuel generation produces a saving of 1.8 tonnes per year of carbon dioxide (CO_2). The first unit was installed in Collydean Primary School, Glenrothes, Scotland, and there are plans for installations in four other primary schools. It is regarded as an ideal system for residential developments (Figure 9.6).

A development from the 1970s has placed the turbine blades inside an aerofoil cowling. A prototype developed at the University of Rijeka, Croatia, claims that this combination can produce electricity 60 per cent more of the time compared with conventional machines. This is because the aerofoil concentrator enables the machines to produce electricity at slower wind speeds than is possible with conventional turbines.

The cross-section of the cowling has a profile similar to the wing of an aircraft which creates an area of low pressure inside the cowling. This has the effect of accelerating the air over the turbine blades. As a result, more electricity is produced for a given wind speed as well as generating

Figure 9.3
Helican turbine on a column at Earth Centre, Doncaster

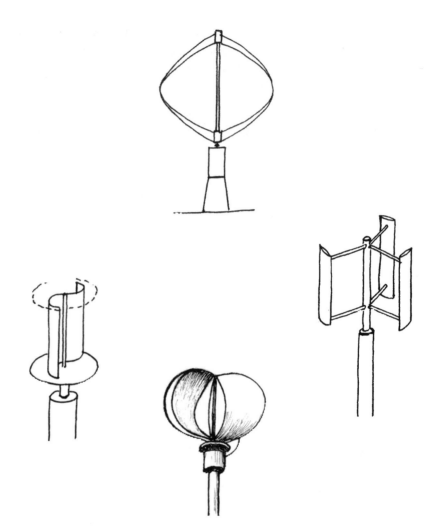

Figure 9.4
Left: S-Rotor; top centre: Darrieus-
Rotor; bottom centre: Lange turbine;
right: H-Darrieus-Rotor

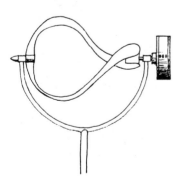

Figure 9.5
Spiral Flugel rotor

at low air speeds compared to a conventional rotor. This amplification of wind speed has its hazards, for example blades can be damaged. The answer has been to introduce hydraulically driven air release vents into the cowling which are activated when the pressure within the cowling is too great. They also serve to stabilise electricity output in turbulent wind conditions, which makes them appropriate for urban sites.

This technology can generate power from 1 kW to megawatt capacity. It is being considered for offshore application. The device is about 75 per cent more expensive than conventional rotors but the efficiency of performance is improved by a factor of five as against a conventional horizontal axis turbine (Figures 9.7 and 9.8).

A mini horizontal axis turbine was introduced in late 2003 called the Windsave. It can generate up to 750 watts at an installed cost of £1 per watt. Its manufacturers claim it could meet about 15 per cent of

Figure 9.6
Swift rooftop wind energy system

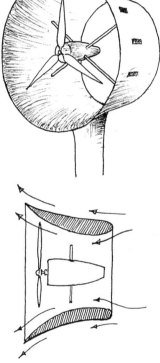

Figure 9.8
Simulation of wind turbines on the Vivo shopping complex, Hamburg

Figure 9.7
Wind turbine with cowling wind
concentrator

the average household electricity demand. It starts generating at a wind speed as low as 3 mph but is most efficient at 20 mph. Producing AC power it can be linked directly to the grid and the householder credited under the Renewables Obligation charges which currently pay a green electricity provider 6 p per kilowatt hour. By using remote metering, each unit can be telephoned automatically each quarter to

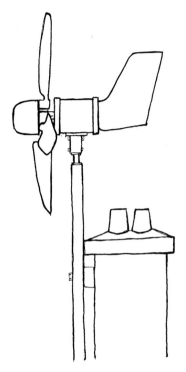

Figure 9.9
Windsave rooftop wind energy system

assess the amount of electricity generated. The power company then collects the subsidy and distributes it back to the home owner on the basis of the total generated. It is this subsidy which justifies a claim that the payback time can be as short as 30 months (Figure 9.9).

Building integrated systems

The Vivo building illustrates one version of a building integrated wind generating system. There is increasing interest in the way that the design of buildings can incorporate renewable technologies including wind turbines. Up to now such machines have been regarded as adjunct to buildings but a concept patented by Altechnica of Milton Keynes demonstrates how multiple turbines can become a feature of the design.

The system is designed to be mounted on the ridge of a roof or at the apex of a curved roof section. Rotors are incorporated in a cage-like structure which is capped with an aerofoil wind concentrator called in this case a 'Solairfoil'. The flat top of the Solairfoil can accommodate PVs. Where the rotors are mounted at the apex of a curved roof the effect is to concentrate the wind in a manner similar to the Croatian cowling (Figure 9.10).

The advantage of this system is that it does not become an over-assertive visual feature and is perceived as an integral design element. It is also a system which can easily be fitted to existing buildings where the wind regime is appropriate. Furthermore it indicates a building which is discretely capturing the elements and working for a living.

The European Union Extern-E study has sought to put a price on the damage inflicted by fossil fuels compared with wind energy. The research has concluded that, for 40 GW of wind power installed by

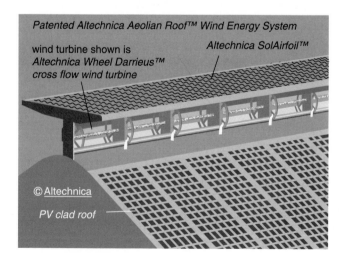

Patented Altechnica Aeolian Roof™ Wind Energy System

wind turbine shown is
Altechnica Wheel Darrieus™
cross flow wind turbine

Altechnica SolAirfoil™

© Altechnica

PV clad roof

Figure 9.10
'Aeolian' roof devised by Altechnica

2010, and with a total investment of Euros 24.8 billion up to 2010, CO_2 emissions could be reduced by 54 million tonnes per year in the final year. The cumulative saving would amount to 320 million tonnes CO_2 giving avoided external costs of up to Euros 15 billion.

This is the first sign of a revolution in the way of accounting for energy. When the avoided costs of external damage are realistically factored in to the cost of fossil fuels, the market should have no difficulty in switching to renewable energy *en masse*.

Conservation of water in housing

Not only is water a precious resource in its own right, there is also an energy component in storing and transporting it and making it drinkable. On average a person in the UK uses 135 litres (30 gallons) of water per day. Of this total about half is used for flushing toilets and personal hygiene. A really thorough home ecological improvement strategy should have three components:

- reduce consumption;
- harvest rainwater;
- recycle grey water.

Reducing consumption

Flushing toilets use about 30 per cent of total household consumption. This can be reduced by changing to a low flush toilet (2–4 litres) or a dual flush cistern. Aerating (spray) taps on basins, sinks and on shower heads make a big impact on consumption. All appliances should have isolating stopcocks so that the whole system does not have to be drained off if one item has a problem. Washing machines and dishwashers vary in the amount of water they consume. This is one of the factors which should influence the choice of white goods.

On average about 200 litres of rainwater fall on the roof of a 100 m^2 house each day in the UK. In many homes this is collected in water butts and used to irrigate the garden. However, it has wider uses. There are several proprietary systems for collecting and treating rainwater so that it can be used to flush WCs and for clothes washing machines. An example is the Vortex water harvesting system which serves roof areas up to 200 m^2 and 500 m^2 respectively. Recycled rainwater must only be sourced from roofs. Storage tanks are either concrete or glass reinforced plastic (GRP). There are controls to ensure that mains water can make good any deficiencies in rainfall. If filtered rainwater is to be used for other domestic purposes, other than drinking, it must be subject to further purification, usually by ultraviolet light. Best use of the filtered rainwater will be made if associated with dual flush WCs. Figure 9.11 shows a typical configuration for rainwater storage.

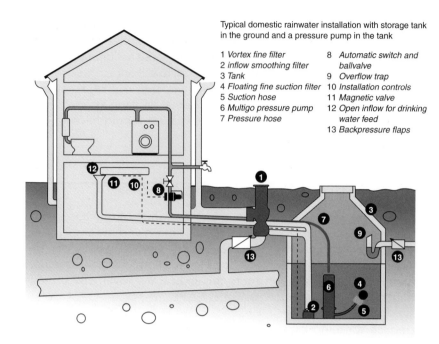

Typical domestic rainwater installation with storage tank in the ground and a pressure pump in the tank

1 *Vortex fine filter*
2 *inflow smoothing filter*
3 *Tank*
4 *Floating fine suction filter*
5 *Suction hose*
6 *Multigo pressure pump*
7 *Pressure hose*
8 *Automatic switch and ballvalve*
9 *Overflow trap*
10 *Installation controls*
11 *Magnetic valve*
12 *Open inflow for drinking water feed*
13 *Backpressure flaps*

Figure 9.11
Rainwater storage system layout
(courtesy of Construction Resources)

It is possible to go a stage further and use rainwater for drinking, but this requires even more rigorous filtration, as employed, for example, in the the Vales' Southwell autonomous house (p. 77). The water from the roof passes through a sand filter in a conservatory. From here it is pumped to storage tanks in the loft and from there through a ceramic/carbon filter to the taps. As an act of faith in the English weather there is no mains backup facility.

A variation on the water recycling strategy is to reuse grey water from wash basins, showers and baths. If waste water from a washing machine is included, then virtually all the waste water can be used to meet the needs of flushing toilets. Again there are systems on the market which serve this function, including water storage.

The Hockerton Housing Project has all these facilities and more because it uses rainwater collected from its conservatory roofs for drinking purposes. The water is stored in 25 000 litre underground tanks where particles have time to settle to the bottom. The water is treated first by passing it through a 5 micron filter to remove remaining particles. Then it is sent through a carbon filter to remove dissolved chemicals. Lastly it is subjected to ultraviolet light to kill bacteria and viruses. The author can vouch for its purity! For the average home this may well be a step too far, but those who feel inspired by this possibility should contact the Hockerton Housing Project at www.hockerton.demon.co.uk.

For the really dedicated there is the composting toilet which eliminates the need for water and drainage. In Europe a popular version is the Clivus Multrum from Sweden. It is a two-storey appliance in that there has to be a composting chamber usually on the floor below the toilet basin. Fan-assisted ducted air ensures an odourless aerobic decomposition process. The by-product from the composting chamber is a rich fertiliser.

Domestic appliances

As the building fabric of a home becomes more energy efficient, the impact of appliances like white goods and TVs becomes a much more significant element of the energy bill. Refrigerators and freezers are particular culprits. In 1999 the European Commission decreed that all white goods, refrigerators, freezers, washing machines, dishwashers etc. should be given an energy efficiency rating from A to G. This has certainly been effective in sending E, F and Gs to the bottom of the best buys. However, whilst A is the top of the scale there is variation within this category which has prompted the introduction of an AA category.

A surprising amount of electricity demand is due to standby electrical consumption. Some appliances like televisions and personal computers have optional standby modes which, nevertheless, are left on power because the consumption involved is regarded as insignificant. Others, like fax machines and cordless telephones need to be permanently on standby. Even appliances with electronic clocks consume power. It has been estimated that a typical household could consume 600 kWh per year on standby alone. For the EU it has been calculated that standby power accounts for 100 billion kWh/year, about one fifth the consumption of a state the size of Germany.

Chapter Ten   Existing housing: a challenge and opportunity

So far the emphasis has been on new buildings, mainly houses, yet these comprise only about 2 per cent of the total building stock at any one time. If buildings are to contribute to carbon abatement in the short to medium term then existing buildings must be targeted.

Currently there is considerable interest in converting redundant industrial buildings to other uses, especially residential. However, the real challenge lies in existing housing. In England and Wales housing is responsible for about 28 per cent of total carbon dioxide (CO_2) emissions.

The UK government is introducing a requirement for houses that come on the market to be accompanied by a 'House Condition Survey', which will include an Energy Efficiency Report. This will not only enable purchasers to compare older houses with new build but will also motivate vendors to upgrade their property in advance of a sale. It is scheduled to come into force in 2006.

The International Energy Agency, which considers energy efficiency worldwide, described UK housing as 'poorly insulated' with 'considerable scope for improvement'. At the same time, government improvement programmes were 'unconvincing' with 'funding low in proportion to the magnitude of the task'. What is the magnitude of the task?

To gauge the scale of the problem we first need to consider the four accredited ways of measuring the energy efficiency of both existing and new homes:

- the SAP method;
- the NHER profile;
- the BEPI profile;
- the carbon dioxide measure.

The official government system of measurement of energy efficiency is the Standard Assessment Procedure (SAP) which comprises a calculation of the heat loss resulting from the form of the building, the thermal properties of its fabric and the level of ventilation. This information is equated with the cost of making good the heat loss by means of the heating system and the cost of fuel. It also takes into account benefits from solar gain. Its scale is from 1 to 120. New homes complying with the Building Regulations according to the SAP method will probably have to be a minimum of SAP 100. The unofficial recommended minimum for reasonable energy efficiency for existing homes is SAP 60.

The National Home Energy Rating (NHER) uses a scale of 1 to 10, and includes such items as the method of space heating, domestic hot water, appliances and lighting and is designed to give an indication of energy costs. The national average NHER is around 4.0.

The Building Energy Performance Index (BEPI) assesses the thermal performance of the fabric of the building taking into account its orientation. It does not include heating systems and does not factor in the cost of energy. The Building Regulations standard equates to a BEPI of 100. Because this measure is confined to the efficiency of the building fabric, this is a more accurate long-term measure of energy efficiency, since appliances and heating systems have a relatively short life and there is no guarantee that replacements will measure up to the previous standard. It is a performance indicator that gives an accurate reading of the energy efficiency of the total fabric and cannot be manipulated to gain a notional but unreal advantage. Thus it gives an accurate picture of the underlying condition of the housing stock.

The Carbon Dioxide Profile indicates the carbon dioxide emissions deriving from the total energy used by a property taking into account the type of fuel. For example, for a given unit of heat, electricity has roughly four times the carbon intensity of gas. It is measured in kg/square metre/year. In the revised Building Regulations 2005, a carbon emission standard will be the only route to compliance.

The English House Condition Survey 1996 found that 84.6 per cent of dwellings were at or below SAP 60 with 8 per cent at or below SAP 20. The current average for England overall is SAP 43.8. This is gradually improving as the ratio of new homes to existing increases. However, in the private rented sector in England 21 per cent are at or below SAP 20, with 12.8 per cent of this sector being at or below SAP 10. Within the <10 category the bottom end is as low as SAP *minus* 25. To put some numbers against these standards, 3.3 million homes in England are at or below SAP 30, 1.6 million are at or below SAP 20 and 900 000 are at or below SAP 10 (*English House Condition Survey*, DETR 1996, December 2000). These numbers are substantially increased when Britain as a whole is considered.

This constitutes a monumental problem which calls for constant pressure on governments to rise to the challenge of upgrading the housing stock. At present the amount of investment in this area of need is totally inadequate and it is being left to enlightened bodies like housing associations to take the initiative.

So, how does this translate into actual home heating habits?

The official standard for adequate heating in a living room is 21°C and in other rooms, 18°C. Only 25 per cent of homes have internal temperatures which meet these standards. The minimum heating regime is 18°C for the living room and 16°C for other rooms.

When the external temperature drops to 4°C, then

- 50 per cent of owner occupied dwellings fail to reach the minimum standard;
- 62 per cent of council homes; and
- 95 per cent of the private rented sector also fail to meet the minimum standard.

These figures are from the DETR House Condition Survey for England.

Many of the owner occupied homes are of 1930s vintage. How do they compare with today's best practice? One crucial measure is carbon dioxide emissions. To achieve adequate space heating a 1930s house is responsible for 4.7 tonnes of carbon dioxide. This compares with 0.6 tonnes in current best practice homes. A 1976 house which was the first to encounter thermal regulations will account for 2.6 tonnes of CO_2 for space heating. Taking into account all fittings and appliances as well as the building fabric, a superinsulated house with best available technology will produce a total of 2 tonnes of CO_2 as against 8 tonnes in total for a 1930s dwelling.

There is a strong social dimension to this state of affairs.

The UK government acknowledges that up to 3 million households in England are officially designated 'fuel poor'. The definition is that they are unable to obtain adequate energy services for 10 per cent of their income. Most of those energy services are of course taken up with space heating. We have the worst record in the EU for extra winter deaths. In the winter of 1999–2000 almost 55 000 died from cold related illnesses between December and March as against the other two four monthly periods. This was the highest winter total since 1976 yet it was a relatively mild winter. In addition there was steep rise in the rate of respiratory and cardiovascular illnesses. About half of this total can be attributed to poor housing.

The main culprit is cold, poorly insulated and damp homes as acknowledged by the government in its document *Fuel Poverty: The New HEES* (DETR 1999):

> The principal effects of fuel poverty are health related, with children, the old, the sick and the disabled most at risk. Cold homes are thought to exacerbate existing illnesses such as asthma and reduced resistance to infections.

Dr Brenda Boardman of Oxford University's Environmental Change Institute has estimated that well over £1 billion per year is spent by the National Health Service on illnesses directly attributable to cold and damp homes. This figure may be significantly higher in that it is impossible to quantify the contribution of poor housing to depressive illnesses. The DTER acknowledges that fuel poor households

> also suffer from opportunity loss, caused by having to use a larger portion of income to keep warm than other households.

This has adverse effects on the social well-being and overall
quality of life for both individuals and communities.

(Fuel Poverty: The New HEES, op. cit.)

This cost will taper off as the upgrading programme gathers
momentum.

A book appeared in 2000 called *Cutting the Cost of Cold* (ed.
Rudge and Nicol, Spon) which should remove any doubts there may
be about the linkage between poor housing and ill health. Increasingly
damp as well as cold is emerging as a major health hazard. Damp generates mould and mould spores can trigger allergies and asthma
attacks. Some moulds are toxic, as in the genus *Penicillium* which can
damage lung cells. It was confidence in the connection between damp
homes and asthma that justified the Cornwall and Isles of Scilly Health
Authority in directing £300 000 via district councils to thermally
improve homes of young asthma patients. This was undertaken as
much as an investment opportunity as a remediation intervention. The
outcome was that the savings to the NHS exceeded the annual equivalent cost of the house improvements. The report on this enterprise,
sponsored by the EAGA Trust, states: 'This study provides the first
evaluation of health outcomes following housing improvements'. It will
surely be the first of many since it provides hard evidence of cost effectiveness. At the opposite end of the country, almost a quarter of all
homes suffer from damp in Scotland (National Housing Agency for
Scotland).

The connection between housing and health has been recognised
by the medical profession in a report *Housing and Health: Building for
the Future* (eds Sir David Carter and Samantha Sharp, British Medical
Association 2003). This is a thorough analysis of the situation from the
medical standpoint.

The remedy

There is no easy way to solve this problem and considerable investment
will be required by central government if fuel poverty linked to substandard housing is to be eliminated. An example of a retrofit package
for housing would consist of:

- improving the level of insulation in walls and roof and, where possible, floor;
- draught-proofing;
- installing Low E double glazing preferably in timber frames;
- installing/converting central heating to include a gas condensing
  boiler;
- installing heat recovery ventilation system.

From the architectural point of view the insulation is the main challenge. It can take three forms:

- external overcladding (enveloping);
- filling the cavity;
- internal dry lining.

Case study

Penwith Housing Association in Penzance, Cornwall, was formed in 1994 to take over the local authority housing from Penwith District Council to make it possible to gain access for funds to upgrade the entire stock. This consisted of a mix of 1940s houses with solid concrete block walls and post-war cavity built homes. The 1940s examples had a SAP rating of 1 and an NHER of 1.1. The application of external insulation, additional roof insulation and double glazing raised this to SAP 26. However, the crucial BEPI rating was raised to 97, i.e. close to Building Regulations standard current at the time. The addition of gas central heating raised the SAP to 76 which dramatically illustrates the effect of fixed appliances to the SAP value.

Being of concrete construction and rendered there was no problem as regards changing the appearance by overcladding. The technique involves applying a render to provide an even and smooth fixing surface to the rigid insulation panels. The panels then receive a waterproofing finish. A mesh is applied to the insulation to provide a key for the external waterproof render which is finished with pebble dash (Figure 10.1).

External cladding has a number of consequences. For example, carrying it round window reveals means that the window frame size is reduced. Roof eaves and verges have to be extended and rainwater/soil vent pipes have to be modified to take account of the deeper eaves.

It is necessary for the insulation boards to receive a finishing coat. In the case of most insulants the finish should offer total waterproofing. A polymer-based render is the most reliable in this respect. This is an adhesive render with an alkali resistant glass fibre mesh as reinforcement. Applied in one or two coats it offers a choice of finishes, for example:

- pebble dash or spar dash;
- textured renders in a range of colours;
- roughcast, also called harling or wet cast.

It is also possible to use cladding which includes

- lightweight natural stone aggregate;
- brick;
- tile, e.g. terracotta;
- weatherboarding.

Figure 10.1
Social housing with cladding over solid
wall construction, Penzance

Benefits

- There is a significant improvement in comfort levels throughout the whole house.
- The walls of the building are protected from weathering, ensuring a longer life.
- There should be absolute protection from penetration by damp.
- The incidence of condensation is reduced to near zero.
- It allows the fabric of the home to act as a heat store – a warmth accumulator.
- It stabilises the structure, preventing cracking due to differential thermal expansion.
- Space heating bills can be reduced by up to 50 per cent.
- The increase in property value as a result of the upgrading usually more than offsets the cost.
- There is normally a significant improvement in appearance.
- The operation can be undertaken without the need to vacate the property.
- There is a significant reduction in carbon dioxide emissions. Government estimates suggest that, over the lifetime of the building, one tonne of CO_2 is saved for every square metre of 50 mm thick insulation.

An example of an individual house application of external cladding is Baggy House in the UK which illustrates the 'Dryvit' system called 'Outsulation' (Figure 10.2).

Where there are overriding reasons for not wishing to overclad with insulation, as, for example, in the case of eighteenth to nineteenth century terraced housing, the alternative is to fix insulation to the inside face of external walls – 'dry lining'. The dilemma is that this reduces internal space. To bring a 140 mm solid external wall near to the current

Figure 10.2
Baggy House, Devon

Buildings Regulations standard would require at least 90 mm of insulation with a plasterboard finish. A suitable insulant is cellular glass fixed to the wall mechanically. The finish is either plasterboard with a skim coat of plaster or plaster applied to metal lathing. There are consequences to using this system, such as the relocation of skirtings and electrical sockets and the reduced size of door and window openings. There is also the risk of cold bridging if the insulation is not continued around the reveals to openings. This could involve the replacement of external doors and windows. However, this is one instance where the best can be the enemy of the good and compromise is reasonable.

Cavity filling

Where there are cavity walls injecting insulation through holes drilled at regular intervals is a common practice. However, caution should be exercised regarding the kind of insulation selected and the *bona fides* of the installation contractor. Post-completion inspections have discovered a number of cases of fraud where only a notional amount of insulation has been injected. Properly installed cavity filled insulation can have a significant impact on the thermal performance. In the Penwith 1960s properties, following cavity filling and extra roof insulation the BEPI was 107 with a SAP of 49. Where central heating was installed the SAP rose to 78 again illustrating why the BEPI is a more useful guide to the long-term energy efficiency of a house since it focuses on the fabric.

Some of the least energy efficient dwellings exist in multi-storey buildings, the most notorious being tower blocks. The team responsible for the innovative Integer House has been commissioned by Westminster Council to raise the energy efficiency of one of its 20 storey tower blocks as a demonstration of best practice in renovation. This will be one to watch. (For further information refer to Smith, P.F. (2004) *Eco-Refurbishment: A Guide to Saving and Producing Energy in the Home*, Architectural Press.)

The Roundwood Estate in Brent is typical of many former council developments with its numerous four storey flats and maisonettes linked by balcony access. The 564 dwellings have been transferred to the Fortunegate Housing Association. They have solid one and a half brick solid external walls and minimal insulation in the roofs. After consultation with the tenants PRP Architects agreed a specification including overcladding external walls with an insulated render system, increased roof insulation, full central heating with combination boilers, and new kitchens and bathrooms with extractor fans. Existing double glazing was considered adequate. The result is that on average each flat will save 1.5 tonnes of CO_2 emissions per year with a reduced fuel bill of £150 per year. At the same time comfort levels have substantially improved.

This is the kind of unromantic but challenging work which will have to be undertaken nationwide if the consequences of fuel poverty are to

Figure 10.3
Roundwood Estate Housing
Association flats, existing and
refurbished

be overcome. An example of a considerable quantity of former council
stock is the balcony access flats in the Roundwood estate. Refurbishment
and overcladding is under way on this estate (Figure 10.3).

As a postscript to this chapter it should be noted that existing
homes that are substantially refurbished are likely to need to comply
with Part L of the Buildings Regulations. As mentioned earlier, Part L is
being revised and this will have the aim of achieving a 25 per cent
improvement in energy efficiency. At the same time, the sole criterion
for compliance will be based on carbon emissions which will close the
loophole of the trade-offs, so much abused in the past. Another change
is that houses will be subject to air tightness standards and will have to
submit to pressure testing.

From January 2007 it is likely that houses for sale will require a
Home Condition Report. This will include an Energy Survey. For new
homes there are currently discussions about enhancing the energy efficiency scale to take account of zero carbon homes.

Low energy techniques for non-domestic buildings

Chapter Eleven

Design principles

Offices in particular have traditionally been extravagant users of energy because, in relation to all other costs, energy is a relatively minor fraction of the total annual budget. In many cases the major electricity cost is incurred by lighting. The 1980s sealed glass box may use energy at a rate of over 500 kWh/m²/year. Currently, best practice is in the region of 90 kWh/m²/year. The aim of the architect under the sustainability banner is to maximise comfort for the inhabitants whilst minimising, ultimately eliminating, reliance on fossil-based energy.

The Movement for Innovation (M4I) has produced six performance indicators as conditions for sustainable design. They are designed to validate or otherwise claims that buildings are 'green'.

1. Operational energy

The energy consumed by a commercial building during its lifetime should be kept to a minimum. The benchmark is currently 100 kWh/m² but this will become more stringent as pressure mounts to limit carbon emissions. Techniques such as high insulation, thermal mass, passive and active solar optimisation, natural light, natural ventilation, on-site electricity generation and seasonal energy storage are components of the green agenda.

2. Embodied energy

Minimising the carbon content of materials in the extraction, manufacture, delivery and construction stages. Promoting the use of recycled materials and designing for reuse after demolition.

3. Transport energy

Avoiding unnecessary transport journeys during construction in terms of the delivery of materials and the removal of site waste. In some cases, like the Wessex Water offices near Bath (see first edition) staff are obliged to use communal transport wherever possible. There is also the matter of location even though this will usually be outside the province of the architect. Access to good public transport should be a prime requisite in deciding location. There have been instances where corporations have relocated from city centres accessible only by public transport to highly energy efficient offices on out of town sites. This has encouraged a much greater use of cars resulting in a net increase in carbon dioxide (CO_2) emissions.

4. Waste

Minimising waste through greater off-site fabrication and modular planning. Sorting and recycling of off-cuts, etc. to avoid landfill costs.

5. Water

Harvesting grey water and rainwater for use in toilets and irrigation. Minimising hard areas to reduce run-off including permeable car park surfaces and porous paviors.

6. Biodiversity

Design landscape to support local flora and fauna. Preserve existing mature trees and generally ensure the well-being of wildlife.

Environmental considerations in the design of offices

The first task is to persuade the clients of the benefits of environmental and energy efficient design. There is now convincing evidence that 'green buildings pay' (see Edwards, B. (ed.) (1998) *Green Buildings Pay*, E & F Spon, the outcome of an RIBA conference).

- It is important that all members of the design team share a common goal and if possible have a proven track record in achieving that goal. From the earliest outline proposals through to construction and installation, the design process should be a collaborative effort. Integrated design principles should be the rule from the first encounter with a client.
- The first aim should be to maximise passive systems to reduce the reliance on active systems which use energy.
- It is important that, at the outset, costs are calculated in a composite manner so that capital and revenue costs are considered as a single accountancy feature. This will help to convince clients that any extra capital expenditure is cost effective, even for buildings to be let or sold on.

- Clients should be required to explain in detail the nature of office routines so that these can be properly matched to operational programmes.
- The claims made for advanced technology do not always match performance. It is important to select *appropriate* technology which achieves the best balance between energy efficiency, occupant comfort and ease of operation and maintenance. At the same time, the best compromise should be reached between optimum performance and the requirements for the majority of the year. To provide significantly greater capacity for just a few days of the year is not best practice.
- Lighting requirements should be clearly assessed to discriminate between general lighting and that required at desktop level.
- On completion building managers should be selected for their ability to cope with the complexities of the chosen building management system (BMS).
- Appropriate monitoring is necessary to be able to assess from day to day how systems are performing. The cost of submeters, hours-run recorders, etc. give valuable returns for a small cost. Energy costs should be identified with specific cost centres.

Passive solar design

Planning and site considerations

Whether it is important to encourage or exclude solar radiation, it is necessary to appreciate the degree to which solar access is available, so that the likelihood of solar heat gain can be determined. At the earliest stage of design one must consider the following parameters in relation to the site:

- the sun's position relative to the principal facades of the building (solar altitude and azimuth);
- site orientation and slope;
- existing obstructions on the site;
- potential for overshadowing from obstructions outside the site boundary.

For the development itself, the following factors need consideration:

- grouping and orientation of buildings;
- road layout and services distribution;
- proposed glazing types and areas, and facade design;
- nature of internal spaces into which solar radiation penetrates.

Chapter 5 referred to the stereographic sun chart and computer programs as a means of assessing the level of insolation enjoyed by a building. Physical models can also be tested by means of the heliodon.

The thermal efficiency of a building can also be affected by its plan form and orientation in respect of the prevailing wind direction. There are a number of guidelines:

- The larger building elevation should not face into the predominating wind direction, i.e. the long axis should be parallel to the wind flow.
- Tall buildings should, where possible, have a facade which is staggered and stepped back away from the wind; protection for pedestrians can be provided by use of canopies and podiums which reduce downdraught at ground level; curved facades moderate the impact of wind, for example the Swiss Re Offices, London, pp. 157–58.
- Sheer vertical faces to tall buildings can generate substantial downdraughts, which can obstruct pedestrian access, and even be dangerous. An example is the 19 storey Arts Tower in the University of Sheffield where the downdraught has knocked people over close to the entrance.
- Buildings can be grouped in irregular arrays, but within each group the heights should be similar and spacing between them kept to a minimum (no more than about a ratio of 2 : 1 in building heights).
- Building layout should avoid creating a tunnelling effect between two adjacent buildings.

Construction technologies

The building envelope

Walls and rainscreens   The glazed curtain wall has advanced considerably since it came into vogue in the 1960s. The repository for knowledge in this context is the Centre for Window and Cladding Technology (www.cwct.co.uk). Metal panel systems are now available with integral insulation, for example EDM Spanwall which uses flat metal sheets pressure bonded to the insulation core. Precast concrete panels also come with integral insulation. Trent Concrete has introduced an insulated concrete sandwich under the name of Hardwall Cladding. The Ocean Terminal at Leith completed in 2001 is a good example of this technology. Often these panels have an exterior finish of stone or reconstructed stone.

Climate facades   The glass curtain wall is a familiar feature of office and institutional buildings dating from the 1950s, though the feature first appeared in the US at the end of the nineteenth century. Liverpool can boast a number of office buildings that point the way to the glass curtain wall such as Oriel Chambers in Water Street, designed by Peter Ellis and completed in 1864.

The technique was conceived at a time when energy was cheap and plentiful and there was no glimmer of global warming. Buildings challenged the environment. Now there is mounting pressure to design buildings which operate in harmony with nature, making the most of solar resources. The demand for increasing energy efficiency led first to the introduction of double glazing. Now things have moved on with the incorporation of a second inside skin of glazing creating what is termed a 'climate facade' or alternatively an 'active facade'.

These are terms for facades that play an active role in controlling the internal climate of offices in which there is an optimum requirement for daylight.

The active facade fulfils a variety of functions. It:

- offers room daylight control;
- acts as an active and passive solar collector;
- offers excess solar heat protection;
- minimises room heat loss;
- serves as a plenum for ventilation supply and extract air;
- facilitates heat recovery.

An example of a climate facade building is the office development at 88 Wood Street in the City of London by the Richard Rogers Partnership (RRP). The requirement was for floor to ceiling glazing which can create a problem of solar gain which is exacerbated by the heat from computers and, in this case, a high services loading. The facade developed by RRP and Ove Arup and Partners consists of a double glazed external skin made up of some of the world's largest double glazed units measuring 3 m × 3.25 m and weighing 800 kg. Then there is a 140 mm gap and a third inner leaf of glass with openable units which completes the facade. Within the cavity are venetian blinds with perforated slats to control sunlight. The aesthetic appeal of the structure is enhanced by the use of extra white glass or 'Diamond White' glass by the manufacturers Saint Gobain.

Air from the offices is drawn into the main perimeter extract ducts within the cavity via plenum ducts within a suspended ceiling and then expelled at roof level. Photocells on the roof monitor light conditions and control the venetian blinds to one of three positions according to the level of glare. When the blinds are closed they act as a heat sink whilst the perforations admit a measure of natural light. The result is that there are substantial savings in the energy normally needed to cool such spaces. There is also a high rate of air change in the building at double the average for a typical office block (Figures 11.1 and 11.2).

Another building with an active facade is Portcullis House, the adjunct to the Houses of Parliament by Michael Hopkins and Partners. Windows are triple glazed with mid-pane retractable blinds designed to absorb solar gain. The outer double glazed element is Low E glass with argon gas. The cavity is ventilated by room extract air, and, at the same time, it acts as a solar collector. The result is a summer solar heat gain of less than 25 W/m^2 across a 4.5 m deep room.

The glazing incorporates a light shelf to maintain daylight levels when solar shading is active. The shelf has a corrugated reflective

Figure 11.1
Offices, 88 Wood Street, City of
London

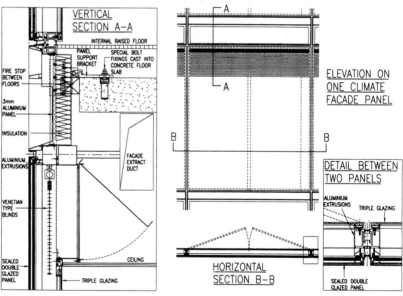

Figure 11.2
Sections through the facade of
88 Wood Street

surface to maximise high altitude sky light but reject short wave low
level radiation. This almost doubles daylight levels in north facing
rooms where adjacent buildings obstruct a view of the sky (Figure 11.3).

A sealed facade does not mean the individual user has no control over ventilation. There are manual trim controls over air supply,

volume, radiator output, blinds, artificial lights and a daylight dimming override.

This is an outstanding example of a building that minimises reliance on services engineering. It is claimed that the integrated approach to the design has resulted in simplified engineering solutions and a considerable saving in energy as against a standard naturally ventilated building.

Another kind of active facade is one which incorporates solar cells. Commercial buildings have perhaps the greatest potential with PV cells integrated into their glazing as well as being roof mounted. Even at the present state of the technology, Ove Arup and Partners estimate that one third of the electricity needed to run an office complex could come from PVs with only a 2 per cent addition to the building cost. The main advantage of commercial application is that offices use most of their energy during daylight hours. The case study of the ZICER building in the University of East Anglia will serve as an example (Chapter 18).

One of the challenges of the next decades will be to retrofit buildings with PVs. In the UK a pioneer scheme is the Northumberland Building for the University of Northumbria in Newcastle where cells have been applied to the spandrels beneath the continuous windows.

To date it has achieved an average daily output of 150 kWh. Based on this figure it is expected that the cost of the PVs will be paid back in three years thanks to a substantial subsidy. After this it will continue to produce electricity free of cost for about 20 years. It is estimated that the annual saving in CO_2 emissions from this building alone will be of the order of 6 tonnes.

Currently the Co-Operative Headquarters building in Manchester is retro-fitting PVs to the south elevation of its circulation tower as part of a refurbishment programme.

Given the abundance of information and advice available, designers should now be able to grasp the opportunities offered by such technologies which also allow exploration of a range of new aesthetic options for the building envelope.

This will increasingly be a preferred option as the cost of fossil fuel rises under the twin pressures of diminishing reserves and the need to curb CO_2 emissions. The Solar Offices of Doxford International by Studio E Architects located near Sunderland is a pioneer example of this tactic in the UK. This is a speculative office development which offers the advantage of much reduced power consumption of 85 kWh/m²/year as against the normal air conditioned office of up to 500 kWh/m²/year. The 73 kW (peak) array of over 400 000 photovoltaic cells on the facade produces 55 100 kWh per annum which represents one third to one quarter of the total anticipated electrical consumption (Figures 11.4 and 11.5).

The Doxford Office is modest compared with the German government In-service Training Centre called Mont Cenis at Herne Sodingen in the Ruhr.

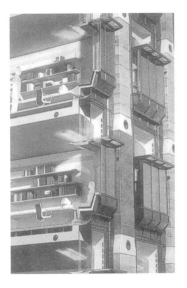

Figure 11.3
Portcullis House; cutaway section of facade

Figure 11.4
Doxford Solar Offices

Figure 11.5
Interior, Doxford Solar Office

The Mount Cenis Government Training Centre is one of the world's most powerful solar electric plants and is a spectacular demonstration of the country's commitment to rehabilitate this former industrial region whilst also signalling the country's commitment to ecological development (Figure 11.6).

After the demise of heavy industry the Ruhr became a heavily polluted wasteland which prompted the government of North-Rhine Westphalia to embark on an extensive regeneration programme covering 800 square kilometres.

The building is, in effect, a giant canopy encompassing a variety of buildings and providing them with a Mediterranean climate. At 168 m long and 16 m high the form and scale of the building has echoes of the huge manufacturing sheds of former times. A timber structural frame of rough hewn pine columns is a kind of reincarnation of the forests from which they originated.

The structure encloses two three-storey buildings either side of an internal street running the length of the building (Figure 11.7). Their concrete structure provides substantial thermal mass, balancing out

Figure 11.6
Mount Cenis In-service Training
Centre, Herne – Sodingen, Germany

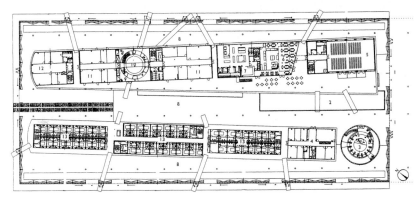

Figure 11.7
Mount Cenis ground floor plan

both diurnal and seasonal temperature fluctuations. Landscaped spaces provide social areas which can be used all year in a climate akin to the Côte d'Azur. Sections of the facade can be opened in summer to provide cross-ventilation.

The building is designed to be self-sufficient in energy. The roof and facade incorporate 10 000 m^2 of PV cells integrated with glazed panels. Two types of solar module were employed: monocrystalline cells with a peak efficiency of 16 per cent and lower density polycrystalline cells at 12.5 per cent. These provide a peak output of 1 megawatt. Six hundred converters change the current from DC to AC to make it compatible with the grid. A 1.2 MW battery plant stores power from the PVs, balancing output fluctuations. The power generated greatly exceeds the needs of the building at 750 000 kWh per year. German policy on renewables makes exporting to the grid a profitable proposition.

This is not the only source of energy generation. The former mines in the area release more than one million cubic metres of methane which is used to provide both heat and power. Capturing the gas in this way results in a reduction of carbon dioxide emissions of 12 000 tonnes.

This complex is an outstanding example of an alliance between green technology and aesthetics. The architects, Jourda and Perraudin, Paris, designed the distribution of PV panels to reflect the arbitrary distribution of clouds by means of six different types of module with different densities creating subtle variations to the play of light within the interior. It all adds up to an enchanting environment of spaciousness, light and shade. At the same time it affords a graphic reminder that regenerated industrial landscapes do not have to be populated by featureless utilitarian sheds.

Floors and ceilings   The undersides of floors have a crucial role to play in determining the effective thermal mass of a structure. Traditionally concrete plank or slab floors had ceilings suspended below them to house services. Now there are increasing examples of the system being reversed with the floor above the slab raised to provide space for ducts and other services. The soffit of the concrete floor is free of finishes, the purpose being to improve the effectiveness of the thermal mass and radiate stored heat in colder temperatures and 'cooling' in hot conditions. In summer, night air is passed through ducts to cool the slab, which then, during the day, radiates cooling into the workplace. Such thermal mass features are sometimes called 'thermal flywheels' or dampeners since they flatten the peaks and troughs of temperature.

One of the most aesthetically and environmentally suitable methods of achieving radiative thermal mass is by barrel vaults, as employed in Portcullis House (Figure 11.8) and Wessex Water Operational Centre near Bath by Bennetts Associates. It is important that the slabs are not carried through to the facade in order to avoid a major thermal bridge. To recapitulate, a thermal bridge is a route whereby cold is able to bypass wall insulation.

A proprietory deck system which incorporates ducts to transport both warm and cool air is Termodeck from Sweden. This was used in the Elizabeth Fry Building in the University of East Anglia to good effect. Air is passed through the ducts at low velocity with stale air drawn into grilles over light fittings and then its heat extracted in a heat recovery unit before being expelled to the open air. There is no recirculation of air, yet this is one of the most energy efficient buildings of the 1990s due to very high levels of insulation and air tightness. For further information see Smith and Pitts, *Concepts in Practice – Energy*, Batsford, 1999.

Whilst the popular way to moderate the peaks and troughs of external temperature as it affects building interiors is to exploit thermal mass, there is an alternative which is to use a phase change material on internal

Figure 11.8
Vaulted floors with exposed soffits,
Portcullis House

surfaces. A system is now on the market which enables lightweight structures to enjoy the benefits of thermal mass. It is based on paraffin wax which is a phase change material. The wax is micro-encapsulated within gypsum plaster. The wax stores heat up to its melting point. This can be adjusted to a range of temperatures according to the requirements of the material that supports it. As the wax stores heat its temperature does not rise until it reaches melting point which is its maximum storage capacity.

Night-time cooling causes the wax to solidify and release the stored heat to warm the interior space. This makes the system particularly suitable for offices which are vacant at night and which can be vented to the outside.

The wax is encapsulated within minute plastic balls to form microcapsules in powder form which is mixed with plaster in a ratio of between 1 : 5 and 2 : 5 by weight. The mix is sprayed to walls. It is claimed that a plaster coating of 6 mm has the same absorbent capacity as a 225 mm masonry wall.

In an office context this material is ideal for facing internal partitions, reducing or even eliminating the need for mechanical ventilation. Up to spring 2004 ten buildings have been equipped with the system which was developed by the Fraunhofer Institute for Solar Energy Systems in Freiburg (e-mail: schossig@ise.fraunhofer.de).

Chapter Twelve
Ventilation

Natural ventilation

Part of the reaction against the sealed glass box concept of offices has been to explore the possibilities of creating an acceptable internal climate by natural means. This has caused a reappraisal of traditional methods including those employed in hot climates for two millennia or more.

Internal air flow and ventilation

Air flow in the interior of buildings may be created by allowing natural ventilation or by the use of artificial mechanical ventilation or air conditioning. The production of buildings using more than one of these options is becoming more frequent. Such buildings are said to be 'mixed-mode'. The overriding principle should be to minimise the need for artificial climate systems and one way to achieve this is to make maximum use of natural ventilation in conjunction with climate sensitive design techniques for the building fabric.

Natural ventilation is possible due to the fact that warm air is lighter than cold air and therefore will tend to rise in relation to cold air. As it rises, colder air is drawn in to compensate: the buoyancy principle. If air flow is to be encouraged to help provide natural ventilation and cooling the following are desirable design features:

- Plan form should be shallow to allow for the possibility of cross-ventilation.
- The most straightforward system of cross flow ventilation is where fresh air is provided with routes through a building from the windward to leeward side. In most office situations this can be considered as a supplement to the main ventilation strategy. Openings on opposite walls to allow cross-ventilation are better than on one or more adjacent walls.
- Building depth should not be more than about five times the floor to ceiling height if cross-ventilation is to be successful.
- For single sided ventilation, depth should be limited to about two and a half times the floor to ceiling height.

- Minimum opening areas should be about 5 per cent of floor area to provide sufficient flow.
- Continuous, secure background ventilation should be available using trickle vents and other devices.
- Windows should be openable, but able to provide *controlled* air flow. This is particularly difficult in high rise buildings but its problems have been addressed in the 40 storey Swiss Re building in the City of London (see pp. 157–159).
- Atria and vertical towers can be incorporated into the design to allow the stack effect to draw air through the building, though care in meeting fire and smoke movement restrictions may determine the limits of what is possible.
- The effectiveness of natural ventilation and cooling can be improved by the use of low energy controlled lighting and low energy office equipment, thus reducing internal heat gain.

The ventilation system most obviously borrowed from the past is the use of the thermal chimney exploiting the buoyancy principle. A thermal chimney which is warmed by the sun accelerates the process, causing cooler air to be drawn into the building at ground level. If the chimney has a matt black finish it will absorb heat and increase the rate of buoyancy. Portcullis House, admirably demonstrates this technology (Figures 12.1 and 12.11). In fact this building is one of the most overt demonstrations of the dynamics of natural ventilation, with external rising ducts carrying the warmed air from the offices to a thermal wheel on the roof before being expelled. Fresh air, in this case, is drawn in at high level assisted by the thermal wheel (Figures 12.11, 12.12 and 12.13).

Figure 12.1
Portcullis House, Westminster, London

Unassisted natural ventilation

Pioneers of natural ventilation are Alan Short and Brian Ford in association with Max Fordham. Their first groundbreaking building in the UK was the Queen's Engineering Building at Leicester de Montfort University (Short Ford and Partners). This building has been well documented and a particularly useful reference is Thomas, R. (ed.) (1996) *Environmental Design*, E & FN Spon.

Maintaining the principle of pure natural ventilation without mechanical assistance is the Coventry University Library, the Lanchester Building, by architects Short and Associates. The environmental strategy was developed in association with Brian Ford. This is a deep plan building making it impossible to employ cross flow ventilation from perimeter windows. There is also the problem of a raised ring road close to the site generating noise and pollution. Accordingly perimeter windows are sealed (Figure 12.2).

The solution was to provide each quadrant of the floor plan with large lightwells doubling up as air delivery shafts. The buoyancy of rising warm air draws fresh air into plenums below floor level to the base of each light tower. From here the air is drawn upwards through preheating coils to be released to rooms at floor level. By now the air has reached 18°C. Additional warmth is provided by perimeter radiators. The air is then drawn into the exit stacks spaced around the external walls. 'Termination' devices at the top of the stacks ensure that prevailing winds will not push air back down the stacks (Figures 12.3 and 12.4).

In a building relying solely on the buoyancy of natural ventilation, control is critical. The building energy management system (BEMS)

Figure 12.2
Coventry University library (courtesy of Marshalls plc)

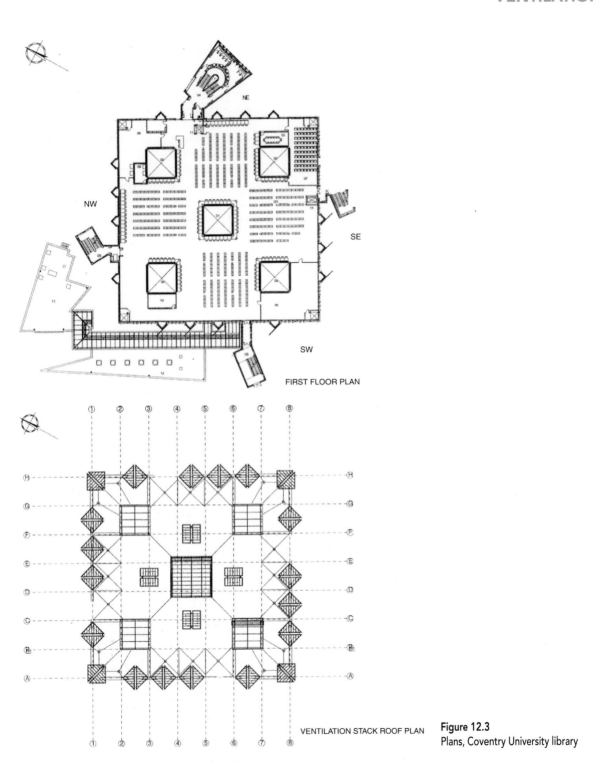

NE

NW

SE

SW

FIRST FLOOR PLAN

VENTILATION STACK ROOF PLAN

Figure 12.3
Plans, Coventry University library

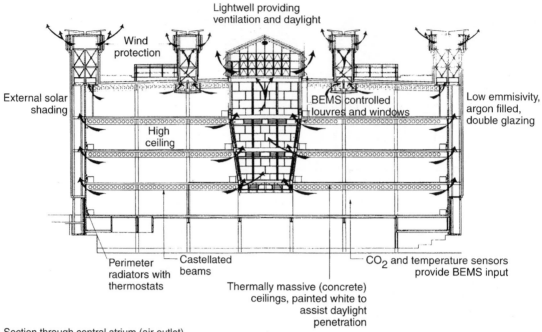

Section through central atrium (air outlet)
■ Warm Exhaust air out

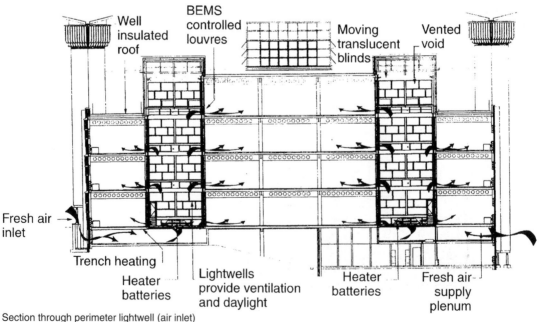

Section through perimeter lightwell (air inlet)
■ Fresh Air intake

Figure 12.4
Air circulation paths

adjusts the outlet opening sizes according to outside temperature and the CO_2 and temperature readings in each zone of the building. It is tuned to meet the optimum fresh air requirement compatible with the minimum ventilation rate (Figure 12.4).

The BEMS controls dampers which allow night air to flow through the building, cooling the exposed thermal mass during the summer. This is a BEMS which is driven by a self-learning algorithm, meaning that it should progressively optimise the system, learning by its mistakes.

Heat losses through the fabric of the building are minimised by good insulations standards: $U = 0.26\ W/m^2K$ for walls and less than $2.0\ W/m^2K$ for windows. The latter comprise Low E double glazing with an argon filled cavity.

The result of avoiding mechanical ventilation and maximising natural light is that the estimated energy demand is 64 kWh/m² per year which represents CO_2 emissions of 20 kg/m². This is around 85 per cent less than the standard air conditioned building.

The building type which presents the most formidable challenge to anyone committed to natural ventilation is a theatre. Short Ford Associates have risen to the challenge in a spectacular fashion. There is a considerable heat load from stage lighting as well as the audience yet the Contact Theatre at Manchester University achieves comfort conditions without help from air conditioning. This is another building by which Alan Short, Brian Ford and Max Fordham have navigated uncharted waters (Figure 12.5).

Figure 12.5
Contact Theatre, Manchester University

The outstanding feature is the cluster of H-pot stacks over the auditorium reaching a height of 40 metres. The H-pot design lifts them above neighbouring buildings to exclude downdraughts from the prevailing south-west winds. Their volume is calculated to accelerate the buoyancy effect and draw out sufficient hot air whilst excluding rain. Things were made more complicated by the fact that this is a refurbishment of a 1963 auditorium, which has been largely preserved. In a theatre ventilation and cooling are the major energy sinks. Consequently the energy load of this building should be a fraction of the norm (Figure 12.6).

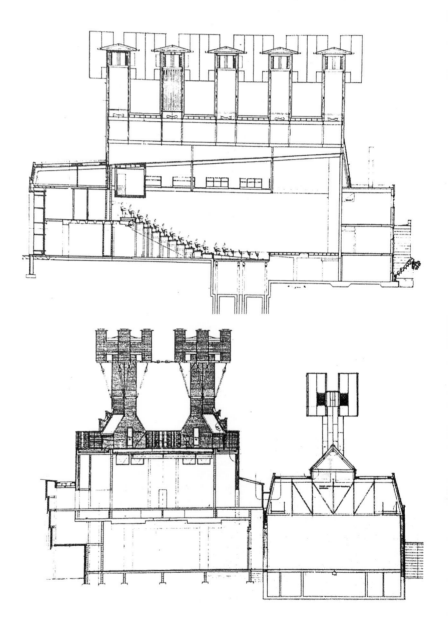

Figure 12.6
Longitudinal and transverse sections,
Contact Theatre

In circumstances like this theatre it may be necessary to incorporate attenuators in the system to minimise external noise.

The stack effect or gravity displacement is dependent on the difference in temperature between the outside and inside air and the height of the air column. There is considerable variation in the relative temperatures over the diurnal and seasonal cycle. During the summer, night-time cooling can be achieved by passing large quantities of fresh air over the structure. Night-time cooling works when the external temperature is lower than the internal one and gravity drives the cooler air down into the building. In the daytime in summer when the internal temperature has become lower than the outside temperature, it is necessary to cool the incoming air, perhaps by evaporative cooling or a heat pump. If heat is transferred from the input duct to the exhaust duct, this further assists buoyancy.

In the UK this system can work economically up to six storeys. Above this duct sizes may become excessively large to cope with the volume of air.

One objection to naturally ventilated buildings is that they draw polluted air into a building. To reduce the chance of this happening in highly polluted areas, fresh air should be drawn into the building at high level, above the diesel particulate matter zone. At the same time, exhaust air which has risen through the stack effect also needs to be expelled at high level, so a means has to be found of ensuring the exhaust air does not contaminate the fresh air.

One way is to employ a terminal design which rotates according to the direction of the wind. In Figure 12.7 a design of terminal is shown which ensures that fresh air is always drawn in from the windward side and exhaust air to the leeward side. A wind vane ensures that the terminal always faces the correct direction. The aerofoil shape of the wind direction terminal produces negative pressure on the leeward side, assisting the expulsion of exhaust air.

In the section, Figure 12.8, the fresh air is delivered through perimeter ducts to provide displacement ventilation. The exhaust air can either exit through perimeter ducts or a climate facade.

Mechanically assisted ventilation

Rotating cowls was the system adopted by Michael Hopkins and Partners with Ove Arup and Partners in the Nottingham University Jubilee Campus (Figure 12.9). This ventilation system is the successor to Hopkins' and Arup's innovations at the Inland Revenue HQ also in Nottingham, and Portcullis House, Westminster. These led to a low pressure mechanical system linked to heat recovery via a thermal wheel which recovers 84 per cent of the exhaust heat.

The mechanical system requires 51 000 kWh per year and this is supplied by 450 m² monocrystalline photovoltaic cells. The ventilation

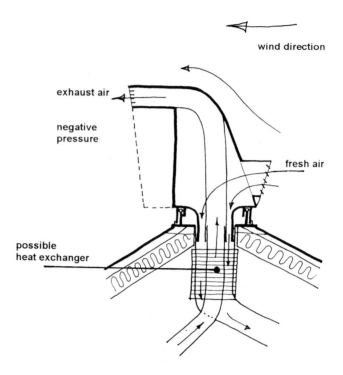

wind direction

exhaust air

negative
pressure

fresh air

possible
heat exchanger

Figure 12.7
Combined function rotary terminal

system uses 100 per cent fresh air throughout the year. Air is introduced directly into the roof mounted air handling units where it passed through electrostatic filters. From here it is blown down vertical shafts into traditional floor voids and thence to teaching rooms via low pressure floor diffusers. Exhaust air uses the corridor as the extract path from where it rises under low pressure via a staircase to the roof air handling unit (AHU) for heat recovery then expelled through the cowl. The vane on the cowl ensures that the extract vent faces the leeward side according to the direction of the wind, as in the traditional oast houses of Kent (Figure 12.10).

In most commercial and institutional buildings it is unlikely that natural ventilation on its own will be adequate. A degree of mechanical assistance is necessary to achieve an adequate rate of movement around the building. Mechanical assistance should not be confused with air conditioning which is a much more complex operation.

Mechanical ventilation involves air flow and movement provision using fans and air and possibly supply/extract ducts. Such a system may be able to act as the heating system in winter. However, in its basic form, no cooling system is incorporated and therefore the lowest air temperature which can be supplied is usually restricted to ambient conditions. Air conditioning involves the cooling of the air using a refrigeration system. More precise control over air temperature and humidity can be achieved this way but usually only within a sealed

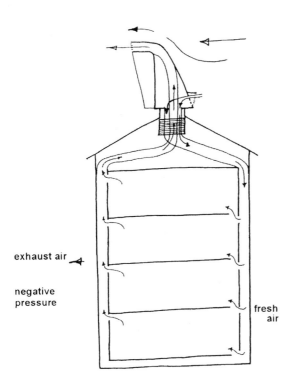

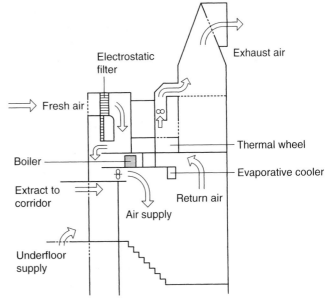

exhaust air

negative
pressure

fresh
air

Figure 12.8
Typical system for a naturally
ventilated office

Figure 12.9
Jubilee Campus, University of
Nottingham

Electrostatic
filter

Exhaust air

Fresh air

Thermal wheel

Boiler

Evaporative cooler

Extract to
corridor

Return air

Air supply

Underfloor
supply

Figure 12.10
Air handling units (AHUs) Jubilee
Campus

building. In many temperate climates, the thermal inertia of a building structure, combined with controlled air flow, should be sufficient to avoid excessive overheating except for a few hours each year. Immediately air conditioning is specified, energy use is likely to increase substantially.

As mentioned the inclusion of mechanical reinforcement of natural ventilation is the first step in the mixed mode direction. There are at least four types of mixed-mode ventilation:

- *Contingency* – mechanical ventilation is added or subtracted from the system as necessary.
- *Zoned* – different ventilation systems are provided for different portions of the building depending upon needs.
- *Concurrent* – natural and mechanical systems operate together.
- *Changeover* – natural and mechanical systems operate as alternatives (but often turn out to be concurrent because of difficulties in zoning or changeover point control).

If mechanical ventilation is to be used to aid summer comfort levels, the following tactics are recommended:

- draw external air from the cool side of the building;
- consider drawing air through cooler pipes or ducts (for instance located underground) to reduce and stabilise its temperature; ground water cooling is becoming increasingly popular;
- ensure supply air is delivered to the required point of use efficiently to provide the most beneficial cooling effect but without uncomfortable draughts;
- ensure extracted air optimises heat removal by taking the most warm and humid air;
- integrate use and positioning of mechanical systems with natural air flow;
- in highly polluted city centre locations, air filtration down to PM5 (particulate matter down to 5 microns) is essential;
- employ night-time purging of the building to precool using lowest temperature ambient air.

The last of these options offers many potential benefits since the air delivered to the space can achieve a lower temperature than ambient external conditions. This is particularly the case where cooler night-time air is passed over the building's thermal mass (often the floor slab) which retains the ability to cool incoming daytime air. Further 'natural cooling' alternatives to air conditioning are summarised on pages 151–154.

An increasingly popular option is 'displacement ventilation'. In this case air at about one degree below room temperature is mechanically supplied at floor level at very low velocity, usually about 0.2 metres per second. This air is warmed by the occupants, computers or light

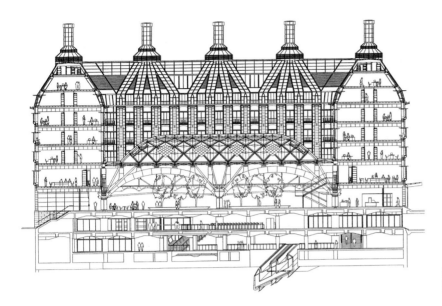

Figure 12.11
Portcullis House, section

fittings, etc. causing it to rise and be extracted at ceiling level. Air quality and comfort levels can be more easily controlled using this system. However, not all rooms may be suitable for this strategy and therefore it should be specified only where appropriate.

Portcullis House is one of the most prestigious buildings to use displacement ventilation (Figures 12.11 and 12.12). A mechanically assisted ventilation system serves a network of linked floor plenums drawing air from ducts in the facade to provide 100 per cent external air to each room. The system incorporates high efficiency heat recovery from solar gain, the occupants, electrical equipment and room radiators. Exhaust air is carried by ducts expressed externally in the steeply pitched roof and expelled through a series of chimneys designed to enhance the stack effect. Heat recovery is by means of a roof mounted rotary hygroscopic heat exchanger or 'thermal wheel' with 85 per cent efficiency which is fed by air return ducts which follow the profile of the roof. This thermal wheel is also able to recover winter moisture from exhaust air, reducing the load on humidifiers (Figure 12.13).

Adjacent to Westminster Bridge, Portcullis House (Figure 12.1) is situated in one of the most heavily polluted locations in London. Ventilation air is drawn in at the highest possible level, well above the high concentration zone of particulate matter from vehicle exhausts. This outside air is fed into the underfloor plenum and the displacement ventilation is assisted by buoyancy action. The brief specified a temperature of 22°C plus or minus 2° so, when necessary, the ventilation air can be cooled by ground water in two bore holes at a steady 14°C. Buoyancy ventilation is assisted by low power fans. The full fresh air system is able to serve all rooms equally, despite the diversity of function. This is essential for a long-life building which may undergo numerous internal changes.

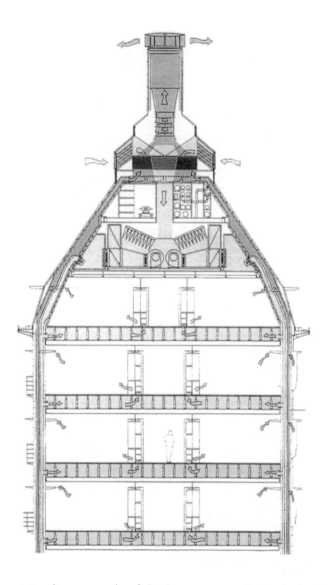

Figure 12.12
Portcullis House, displacement ventilation

An outstanding example of displacement ventilation being inserted into a refurbished building is afforded by the Reichstag. By a slender majority the German Parliament decided to move to Berlin and to rehabilitate the Reichstag. Norman Foster was invited to submit a design in a limited competition which he won.

The debating chamber uses displacement ventilation drawing air again from high level above low level pollution such as PM10s (it is now considered that PM5 should be the health threshold). The chamber floor comprises a mesh of perforated panels covered by a porous carpet. The whole floor, therefore, is a ventilation grille. Large ducts under the floor enable air to be moved at low velocity, which reduces noise and minimises the power for fans (Figure 12.14).

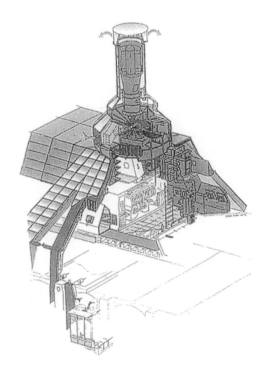

Figure 12.13
Portcullis House, ventilation pathways
and detail of the thermal wheel

Finally, the critical design issues concerning mechanical ventilation involve:

- the sizing and routing of ducts to minimise resistance and thus keep fan size to a minimum;
- the positioning of diffusers in relation to plan and section of rooms;
- the size of diffusers to minimise noise;
- the inclusion of devices to stop the spread of fire.

Cooling strategies

Cooling strategies begin at the level of the site. Vegetation, especially trees, provides both shade and evaporative cooling through moisture expiration through leaves. Pools, fountains, waterfalls/cascades, sprays and other water features all add to the evaporative cooling effect. In studies of 'heat island effect' generated by buildings it was found that clusters of trees within the heat island can produce a localised drop in temperature of 2–3°C.

Chilled ceilings are a method of providing cooling not necessarily associated with air flow systems. The advantages of the system are, first, that thermal stratification affects in a room are reduced and, second, that a chilled ceiling counterbalances the effect of thermal buoyancy, that is, rising warm air. The ceiling may be chilled using a refrigerant. The more

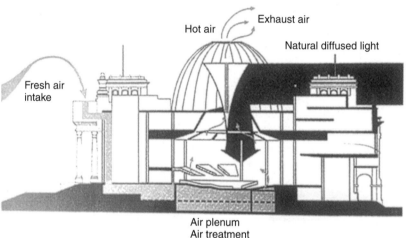

Figure 12.14
Displacement ventilation and natural light in the Reichstag

environmentally benign method is to employ mechanical night-time cooling to precool exposed floor slabs. An alternative system involves embedding pipes in concrete floors to carry cooling water, usually from a ground source.

Evaporative cooling

Another case of 'nothing new under the sun' is evaporative cooling. One of the earliest cases of this being incorporated in a building is the Emperor Nero's megalomanic 'Golden House' which covered most of the centre of Rome. At its centre was the domed octagon room and in one of its sides a waterfall was inset, supplied by a mountain stream. No doubt it performed the dual role of architectural feature and cooling device.

Evaporative cooling works on the principle that molecules in a vapour state contain much more energy than the same molecules in a liquid state. The amount of heat required to change water into vapour is the latent heat of evaporation. This heat is removed from the water, hence 'evaporative cooling', and transferred to the vapour. So, evaporation causes surfaces to cool (Thomas, R. (ed.) (1996) *Environmental Design*, E & FN Spon).

Evaporative techniques include:

- air that does not already have a high moisture content can be cooled by allowing water to evaporate into it;
- as stated, direct evaporation occurs when air passes through tree foliage, fountains and across pools;
- evaporative cooling is produced if incoming air to a building passes over a dampened surface, or through a spray or damp material across windows;
- direct evaporative cooling is best in dry climates where average relative humidity at noon in summer does not exceed 40 per cent;
- in the case of indirect evaporation, the air does not come into direct contact with the moisture, but can be allowed to pass through tubes or pipes which have their outer surfaces moistened.

An example of a design which incorporates evaporative cooling is the Jubilee Campus at Nottingham University. Sloping glazing directs air which has previously passed across an extensive open air pool into an atrium between teaching and office units. Orientation ensures that the prevailing wind is in the right direction (Figure 12.15).

Figure 12.15
Directed evaporative cooling, Jubilee Campus

Additional cooling strategies

- Shading should be compatible with daylight provision and passive solar gain, at the same time causing minimum interference with external views.
- Use heat absorbing and heat reflecting glasses.
- In traditional Mediterranean building, the outer surfaces were painted light colours to reflect a portion of the heat gain; we can learn from this.

The ecological tower

Surely an oxymoron? The orthodox 'green' would rule out anything above about 12 storeys since this is the height at which natural ventilation in the western European climate zone is said to become impracticable. Tower blocks usually require a heavy engineering services system. Also the construction energy costs rise significantly every five floors or so.

However, the ecological tower block has its advocates, most notably Ken Yeang from Kuala Lumpur. He pioneered the idea of gardens in the sky coupled with natural ventilation. To cope with the wind speeds (up to 40 metres per second at 18 storeys) he uses wing wind walls and wind scoops which deflect the wind into the centre of the building.

The first manifestation of these principles in the west was the Commerzbank in Frankfurt (Figure 12.16). This began life as a limited competition for an office headquarters comprising 900 000 square feet of office space and 500 000 square feet of other uses. The brief was clear that it should be an ecological building in which energy efficiency and natural ventilation played a crucial role. At that time the Green Party was in control of the city. In the winning design by Norman Foster Associates, a 60-storey three-sided building wraps round an open central core ascending the full height of the building (Figure 12.17). The most remarkable feature of the design is the incorporation of open gardens. The nine gardens each occupy four storeys and rotate round the building at 120 degrees enabling all the offices to have contact with a garden.

The gardens are social spaces where people can have a coffee or lunch and each one 'belongs' to a segment of office space accommodating 240 people. As the architects put it: 'we're breaking the building down into a number of village units'. This is extremely important in reducing the scale of the place for its occupants. The gardens feature vegetation from North America, Japan and the Mediterranean according to their height above ground.

The natural ventilation enters through the top of the gardens passing into the central atrium. The atrium is subdivided into 12-storey units and within 12 floors there is cross-ventilation from the gardens in

Figure 12.16
Commerzbank, Frankfurt

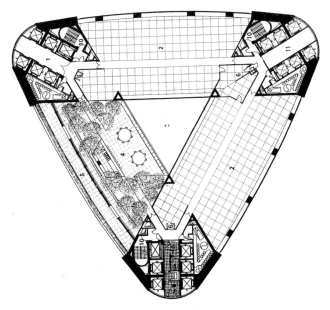

Figure 12.17
Commerzbank typical floor plan

the three directions (Figure 12.18). Air quality is good, enhanced as it is by the greenery. It is estimated that the natural ventilation system will be sufficient for 60 per cent of the year. When conditions are too cold, windy or hot, the building management system activates a backup

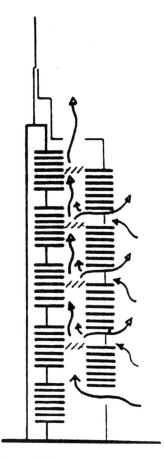

Figure 12.18
Natural ventilation paths in the Commerzbank

ventilation system which is linked to a chilled ceiling system that operates throughout the building.

The curtain wall design is on *Klimafassade* (climate facade) principles. Air enters at each floor in the facade into a 200 mm cavity where it heats up and passes out through the top of the cavity, which is, in effect, a thermal chimney. The climate facade consists of a 12 mm glass outer skin that has been specially coated to absorb radar signals, presumably from the airport. The inner skin of the facade is Low E double glazing giving the overall system a high U-value. There are permanent vents in the outer skin whilst the inner double glazed element has openable vents which can be overriden by the BMS when circumstances demand it. Motorised aluminium blinds in the cavity provide solar shading. It is calculated that the ventilation system will use only 35 per cent of the energy of an air conditioned office.

This is a remarkable attempt to create an extremely high tower block which minimises its environmental impact whilst also providing optimum comfort and amenity for its occupants. It also demonstrates how bioclimatic architecture is subject to the vagaries of political fortune. If the Greens had not had their brief moment of glory it is likely that this building would never have happened.

In 2004 Number 30 St Mary Axe, the London headquarters of the international reinsurers Swiss Re, was completed (Figure 12.19). It is claimed by its architects Foster and Partners to be the first environmental skyscraper in the City. At 40 storeys its circular plan and cone-like shape differentiate it from all other high buildings in London. The question is whether this is a piece of architectural whimsy or a form that arises from a logical functional brief. There is no doubt as to its genetic origin which is the Commerzbank in Frankfurt with its triangular plan and four-storey atria which rotate around the plan (Figures 12.19–12.21).

The idea of an atrium space easily accessible at all levels has now evolved into six spiral light wells that have a platform at every sixth floor. The spirals are accentuated in darker glass on the elevation. Triangular in plan they serve to provide both light and ventilation. The curved aerodynamic shape ensures then even high winds slide off the surfaces making minimum impact. This, in turn, has made it possible to incorporate motorised opening windows in the atria to assist natural ventilation. Floors between the break-out spaces have balconies to the atria. The 39th floor is a restaurant offering spectacular views for the privileged few.

According to the services engineers Hilson Moran, the ventilation system would be boosted by air pressure variation produced by the circular form driving the natural ventilation cycle. The atria/lightwells provide natural ventilation and act as 'lungs' for the building, providing natural ventilation for 40 per cent of the year. Overall the ventilation system is mixed mode employing air conditioning which is perhaps inevitable in a building of this height and location. However, the energy

Figure 12.19
Swiss Re Insurance Group
headquarters, London

impact of the air conditioning is reduced by a series of heat recovery units. Both natural and mechanical ventilation systems are controlled by an intelligent building management system.

The external skin is a climate facade consisting of an external double glazed external screen and single internal glazing. The space between serves as a ventilated cavity, removing warm air in summer and providing insulation in winter. Solar controlled blinds are positioned within the cavity.

A circular plan has the advantage of maximising daylight in the office floors which are situated around the perimeter with circulation taking up the core of the building.

Altogether the environmental attributes of the design result in an estimated energy consumption of 150 kWh/m² per year which repre-sents a 50 per cent saving compared with a traditional, good practice design, fully serviced office development of similar size.

This building highlights one of the dilemmas of bioclimatic archi-tecture, namely that a bespoke building may only be partly used by the building owner. In this case Swiss Re will undertake rigorous energy

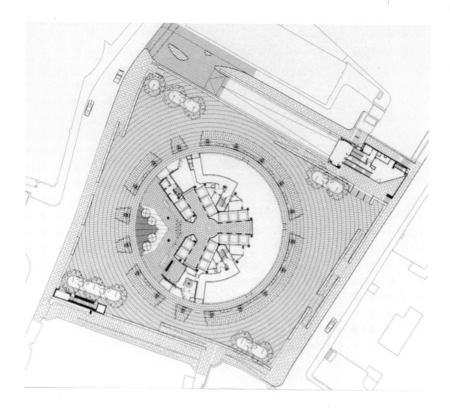

Figure 12.20
Ground floor plan and piazza

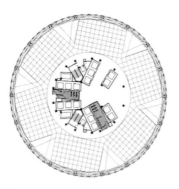

Figure 12.21
Upper floors with triangular atria

management. However, much of the tower will be let out with no guarantee of a similar quality of energy management. The worst case scenario is that the system will be allowed to default to air conditioning which will negate the energy efficiency targets of the designers.

Nearby, in Aldgate, Nicholas Grimshaw and Partners are constructing a 49-storey office building, the Minerva Tower (Figure 12.22).

Like the previous examples in the book this will maximise natural ventilation as part of a mixed-mode ventilation strategy within the constraints of a high rise building. The services engineers, Roger Preston and Partners, reckon that if the natural ventilation capacity is used to the full, it should produce a two thirds energy saving against a conventional sealed air conditioned equivalent. Again the design makes maximum use of the climate facade principle which adds about 3 per cent to the cost and reduces the floor plate. When the energy savings are capitalised it quickly becomes clear that the extra cost is soon recovered, offering considerable revenue benefits thereafter.

Up to the seventh floor occupants can open windows behind a protective glass screen. Above this level the climate facade comes into its own. This moderates the problems associated with high rise buildings: high wind velocity, pollution and noise. The natural ventilation works by allowing occupants to operate double glazed windows which open into a 650 mm space sealed from the outside by a single skin of

Figure 12.22
Minerva Tower

glazing. Vents at the top and bottom of this void allow access for fresh air. This means that, even at a height of 200 m, air velocity can be moderated by vents, allowing it to enter the office space at an agreeable velocity. The designers are optimistic that the tower will be able to operate in natural mode for about two thirds of the year, with mechanical ventilation only necessary in extremely hot, cold or windy conditions.

The seasonal variations in the operation of the climate facade are shown in Figure 12.23.

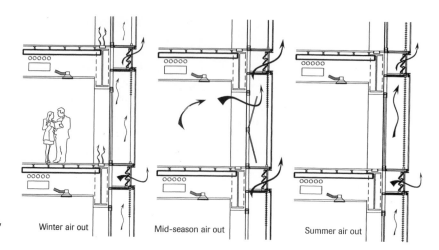

Figure 12.23
Natural ventilation in a climate facade, Minerva 2

Winter air out   Mid-season air out   Summer air out

Summary

Ventilation and air movement – recommendations

- Help cool occupants by increasing air movement during day time.
- Cool the structure of building using cooler air normally available at night.
- Plan the siting of building openings to enhance natural ventilation.
- Investigate the use of wing walls to improve air flow through openings.
- Allow stack effect flow paths to produce ventilation air movement.
- Consider the use of solar chimneys to enhance stack air movement.
- Wind towers and wind catchers can be used to derive additional air flow.
- Internal fans – box, oscillating and ceiling types – should be available when alternative air flow is insufficient.

Absorption of heat gain

- Absorption cooling uses natural sources of heat to drive simple absorption refrigeration systems.
- Lithium bromide and ammonia-based refrigerants are most frequently used.
- Heat is removed from the building by air or liquid cooled by the absorption system.

Radiative loss of heat

- Radiant heat loss from building surfaces can be improved by consideration of the geometry of the building in relation to the sky and other structures.

- Exposed roof surfaces may allow night-time cooling in suitable climates.

Earth cooling strategies

- The temperature of the earth below ground is generally cooler and more stable than the air above ground.
- The earth is used to absorb heat either by building wholly or partly underground or by passing air through ducts or passages, usually one to three metres below the surface, prior to supply to the building.

Air conditioning

Air conditioning systems have high energy demands for heating and particularly cooling systems. In addition the rates of air flow are often substantially higher than with simple mechanical ventilation systems, thus requiring heavy duty energy guzzling fans. The additional proportion of energy consumption is not matched by a proportional increase in comfort. The system is often operated for large fractions of the day when a suitable building design combined with an appropriate environmental control strategy would obviate the need for such air conditioning. The extravagant use of air conditioning is particularly noteworthy in the temperate climate of the United Kingdom.

There are of course some circumstances in which air conditioning is necessary. However, its use should be justified by the particular circumstances. In general it can be asserted that climate-sensitive design can eliminate the need for air conditioning in most instances.

Where air conditioning is deemed necessary, it likely to be of prime importance in only a fraction of the whole building and therefore designers should design for appropriate compartmentalisation with the conditioned area sealed from the remainder of the building.

Chapter Thirteen

Energy options

Electricity is the ultimate convenience source of energy which disguises the fact that, with present methods of production and the fuel mix, it is highly energy *inefficient*. At its point of use, that is, as delivered energy, it is around 30 per cent efficient. Energy is defined as 'primary' and 'delivered'. Primary energy is that which is contained in the fuel in its natural state; delivered energy is that which is in the fuel at the point of use.

At present fossil-based energy is relatively cheap because, as indicated earlier, it does not carry its external costs such as the damage to health, to forests, to buildings and above all to climate. It may soon become politically necessary to incorporate these costs into the price of fossil fuels which will have huge economic consequences. Meanwhile the biggest carbon dioxide (CO_2) abatement gains are to be realised in cutting demand especially in buildings. Even at the current price of energy green buildings can be cost effective.

It is worth noting the relative CO_2 emissions between different forms of fossil-based energy:

	kg/kWh delivered
Electricity	0.75
Coal	0.31
Fuel oil	0.28
Gas	0.21

Much has been made of the UK's switch to gas fired electricity generation, yet still electricity accounts for 750 grams of CO_2 in the atmosphere for every kilowatt hour.

An increasingly popular way of servicing commercial and institutional buildings is by combine heat and power (CHP). It can be one of the more efficient ways of using energy. A typical distribution of total energy output from a CHP system is

Electricity	25%
High grade heat	55%
Medium grade heat	10%
Low grade heat	10%

This is called the 'energy balance' of CHP and it is attractive for two main reasons:

- Most of the energy of the fuel is useful.
- It can be adapted to low to zero carbon applications.

A CHP system is flexible. At present most CHP installations operate with gas or diesel reciprocating engines or turbines for larger installations. However, even relatively small installations will soon be able to switch to gas fired micro-turbines. Later in the decade there will probably be a considerable rise in the use of fuel cells. This is the technology of the future.

The fuel cell

Fuel cells are electrochemical devices that generate DC electricity similar to batteries. Unlike batteries they take their energy from a continuous supply of fuel, usually hydrogen. The fuel cell is not an energy storage device but may be considered as an electrochemical internal combustion engine. It is a reactor which combines hydrogen and oxygen to produce electricity, heat and water. Thus its environmental credentials are impeccable. The problem at the moment is that it is an expensive way of producing energy. Each installed kilowatt costs $3000 to $4000; whereas a combined cycle gas turbine system costs $400 per kilowatt. The reason for this cost difference is that the fuel cell uses platinum as a catalyst. However, experts think that the quantity of platinum can be cut by a factor of 5, which will bring about a significant reduction in cost. There will also be considerable reductions as mass production begins to bite. The latest prediction is that the cost should fall to between $600 and $1000 per kilowatt.

Fuel cells are efficient, clean and quiet with no moving parts and are ideal for combined heat and power application. For static cells in buildings perhaps the most promising technology is the solid oxide fuel cell which operates at around 800°C. Most fuel cells work with hydrogen. At present the most cost-effective way to obtain the hydrogen is by reforming natural gas. According to Amory Lovins 'A reformer the size of a water heater can produce enough hydrogen to serve the fuel cells in dozens of cars' (*New Scientist*, 25 November 2000, p. 41). In that case it will not be long before it will be possible to buy a fuel cell and reformer kit for the home which will make it independent of the grid providing heat and power much more cheaply than is possible at present. Considerable research effort is being directed into improving the efficiency and lowering the cost of fuel cells because this is the technology of the twenty-first century and huge rewards await whoever makes that breakthrough. According to David Hart of Imperial College 'If fuel cells fulfil their potential, there is no reason why they shouldn't replace almost every battery and combustion engine in the world' (*New Scientist*, Inside Science 'Fuelling the Future', 16 June 2001).

At present there are five versions of fuel cell technology. The proton exchange membrane system is the most straightforward and serves to explain the basic principles of the fuel cell.

Proton exchange membrane fuel cell

Sometimes called the polymer electrolyte membrane fuel cell (PEMFC in either case) it is also referred to as the solid polymer fuel cell. This is one of the most common types of cell being appropriate for both vehicle and static application. Of all the cells in production it has the lowest operating temperature of 80°C. The cell consists of an anode and a cathode separated by an electrolyte, usually Teflon. Both the anode and cathode are coated with platinum which acts as a catalyst. Hydrogen is fed to the anode and an oxidant (oxygen from the air) to the cathode. The catalyst on the anode causes the hydrogen to split into its constituent protons and electrons. The electrolyte membrane allows only protons to pass through to the cathode setting up a charge separation in the process. The electrons pass through an external circuit creating useful energy at around 0.7 volts then recombining with protons at the cathode to produce water and heat (Figure 13.1).

To build up a useful voltage cells are stacked between conductive bi-polar plates, usually graphite, which have integral channels to allow the free flow of hydrogen and oxygen (Figure 13.2).

The electrical efficiency of the PEMFC is 35 per cent with a target of 45 per cent. Its energy density is 0.3 kW/kg compared with 1.0 kW/kg for internal combustion engines.

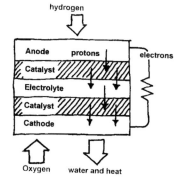

Figure 13.1
Basic structure and function of the proton exchange membrane fuel cell

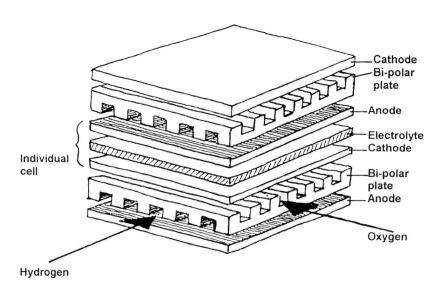

Figure 13.2
Fuel cell stack

One problem with the PEMFC is that it requires hydrogen of a high degree of purity. Research activity is focusing on finding cheaper and more robust catalysts as well as more efficient ion exchange polymer electrolytes.

Phosphoric acid fuel cell (PAFC)

Similar to PEMFCs this cell operates in the middle temperature range at around 200°C. This means it can tolerate some impurities. It employs a phosphoric acid proton conducting electrolyte and platinum or platinum–rhodium electrodes. The main difference from a PEMFC is that it uses a liquid electrolyte.

The system efficiency is currently in the 37–43 per cent range, but this is expected to improve. This technology seems particularly popular in Japan where electricity costs are high and dispersed generation is preferred. A 200 kW unit which uses sewage gas provides heat and power for Yokohama sewage works. The largest installation to date for the Tokyo Electric Power Company had an output of 11 megawatts – until it expired.

PAFC units have been used experimentally in buses. However, it is likely that its future lies in stationary systems.

The *New Scientist* editorial referred to above predicts that 'Larger, static fuel cells will become attractive for hotels and sports centres, while power companies will use them as alternatives to extending the electricity grid.' An example of this is the police station in Central Park, New York, which found that installing a PAFC of 200 kW capacity was cheaper than a grid connection requiring new cables in the park (David Hart, op. cit.). One year after this prediction the Borough of Woking, Surrey, UK, installed the first commercial PAFC fuel cell to operate in the UK. It also has a capacity of 200 kW and provides heat, cooling, light and dehumidification for the Pool in the Park recreation centre. The fuel cell forms part of Woking Park's larger combined heat and power system (see p. 242).

Solid oxide fuel cell (SOFC)

This is a cell suitable only for static application, taking several hours to reach its operating temperature. It is a high temperature cell, running at between 800 and 1000°C. Its great virtue is that it can run on a range of fuels including natural gas and methanol which can be reformed within the cell. Its high operating temperature also enables it to break down impurities. Its high temperature also removes the need for noble metal catalysts such as platinum.

It potentially has a wide range of power outputs, from 2 to 1000 kW.

In contrast to PEMFCs the electrolyte conducts oxygen ions rather than hydrogen ions which move from the cathode to the anode. The

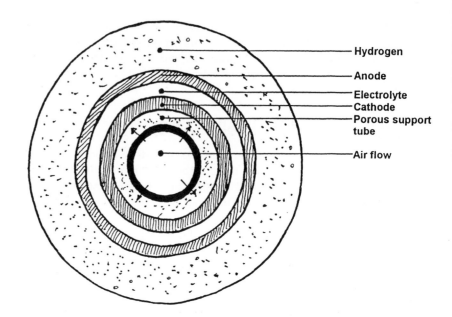

Figure 13.3
Solid oxide fuel cell in its tubular
configuration

Hydrogen
Anode
Electrolyte
Cathode
Porous support
tube
Air flow

electrolyte is a ceramic which becomes conductive to oxygen ions at
800°C. SOFCs are often structured in a tubular rather than a planar form
(as in the PEMFC) to reduce the chance of failure of the seals due to
high temperature expansion. Air (oxygen) flows through a central tube
whilst fuel flows round the outside of the structure (Figure 13.3).

According to David Hart of Imperial College 'Solid oxide fuel cells
are expected to have the widest range of applications. Large units
should be useful in industry for generating electricity and heat. Smaller
units could be used in houses.

Alkaline fuel cells (AFC)

This fuel cell dates back to the 1940s and was the first to be fully developed in the 1960s. It was used in the Apollo spacecraft programme. It
employs an alkaline electrolyte such as potassium hydroxide set between
nickel or precious metal electrodes. Its operating temperature is 60–80°C
which enables it to have a short warm-up time. However, its energy
density is merely one tenth that of a PEMFC which makes it much bulkier
for a given output.

Molten carbonate fuel cell (MCFC)

This is a high temperature fuel cell operating at about 650°C. The
electrolyte in this case is an alkaline mixture of lithium and potassium

carbonates which becomes liquid at 650°C and is supported by a ceramic matrix. The electrodes are both nickel based. The operation of the MCFC differs from that of other fuel cells in that it involves carbonate ion transfer across the electrolyte. This makes it tolerate both carbon monoxide and carbon dioxide. The cell can consume hydrocarbon fuels that are reformed into hydrogen within the cell.

The MCFC can achieve an efficiency of 55 per cent. The steam and carbon dioxide it produces can be used to drive a turbine generator (cogeneration) which can raise the total efficiency to 80 per cent – up to twice that of a typical oil or gas fired plant. Consequently this technology could be ideal for urban power stations producing combined heat and power. The Energy Research Corporation (ERC) of Danbury, Connecticut, USA, has built a 2 megawatt unit for the municipality of Santa Clara, California, and that company is currently developing a 2.85 megawatt plant.

Development programmes in Japan and the US have produced small prototype units in the 5–20 kW range, which, if successful, will make them attractive for domestic combined heat and power.

The main disadvantage of the MCFC is that it uses as electrolytes highly corrosive molten salts that create both design and maintenance problems. Research is concentrating on solutions to this problem.

In March 2000 it was announced that researchers in the University of Pennsylvania in Philadelphia had developed a cell that could run directly off natural gas or methane. It did not have to be reformed to produce hydrogen. Other fuel cells cannot run directly on hydrocarbons which clog the catalyst within minutes. This innovative cell uses a copper and cerium oxide catalyst instead of nickel. The researchers consider that cars will be the main beneficiaries of the technology. However, Kevin Kendall, a chemist from the University of Keele, thinks differently. According to him 'Millions of homeowners replace their gas-fired central heating systems in Europe every year. Within five years they could be installing a fuel cell that would run on natural gas . . . Every home could have a combined heat and power plant running off mains gas' (*New Scientist*, 18 March 2000). That prediction should perhaps be raised to 2010.

International Fuel Cells (US) is testing a cell producing 5 kW to 10 kW of electricity and hot water at 120–160°C for heating. This is a residential system which the US company Plug Power, which is linked to General Electric, is marketing as the 'GE HomeGen 7000' domestic fuel cell.

Professor Tony Marmont, the initiator of the fuel cell in his West Beacon farm, considers a scenario whereby the fuel cell in a car would operate in conjunction with a home or office. He estimates that a car spends 96 per cent of its time stationary so it would make sense to couple the car to a building to provide space and domestic hot water heat. The electricity generated would be sold to the grid. The car would be fuelled by a hydrogen grid. Until that is available a catalyser within the car would reform methanol or even natural gas from the mains to provide the hydrogen.

The reason for the intensification of research activity is the belief that the fuel cell is the energy technology of the future in that it meets a cluster of needs, not least the fact that it can be a genuine zero carbon dioxide energy source. It could also relieve us of reliance on a national grid which, in many countries, is unreliable. Perhaps the greatest beneficiaries will initially be rural communities in developing countries who could never hope to get access to a grid supply. Access to energy is the main factor which divides the rich from the poor throughout the world. A cheap fuel cell powered by hydrogen electrolysed from PV, solar-electric or small-scale hydroelectricity could be the ultimate answer to this unacceptable inequality.

There is little doubt that we are approaching the threshold of the hydrogen-based economy. Ultimately hydrogen should be available 'on tap' through a piped network. In the meantime reforming natural gas, petrol, propane and other hydrocarbons to produce hydrogen would still result in massive reductions in carbon dioxide emissions and pollutants like oxides of sulphur and nitrogen. The domestic-scale fuel cells will have built-in processing units to reform hydrocarbon fuels and the whole system will occupy about the same space as a central heating boiler.

The fuel cell will really come into its own when it is fuelled by hydrogen produced from renewable sources like solar cells, wind- and marine-based renewables. If tidal energy is exploited to its full potential there will be peak surpluses of electricity which could serve to create hydrogen via electrolysis.

The first domestic scale fuel call was installed in the experimental Self-Sufficient Solar House created by Fraunhofer Institute for Solar Energy Systems in Freiburg in 1994. Its hydrogen was electrolysed from PVs on its roof and stored in an outside tank (Figure 5.6).

In the US there are growing problems in some areas over the reliability of the power supply and this is increasing the attractiveness of fuel cells. In Portland, Oregon hydrogen extracted from methane from a sewage works generates power sufficient to light 100 homes. The same happens in California where sewage from the Virgenes Municipal Water District in Calabasas reforms methane into hydrogen to supply a fuel cell that provides 90 per cent of the power needed to run the plant. If it were available to the grid it would power 300 homes.

The US Department of Energy plans to power two to four million households with hydrogen and fuel cells by 2010 and ten million by 2030. If the hydrogen is obtained from sewage, livestock waste, underground methane or water split by PV/wind electrolysis then this programme will certainly be one to be emulated by all industrialised countries.

Fuel cells reliant on renewable energy will be heavily dependent on an efficient electricity storage system. At present this is one of the main stumbling blocks to a pollution-free future.

The main barrier to the widespread adoption of fuel cells is the cost. The US Department of Energy estimates that the current cost of a fuel cell is ~$3000 per kilowatt. A UK firm ITM Power of Cambridge is claiming that it should be able to reduce this to ~$100/kW by developing a simplified fuel cell architecture based on a patented unique family of ionically conducting polymers which are cheap to produce. Production costs will be considerably reduced due to its patented one-stop manufacturing process. A complete fuel cell stack would be made in a single process. It plans to have domestic-scale fuel cells on the market in 2005.

Storage techniques – electricity

Flywheel technology

The use of flywheel technology to store energy has been pioneered in vehicles. Braking energy is used to power a flywheel which then supplements acceleration energy. The development thrust, however, has come from space technology. Its true potential lies in the storage of energy over a much longer term and in larger quantities as friction problems are overcome. An experimental project is underway on the Isle of Islay which is also the site of the pioneer wave energy projects (Chapter 3).

The Japanese are taking the technology further by developing a levitating flywheel using high temperature superconducting ceramics to repel magnetic fields. The flywheel is made to rotate by electromagnetic induction to a speed of 3600 revolutions per minute which represents an energy storage capacity of 10 000 watt hours. Energy can be drawn off by the permanent magnets in the disc inducing an electric current in a coil. If situated in a vacuum, the energy loss over a 24 hour period would be negligible (*New Scientist*, 13 July 1991, p. 28).

Hydrogen storage

Hydrogen has an image problem thanks to regular replays of the Hindenberg disaster. The traditional storage method is to contain it in pressurised tanks (see Freiburg House, Figure 16). Up to 50 litres can be stored at 200 to 250 bar. Larger-scale operations need pressures of 500–600 bar.

It can be liquefied, but this requires cooling to $-253°C$ which is highly energy intensive. In this form it has a high energy to mass ratio – three times better than petrol but it requires heavily insulated tanks.

Bonded hydrogen is one of the more favoured options. Metal hydrides such as FeTi compounds store hydrogen by bonding it chemically to the surface of the material. The metal is charged by injecting hydrogen at high pressure into a container filled with small particles.

The hydrogen bonds with the material producing heat in the process. The hydrogen is released as the heat and pressure dissipate.

Regenerative fuel cell

A technology which is about to receive its first large-scale demonstration is based on a technology called 'Regenesys'. It converts electrical energy to chemical energy which is reversible and is capable of storing massive amounts of electricity.

National Power in the UK is constructing a 360 GJ installation with a rated power output of 15 MW which will feed directly into the grid.

In the opinion of the Royal Commission on Environmental Pollution, hydrogen and regenerative fuel cells will be in widespread operation by the middle of the century. If global warming and security of energy supply issues simultaneously become critical then viable large-scale storage technologies will arrive much sooner.

Photovoltaic applications

Commercial buildings have perhaps the greatest potential for PV cells to be integrated into their glazing as well as being roof mounted. Even at the present state of the technology, Ove Arup and Partners estimate that one third of the electricity needed to run an office complex could come from PVs with only a 2 per cent addition to the building cost. The main advantage of commercial application is that offices use most of their energy during daylight hours. The case study of the Zicer building in the University of East Anglia will serve as an example (Chapter 18).

One of the challenges of the next decades will be to retrofit buildings with PVs. A pioneer example is the Northumberland Building for the University of Northumbria in Newcastle where cells have been applied to the spandrels beneath the continuous windows (see Smith, P., and Pitts, A.C. (1997), *Concepts in Practice Energy*, Batsford).

Given the abundance of information and advice available, designers should now be able to grasp the opportunities offered by such technologies which also allow exploration of a range of new aesthetic options for the building envelope.

The most extensive use of PV technology has been in the commercial and institutional sector. Reference was made earlier to the solar offices at Doxford with its complete southerly facade supporting 400 000 PV cells.

More recently the technology has been incorporated into an atrium roof at Nottingham University's Jubilee Campus (Figure 13.4).

However, much more ambitious PV programmes have been carried out on the continent. In Chapter 11 the example of the Mont Cenis training centre in Germany was cited as an ambitious use of PVs. It is a multi-use complex, principally an Academy for Further Education, a hotel, offices and a library. These are contained within a glazed envelope 180 m by 72 m and 16 m high. Of the 12 000 m^2 of roof, 10 000 m^2 are

Figure 13.4
Photovoltaic cells, Jubilee Campus,
Nottingham University

devoted to PV cells producing more than twice the energy demand of the building (Figure 13.5).

The PV market is growing dramatically – 43.8 per cent in 2002 with most going to grid connected supply in Japan, Germany and California. This is a technology which is seen to have enormous potential and therefore is attracting considerable research effort. The Sunpower Corporation is manufacturing a solar cell which achieves an efficiency of over 20 per cent as verified by the US National Renewable Energy Laboratory. This laboratory has also verified the bench efficiency of 36.9 per cent achieved by Spectrolab's Improved Triple Junction solar cell. Efficiencies of over 40 per cent are confidently predicted. As economies of scale also bring down costs, the impact on the electricity market could be dramatic with the potential for every home to become a micro-power station. Before these developments had occurred, Hermann Scheer calculated that Germany's aggregate demand of 500 TWh/year could be met by installing PVs on 10 per cent of roofs, facades and motor-way sound barriers (*The Solar Economy*, p. 64, Earthscan 1999).

Heat pumps

Heat pumps are an offshoot of refrigeration technology and are capable of providing both heat and cooling. They exploit the principle that

Figure 13.5
PV roof over the Mont Cenis complex,
Herne Sodingen, Germany

certain chemicals absorb heat when they are condensed into a liquid and release heat when they evaporate into a gas.

There are several different refrigerants that can be used for space heating and cooling with widely varying global warming potential (GWP). Refrigerants which have an ozone depleting potential are now banned. Currently refrigerants which have virtually zero GWP on release include ammonia which is one of the most prevalent.

The heating and cooling capacity of the refrigerant is enhanced by the extraction of warmth or cooling from an external medium – earth, air or water.

The most efficient is the ground source heat pump (GSHP) which originated in the 1940s. This is another technology which goes back a long way but which is only now realising its potential as a technology for the future.

It exploits the stable temperature of the earth for both heating and cooling. The principle of the GHP is that it does not create heat; it transports it from one area to another. The main benefit of this technology is that it uses up to 50 per cent less electricity than conventional electrical heating or cooling.

At present ground coupled heat pumps have a coefficient of performance (COP) between 3 and 4 which means that for every kilowatt of electricity they produce 3 to 4 kilowatts of useful heat. The theoretical ultimate COP for heat pumps is 14. In the near future a COP of 6 is likely.

Most ground coupled heat pumps adopt the closed loop system whereby a high density polyethylene pipe filled with a mix of water and antifreeze, which acts as a heat transporter, is buried in the ground. It is laid in a U configuration vertically and a loop horizontally. The vertical pipes descend up to a 100 m depth; the horizontal loop is laid at a minimum of 2 m depth.

The horizontal type is most common in residential situations where there is usually adequate open space and because it incurs a much lower excavation cost than the alternative. The only problem is that, even at a 2 m depth, the circuit can be affected by solar gain or rainfall evaporation. In each case the presence of moving ground water improves performance.

Usually the lowest cost option is to use water in a pond, lake or river as the heat transfer medium. The supply pipe is run underground from the building and coiled into circles at least 2 m below the surface.

Heat pumps have been compared to rechargeable batteries that are permanently connected to a trickle charger. The battery is the ground loop array which has to be large enough, together with a matched compressor, to meet the heating/cooling load of a building. The energy trickle comes from the surrounding land which recharges the volume of ground immediately surrounding the loop. If the energy removed from the ground exceeds the ground's regeneration capacity, the system ceases to function, so it is essential that demand is matched to the ground capacity (from Dr Robin Curtis, GeoScience Ltd).

Pencoys Primary School in Cornwall is an example of a PFI project by W.S. Atkins which supplements its energy with GS heat pumps. The system has 15 shafts sunk to a depth of 45 m. The heat pumps produce water at 45–50°C which is stored in two 700 litre insulated buffer tanks. A secondary circuit serves to provide underfloor heating at about 50°C. The system has a coefficient of performance of 4. The heat pumps operate mainly at night using off-peak electricity to minimise costs. The stored heat together with internal heat gains and the thermal mass of the building provide space heating for most of the time. In really cold weather immersion heaters in the storage vessels boost heat output.

At current energy prices the system is more expensive to run than a conventional boiler installation. However, gas prices will probably continue to rise due to security of supply problems. This, plus the climate change levy, will enable the system to overtake a standard boiler option in economy of running costs in the near future. The system was designed by GeoScience.

GeoScience was also involved in the design of one of the first business parks in the UK to exploit this technology, namely the Tolvaddon Energy Park in Cornwall which exploits geothermal energy with 19 heat pumps that pump water around boreholes to a depth of 70 metres. This project was only made viable because of support from the Regional Development Agency (RDA) for the South West which required that this business park should be a demonstration of heat pump technology.

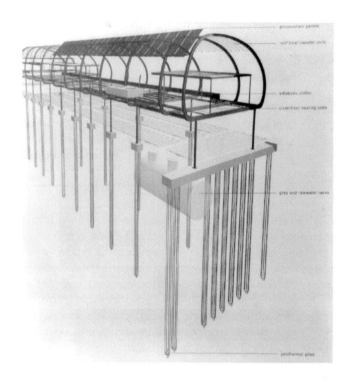

Figure 13.6
Building of the Future, London

Where buildings require piled foundations, an economical option is to integrate ground source heat pumps into the foundations as demonstrated by the 'Building of the Future', Primrose Hill, London, by Richard Paxton Architects (Figure 13.6). This is a mixed office and residential development totalling 1000 m². The GS heat pumps utilise four plastic pipe loops connected to the reinforcement steel of the piles. These supply both heating and cooling to the floors depending on the season. A secondary coil is positioned in the roof and linked to the central manifold. This supplements the heating when necessary but also serves as a night cooling system by dumping heat in summer. A gas boiler and evaporative (adiabatic) mechanical cooling act as backup to the heat pumps.

In addition, PVs on the roof meet most of the electricity needs of the building. In all it is expected that energy costs compared with conventional heating and cooling will be reduced by about 30 per cent (Figure 13.6).

Energy storage – heating and cooling

Sources of natural energy are intermittent. To obtain continuous flows of energy using such sources therefore requires systems of storage. As stated earlier, this is not a new concept since, in the Middle Ages, tide mills stored water at high tide in order to release it at an appropriate rate to turn the water wheel during the ebb tide.

Energy storage offers an efficiency and cost gain in two respects. First, in buildings that optimise solar gain, surplus solar energy can be used to charge a storage facility to be used later for space heating. Second, storage can help to flatten the peaks of electricity costs by charging the store with off-peak electricity and using the stored power to reduce demand at peak periods.

The storage potential of energy is available for three purposes: heating, cooling and the storage of electricity.

Heat storage

The most straightforward method of storage is by means of a network of pipes carrying solar heated air though a reasonably dense medium such as bricks, concrete blocks or water. The storage container is heavily insulated. If sufficient space is available below a building, enough heat can be stored to supplement space heating through the whole of the heating season, hence the term 'seasonal storage'. Alternatively, off-peak or PV derived electricity may be used as the heating element. More sophisticated is the use of a phase change material such as sodium sulphate which works on the principle of the latent heat of fusion. Called eutectic or 'Glaubars' salts this medium turns from solid to liquid at around 30°C and then gives off heat as it solidifies.

Cool storage

As the automatic inclusion of full air conditioning is increasingly being questioned, the problem of space cooling enters a new dimension. Again the principle is to use spare energy, off-peak or PV electricity, to refrigerate a medium. At its crudest, the medium may be the earth beneath a building. A more practicable method is to use phase change and the latent heat of fusion as above to provide high density storage. One option called the STL storage system comprises a storage vessel containing spherical polyethylene nodules filled with a solution of eutectic salts and hydrates. This system is ideal in situations where there is cyclic demand since it facilitates cooling (or heating) when energy costs are at their lowest or a plant is shut down. In conjunction with air conditioning, this system can result in a dramatic lowering of the required capacity of the chiller unit. The system may be given a lift in efficiency by the use of heat pumps which provide either cooling or warmth on the principle of a refrigerator.

As indicated earlier, the building fabric can be a significant energy storage system on the basis of thermal mass. Heat absorbed by the structure flattens the peaks and troughs of temperature. Exposed concrete floors have been cited as an efficient storage medium for convective and radiative heat transfer. It is worth noting again that it is the outer 100 mm of the fabric which comprise the effective thermal mass. The effectiveness of the underside of the floor is negated by suspended ceilings. However, a compromise solution is perforated tiles which have an open area of 42 per cent which is sufficient to allow 91.6 per cent overall heat transfer whilst concealing services.

Seasonal energy storage

A marriage between solar energy and the thermal constancy of the ground offers an opportunity to make significant reductions in both the heating and cooling loads generated by buildings. Known as 'aquifer storage' the principle is that, in summer, buildings absorb considerable amounts of surplus heat which can either be vented to the atmosphere or used to provide a reservoir of warmth for the winter. The energy storage system comprises two wells drilled into the water table below the building, one warm the other cold. The system relies on the fact that ground water is a constant (10–12°C in the UK).

This system should be distinguished from the tanked seasonal storage at Frierichshafen described earlier which is fed by solar thermal panels.

In summer water from the cold well is pumped into the building and, via a heat exchanger, cools the ventilation system. As it passes through the building it absorbs heat ending up at around 15–20°C. It is then returned to the warm well. In winter the system is reversed and warm water heats the ventilation air. It loses heat to the building and returns to the cold well at about 8°C to be stored for summer cooling (Figure 13.7).

Figure 13.7
Principles of seasonal storage
(courtesy of CADDET)

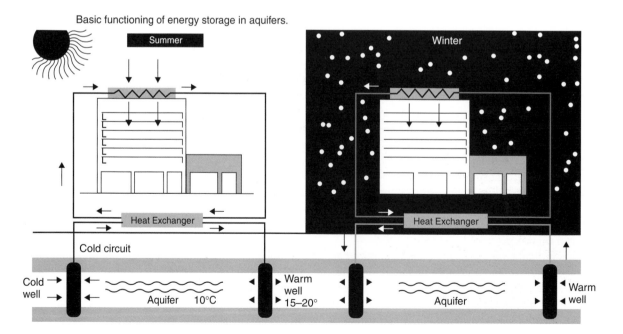
Basic functioning of energy storage in aquifers.

The Netherlands are leading the way in this technology with 19 projects completed or under way with a projected annual primary energy saving of 1.5 million cubic metres of natural gas equivalent. Recent buildings to benefit from this technology include the Reichstag in Berlin and the city hall and Schiphol Airport offices in The Hague.

In the case of the Reichstag surplus heat is stored interseasonally in a natural aquifer 400 m below ground. Aquifers at 40 m depth are used for cooling.

The Sainsbury supermarket at Greenwhich Peninsular, completed in September 1999, employs earth sheltered walls to regulate temperature on the sales floor. Ventilation air is passed through underground ducts to maintain cooling. Also there are two 75 m deep boreholes, one absorbing heat from refrigeration equipment, the other providing ground cooling.

Electricity storage

Batteries

Battery technology is still the most common method of storage, but the promised breakthrough in this technology has yet to materialise. Still in general use is the traditional lead acid battery which is heavy, expensive and of limited life. Even the ground-breaking Freiburg zero electric house relied on lead acid batteries for its fall-back position. The PV hydrogen fuel cell copes with most of the year (Figure 13.8).

Lighter but more expensive are nickel–cadmium batteries which have the advantage of rapid charging achieved by low internal resistence.

Figure 13.8
Banks of lead acid batteries in the Freiburg Solar House

The car industry is particularly interested in this form of storage. There are, of course, serious environmental hazards associated with cadmium.

One of the most promising batteries is the Ovonic nickel–metal hydride battery. It can be discharged and recharged up to 10 000 times. As an indication of its efficiency, a lead acid battery could give a vehicle a range of 190 kilometres. The Ovonic battery would raise this to 480 kilometres. This order of improvement makes it an attractive storage proposition for buildings employing PV generation (Ball, P. (1997) *Made to Measure*, Princeton, p. 258).

Building management systems

Digital control mechanisms and the availability of system controls to operate them have developed rapidly since the 1970s. The incorporation of computers, modern multiple-parameter optimisation techniques and intelligent control have enhanced the opportunity to provide very sophisticated environmental control systems in buildings. Often the environmental data collection and control system is incorporated within an overall building management system (BMS) which also deals with communication networks, security, fire protection, lift operation, occupancy related scheduling and a number of other functions. Frequently, the system is under the control of a facilities manager. The portion of the system dealing with energy is the building energy management system (BEMS), which may in some circumstances operate autonomously. The location of the control system need not be on-site and the supervision of the system may well be located centrally for multiple building complexes or for a series of similar buildings in outlying areas.

BMS/BEMS are generally designed to operate to control heating, lighting, ventilation and air conditioning systems in terms of engineering the status of the internal environment. They can also be used to control more passive features such as window opening and shading device position.

The incorporation of whole building systems control has often been accompanied by centralisation of the decision-making power. As a result, though the building as a whole has the potential to optimise its energy and environmental performance to achieve some centrally defined goal, the ability of the occupants to influence their own environment has been degraded. This has left people with the feeling that if they do not match the typical occupant profile, they have to accept the discomfort. Further, there is evidence to show that occupants are more tolerant of less than perfect environmental conditions if they have some control over their immediate environment.

Poor occupant satisfaction with environmental control systems has also been associated with complaints of sick building syndrome. Further difficulties can arise if the facilities manager lacks either the time or the expertise to understand the complexities of the BMS analyses and thus does not appreciate the subtleties of the system or how the system can be fine tuned to create maximum energy savings.

Control of environmental conditions inside buildings is certainly of crucial importance in reducing energy consumption as well as affecting the well-being and efficiency of the occupants. Overcomplexity also affects the occupants who may revert to the option requiring least effort which may also be the least energy efficient. The combination of inadequate user control or central management can, as mentioned earlier, negate the benefits of the whole system.

Tools for environmental design

The three main categories of passive solar design, along with their subdivisions, are most usually applied within domestic-scale designs. However, similar principles have been analysed with reference to commercial developments. One assessment method that addresses this sector is the Lighting and Thermal Value of Glazing Method – the 'LT Method', developed in the UK. This method reduces a building to an orthogonal plan with core and perimeter zones. The perimeter zone is that which is subject to significant external climatic influences on its lighting, heating and cooling requirements. The perimeter zones are classified by orientation and depth, and are defined as passive zones. The technique gives annual comparisons and is relatively quick and easy to use.

The LT Method, which has so far been developed for use in the European climate, permits a straightforward prediction of likely energy use for lighting, heating and (if specified) cooling services on an annual basis. Such an approach, whilst being somewhat simplistic, does provide a quick guide to energy consumption by indicating optimum window size and orientation at the initial design stage. It is therefore valuable in determining the basic plan form. A number of variations of this method now exist to deal with a variety of building types. The system is described in Baker, N.V. (2000) *Energy and Environment in Non-domestic Buildings*, Cambridge Architectural Research Ltd, The Martin Centre, University of Cambridge.

For more complex analysis a number of programme suites now exist. The one which has been adopted as the European Reference Model is the Environmental Systems Performance Model produced by Integrated Environmental Solutions (IES) which can be linked to Autocad. This model is perhaps more appropriate at a post-graduate level.

At the time of writing one of the most sophisticated and comprehensive computer modelling systems also comes from IES (www.ies4d.com). Its programs facilitate a full dynamic thermal modelling of a building and consequent energy consumption (APACHE-calc and APACHE-sim).

Earlier, reference was made to its 'Suncast' program which generates shadows from any sun position. It has the advantage that its programs are graded in complexity and so can be introduced at undergraduate level.

In the non-domestic sector the benefits of, and problems associated with, solar radiation are summarised in Baker, N.V. (2000) *Energy and Environment in Non-Domestic Buildings*, Cambridge Architectural Research Ltd, The Martin Centre, University of Cambridge.

As a postscript to this chapter it is useful to summarise the conclusions of a report by Arup referred to earlier on building performance in the context of climate change up to 2080.

Report by Arup Research and Development for the DTI's Partners in Innovation Programme 2004

Report on offices

The datum for the research was the weather in 1989 which was extrapolated to 2020, 2050 and 2080 using data from the UK Climate Impacts Programme (UKCIP). The research used a median of four UKCIP climate change scenarios based on progress in abating CO_2 emissions. It predicts that temperatures in the south of England could be up to 8°C warmer by 2080 reaching 40°C. Above 28°C occupants experience increasing discomfort.

The report predicts that a 1960s office that is naturally ventilated will be unusable between June and August by 2080 with internal temperatures reaching 39°C. That is 3 degrees hotter than the July average for a street in Cairo. Natural ventilation is employed in 70 per cent of UK offices. This raises questions about current recommendations regarding night cooling of offices as the external air temperatures get hotter. It suggests that even offices which are air conditioned to current climate extremes will be inadequate.

The report recommends that air conditioning systems should be driven by renewable electricity – PVs etc. 'Air conditioning needs to be combined with passive cooling systems to provide a greener and more cost-effective solution' (Jake Hacker, project leader for the research). Such mixed mode solutions are the way for the future.

The report makes the sobering remark that even the BRE low energy office in Watford fails to meet BRE's own benchmark for comfort from 2020 onwards.

Lighting – designing for daylight

Chapter Fourteen

As one of the largest energy sinks for commercial and industrial buildings, lighting justifies special treatment. Furthermore, with buildings becoming increasingly energy efficient in terms of space heating so the lighting load becomes of greater significant. It will be some time before we realise the revolution in lighting promised by developments in light emitting diodes.

Current wisdom has it that office design should optimise natural lighting. One reason for this is that lighting is often the largest single item of energy cost, particularly in open plan offices. Another factor is that occupants tend to prefer natural light, especially since certain forms of artificial lighting have been implicated as the source of health problems.

Energy efficient buildings should make as much beneficial use of naturally available light as possible. Lighting is important because of the influence it has over occupant experience. Until about 50 years ago, the use of windows and plan form of buildings was very much influenced by the limits of natural light admission. The development of the fluorescent tube lamp made the deep plan office a feasible proposition but at the expense of noise pollution and frequency band discomfort. There was the added psychological penalty of reducing access to daylight and external views. It is only relatively recently that the importance of these benefits have been acknowledged.

Principal factors influencing levels of daylight are:

- orientation of windows;
- angle of tilt of windows;
- obstructions to light admission (e.g. nearby buildings);
- reflectivity of surrounding surfaces.

Factors which relate to the exploitation of daylight include:

- Windows provide external views and time orientation for occupants.
- Occupants are more accepting of variable illumination when daylight is the light source.
- Natural light produces a true colour rendering.

However, it would be unusual to expect to supply all lighting requirements using daylight in non-domestic buildings.

Design considerations

In order to achieve successful daylighting design, the following aspects should be considered:

- The amount of glazing has a clear influence on the amount of daylight available, but more window area is not always better, it may simply increase contrast.
- Large windows admit light but also provide heat gain and heat loss routes and thus potential thermal discomfort, especially from cold draughts near the windows.
- Allocation of rooms to facades should be appropriate to the activity – to do this successfully will require consideration of the issues at the building planning stage.
- The amount of sky which can be seen from the interior is a critical factor in determining satisfactory daylighting.
- High window heads permit higher lighting input as more sky is visible.
- External obstructions/buildings which subtend an angle of less than 25° to the horizontal will not usually exclude use of natural daylight.
- If there are many external obstructions the room depth should be reduced.
- Daylight normally penetrates about 4–6 m from the window into the room.
- Adequate daylight levels can be achieved up to a depth of about 2.5 times the window head height.
- Rooflights give a wider and more even distribution of light but also permit heat gains which may cause overheating.
- Generally rooflights provide about three times the benefit of an equivalently sized vertical window.
- Rooflight spacing should be one to one-and-a-half times the ceiling height.
- Where single sided daylighting is proposed, the following formula gives a limiting depth (L) to the room:

$$(L/W) + (L/H) <= 2/(1 - R_b)$$
where L = room depth, m
W = room width, m
H = height of top of window, m
R_b = average reflectance of internal surfaces

(Adrian Pitts in Smith, P. and Pitts, A.C. (1997) *Concepts in Practice – Energy*, Batsford).

- In non-domestic buildings, the window area should be about 20 per cent of the floor area to provide sufficient light to a depth of about 1.5 times the height of the room.
- Internal reflectances should be kept as high as possible.

Examples

One of the most dramatic techniques for channelling daylight into the deep interior of a building has been devised by Foster Associates for the Reichstag building.

The original design was for an all encompassing canopy but this proved much too expensive. Initially Norman Foster opposed the idea of reinstating a dome since this was emblematic of an era best forgotten. However, he yielded to pressure and used the dome as an opportunity to create something dramatic.

It is effectively a double dome, with the lower portion sealed from the upper space (echoes of Wren at St Paul's Cathedral). The upper cupola is a public space which permits views into the chamber. The spectacular feature is the cone designed by Claude Engel which is sheathed in 360 mirrors that reflect daylight into the lower chamber. Sun-tracking shading prevents direct sunlight from reaching the chamber. The cone houses air extract and heat exchange equipment. The motorised shading and the heat exchange equipment is powered by photovoltaics (Figure 14.1).

Figure 14.1
Reflective cone in the Reichstag

The atrium

The atrium has become an almost universal feature of commercial buildings. Occasionally the incorporation of an atrium can transform existing buildings, as in the case of the city campus of Sheffield Hallam University (Figure 14.2). There is no doubt that much of the appeal of atria lies in their aesthetic attributes. However, they have a practical justification by creating opportunities for introducing natural light and ventilation often deep into a building.

The shape and form of the atrium also has an important effect on the availability of natural lighting in the spaces adjacent to the atrium. There are several factors to consider.

- The structure of the atrium roof can reduce its transparency by between 20 and 50 per cent. This is an important factor if the ground level is meant to be predominantly naturally lit.
- The offices enclosing the atrium will benefit from a measure of natural light as well as external views. Access to natural light will be improved significantly if the sides of the atrium are stepped outwards.

Figure 14.2
Atrium between existing buildings,
Sheffield Hallam University

- The surface finish in respect of colour and reflectance of the atrium walls will influence the level of daylight reaching the lower floors.

Light shelves

Light shelves have been in use for some time and serve the dual purpose of providing shade and reflected light. Sunlight is reflected from the upper surface of the light shelf into the room interior and particularly onto the ceiling where it provides additional diffuse light thus helping to provide uniform illumination. Under conditions of an overcast sky, light shelves cannot increase the lighting level. They operate most effectively in sunlight. In this context ceilings are usually designed to be higher than normal for best operation (Figure 14.3).

Some degree of control is possible by modifying the angle of the light shelf; either internally or externally or in combination. Problems with low angle winter sunlight penetration can give rise to glare. Difficulties can be experience in cleaning the light shelves, especially the external type.

Earlier, Portcullis House illustrated this feature with a level of sophistication involving a corrugated reflective surface to maximise high altitude reflection whilst rejecting low altitude short wave solar radiation. This almost doubles the daylight levels in north facing rooms.

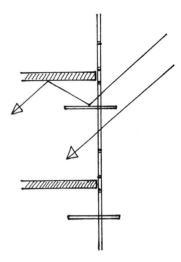

Figure 14.3
Basic principle of the light shelf

Prismatic glazing

Whilst the systems so far discussed rely on the reflection of light, prismatic glazing operates by refracting incoming light. The system consists of a panel of linear prisms (triangular wedges) which refract and spread the incoming light to produce a more diffuse distribution. The view out is substantially restricted, but the system can be used as an alternative to the reflective louvre system without some of its drawbacks. Glare can be somewhat reduced too. Maintenance is virtually eliminated if the system is installed between the panes of double glazed units.

Light pipes

Light pipes gather incoming sunlight sometimes using a solar tracking system. The light is concentrated using lenses or mirrors and is then transmitted to building interiors by 'pipes'. The pipes can be hollow shafts or ducts with reflective internal finishes, or may use fibre optic cable technology. A special luminaire is required to provide distribution of the light within the building.

The system is heavily reliant on the availability of sunlight and for critical tasks or areas a backup artificial light source is required. Examples of the technology are to be found in the roof of the concourse at Manchester Airport, UK, and the experimental low energy house at Nottingham University (Figure 14.4).

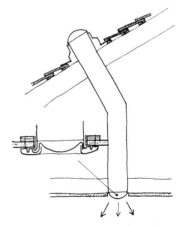

Figure 14.4
Section through a sunpipe

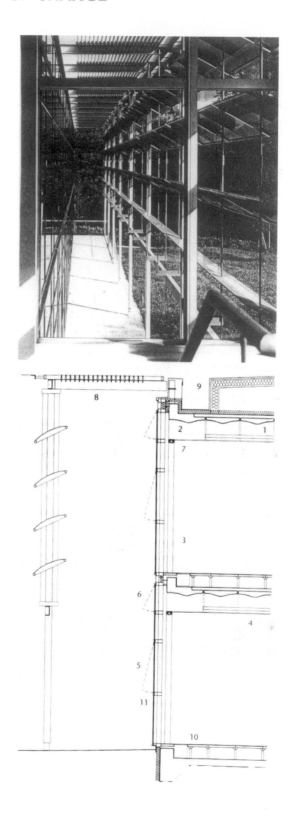

Figure 14.5
Solar shading, Wessex Water Divisional
Headquarters

Holographic glazing

Holographic glazing is still under development but potentially offers advantages over prismatic glazing. A diffraction process is also used, but in this case the light output can be more finely tuned to produce particular internal light patterns. There are some limitations set by the angle of incoming light to which the holographic pattern is tuned.

Solar shading

In considering climate facades solar shading featured as an integral element in the triple glazing. More common are external shading devices which are confined to the southerly elevation. These are featured in Portcullis House. More recently the Wessex Water building features some of the most complex solar shading devices yet encountered (Figure 14.5).

The Millennium Galleries opened in Sheffield in 2001 have some of the most elaborate solar shading which can be rotated through 90° to achieve levels of solar exclusion up to total internal blackout (Figure 14.6).

Figure 14.6
Variable solar shading, Millennium Galleries, Sheffield

Chapter Fifteen   Lighting – and human failings

Artificial lighting is a major factor in deciding the quality of the internal environment of offices. It is also a serious contributor to carbon dioxide, (CO_2) emissions accounting in the US, for example, for up to 30 per cent of total electricity use (*Scientific American*, March 2001). For these reasons it is a subject that warrants special attention.

Design studies suggest that considerable energy savings can be made by maximising natural light, particularly if it is linked to automatic controls. Passive solar studies claim that efficient and well-controlled lighting would reduce energy/carbon dioxide costs by more than any other single item.

There is still reluctance to accept any additional capital cost to achieve sustainable design despite the prospect of significant revenue savings. Even in terms of capital cost alone energy efficiency can make savings. For example, high frequency lighting, good reflecting luminaires and infra-red controls can save money because fewer fittings are required with lower heat production, in turn leading to a reduced cooling load. At the same time there is the chance to install fewer switch drops reducing cabling and simplifying fitting-out. This lighting strategy could also reduce the contract period with obvious benefits in terms of an earlier occupancy date.

Post-occupancy analysis has thrown some doubt on these assumptions (Bordass, W., PROBE studies). Changes in office design and work routines has caused a reappraisal of the maximisation philosophy. In addition, a build-up of user appraisal has shown that, in many cases, the claimed benefits of maximising natural lighting have turned into clear dis-benefits. As a result, recent occupancy studies have shown that artificial lights are left on much more than predicted. There are many reasons for this, and this chapter will review some of the most prominent.

When the original research into alternatives to the permanently artificially lit office space was carried out, work in offices was largely paper based. At the same time, research and guidance in the past has been simplistic and inadequately focused on the real contexts in which people make decisions. For example, it is possible for a single decision by an individual to put a whole system into an energy wasting state. Insufficient consideration is given to the fact that anomalous situations are often difficult to correct and it is easier to adopt the 'inertia solution'.

Now computers are the universal office tool and excessive daylight can be a severe nuisance due to reflection from VDU screens. If lighting controls are not tuned to each individual workstation, this can result in greater energy use than in a conventional office. For example, it has been found that all lights can be on because one person has drawn the blinds to avoid glare. Even where lights are zoned according to daylight penetration, these often do not relate to workstations with the result that lights are on all day to compensate.

A lesson which is being gradually learnt is that individuals will always select the least cost option in terms of effort. It is not that people are inherently lazy, but that they will tend to resent expending effort on activities which they regard as the responsibility of management. For example, it is often easier to switch on lights than adjust blinds, and that is what happens when natural light levels fluctuate. The common 'inertia response' is to close the blinds and switch on the lights. Where daylight results in glare, individuals will adjust the blinds and artificial lighting to avoid discomfort and achieve an even distribution of lighting regardless of energy consumption.

In cellular offices individuals take more responsibility for adjusting their light levels and optimising the relationship between artificial and natural lighting. In open plan situations where no individual is responsible, blinds tend to be left closed if that was their position on the previous day, regardless of external conditions.

Photoelectric control

Where lights are operated electronically according to natural light levels, the systems can be either closed or open loop. A closed loop system controls the lighting to top up the daylight to achieve a given minimum acceptable illuminance level. Open systems measure external incident daylight to dim lights but with no feedback of the actual levels of realised illuminance.

Blinds can override the controls of both open and closed systems. Complaints at the lack of finesse of such systems can result in management abandoning photoelectric control altogether. Where sensors in closed systems are near windows, it is not uncommon to find occupants closing the blinds to activate the lights. Furthermore, in many cases there are not enough sensors and lighting zones to take account of localised variations in daylight due to orientation or shading. As a rule of thumb, to avoid the need to make small-scale adjustments, lights should not go off until the illuminance level is about twice the design level.

Glare

Another rule of thumb which is observed by designers is that 'if you can't see the sky the daylight level is inadequate'. The result is tall windows to give maximum daylight penetration. This carries the attendant risk of glare unless workstations are properly positioned in relation to the window. In most cases this will mean desks at right angles to the external wall and the VDU viewing axis parallel to the window plane.

One option is to resort to automatic blinds. Occupiers sometimes complain that the spontaneous action of the blind is an irritant and represents a denial of individual choice. Local manual override is the preferred answer.

Recent developments in glass technology referred to earlier in terms of electrochromic glass offer solutions to these problems, especially if it can be controlled on an individual pane basis.

Another problem that occurs is that lighting and blinds controls are not co-ordinated. Lights tend to stay on regardless of the position of the blinds. The operation of externally positioned blinds can be frustrated by adverse weather conditions, especially high winds.

Dimming control and occupancy sensing

Closed loop systems are designed to provide a constant level of desktop illuminance. However, as the level of outside light fluctuates, so individuals may wish to vary desktop light levels to minimise contrast. On a bright day a constantly lit desk would appear gloomy.

There are obvious advantages to light switching which is responsive to a human presence, but even this technology is not devoid of problems. The adjustment of the sensors is a matter of fine tuning. For example, they may not be sufficiently sensitive to the movements of people engaged in high concentration tasks. Alternatively they may be so sensitive that passers-by trigger the switch causing a distraction. In practice it is often difficult to locate sensors to suit occupancy patterns and work requirements especially in open plan offices where workstations may frequently be relocated. The ideal solution is to rely on manual switching for the 'on' and automatic switching for the 'off'.

Occupancy sensors achieve their optimum value in service areas and circulation spaces. These are areas which are frequently overlooked yet they can use more energy pro rata than office spaces. One common fault is that the positioning of switches and sensors does not take account of the contribution of natural light. This is a particular fault in offices with atria. In some of the worst cases activating lights in an office area can switch on all lights along the exit route and in extreme instances, throughout the whole circulation area. A balance should be struck between optimum safety and the profligate use of energy.

Switches

A common failing is that switches are not positioned logically in terms of their relation to the fittings and behaviour patterns of occupants. Switches remote from fittings lead to uncertainty as to the status of the lights. The answer would be to include a red 'live' light in the switch.

Remote infra-red switching is an efficient and effortless system, provided the operation zone focuses down to the size of an individual workstation. Where switching is not ergonomically appropriate the tendency once again is for lights to be left on permanently.

System management

One major reason why certain high profile energy efficient buildings fail to meet expectations is because of deficiencies at the level of system management. It may be that system interfaces are not well understood by staff. Even service managers and suppliers are occasionally not as well informed as they should be. The problem is exacerbated if the original software source is no longer available.

System complexity is another problem. If services managers are not conversant with the intricacies of a system, they will tend to operate it at or near its optimum on the principle that overkill masks lower order problems and safeguards one's back. Also, overcomplex systems discourage interference and adjustment in case the outcome is worse and defies a remedy. Calling out specialists to make adjustments can be expensive thus tempting managers to prefer to operate the system below its design efficiency.

Complex systems can also be inflexible. In some cases the system's programme no longer serves the functions of the building. In extreme cases this has led to the complete abandonment of the system.

In some cases the fault for poor system performance lies with office managers who fail to inform the staff of the operational characteristics, cost and energy implications of the system. For example, in one instance, staff were not told of the fact that pressing a switch twice would turn on extra lights. The human factor is of prime importance. Good communication between management and staff can achieve a satisfactory performance from a less than perfect system. Inadequate communication can undermine the virtues of the best possible system design.

There is also the situation that office managers sometimes fail to address the more subtle needs of staff, gearing the system to crude averages with the result that nobody is satisfied.

The increasing popularity of flexible working hours is causing difficulties. Light controls may have been designed for fixed working hours and set lunch times. This is another instance where the complications and cost of modifying the system to respond to new work practices may be unacceptable and therefore the system is abandoned. There has been a case where all lights in an office were operated from a central control desk. The desk only operated from 09.00 to 17.30 hours. Since staff became able to work flexible hours, it meant that those working after 17.30 were obliged to leave the lights burning all night.

Another potential source of conflict between design and operation is when a single occupancy office reverts to multiple occupancy. It is usual for the principal tenant to have overall control of the services. Variable working patterns and conflicting needs often means that lights are left on unnecessarily.

A relatively recent trend in the production of buildings is for the design to be separated from the fitting-out. The architect and services designer may produce an elegant energy-efficient concept which can be totally vitiated by the fitting-out contractor who has not been informed of the energy saving features and consequent operational constraints of the design. Even worse is the situation where the sub-contractor deliberately ignores the design objectives of the architect and engineer in order to keep down costs. The problem of discontinuity between design intention and fitting-out can be particularly acute in the case of refurbishments.

Air conditioned offices

These present a different set of problems for designers. The psychological effect of a space hermetically sealed from the outside world is to suggest an environment designed to overcome nature and be wholly distinct from it. As a result, the inhabitants tend to regard it as natural that all the services should be fully used all the time. If, in addition, the facades feature solar tinted glass, even more lighting is used to compensate for the constantly gloomy outlook.

Lighting – conditions for success

Open plan installations which offer occupant satisfaction and energy efficiency usually satisfy four conditions:

- The design is straightforward and comprehensible, avoiding over-complexity.
- They have intelligible local controls with clear user interfaces.
- The system is robust and reliable.
- There is responsive and intelligent office and services management.

It is still comparatively rare to encounter an open plan office which achieves low lighting energy consumption combined with high daylight use and which produces a high level of occupant satisfaction.

Those that achieve low lighting energy consumption tend to display the following characteristics.

- There is an assertive client who has formulated the system's requirements clearly and insisted from the outset on effective lighting controls.
- Following commissioning there is intelligent management of the system combined with responsive management at office level.
- Glare is reduced to a minimum by means of light shelves, overhangs, splayed reveals and deeply recessed windows.
- The interior layouts position most desks at right angles to windows.
- Control systems are capable of responding to individual requirements with good switching design (often infra-red) and controls which are user friendly and take account both of daylight levels and workstation layout.
- There should be efficient lighting throughout with high frequency control gear and good optics.
- Design luminance should be set to achieve about 400 lux with lower levels in circulation areas.
- It is an advantage to have variety in lighting but without excessive contrast or the 'oppressive feel' generated by installations with 100 per cent Category 1 luminaires.
- There will be good levels of daylight in perimeter work areas without causing excessive glare in interior spaces.
- Blinds will be easy to operate with a good range of adjustment and which need to be fully closed only in exceptional circumstances.
- Interior fittings and furnishings are light in colour and tonal value with tall fittings kept to a minimum.
- VDUs can be easily moved to avoid glare.
- Circulation lighting is low energy and well planned and controlled with full account taken of contributions from daylight. An important added advantage in corridors etc. is the occasional external view.
- Daylight within circulation spaces has the effect of putting a brake on the use of artificial lighting in the office areas.
- The system has a high degree of inherent flexibility so that it can be finely tuned and retuned to user needs.

Summary of design considerations

- Design of artificial lighting systems should not be extravagant, lighting levels should be designed be to as low as is permitted whilst still achieving the standard required.
- Task lighting should be used for specific workstations in order to reduce the level of general background lighting.
- Energy efficient lamps should be specified – usually high frequency fluorescent or alternative discharge lamps; compact fluorescent lamps should be specified where appropriate.

- Appropriate luminaires, giving energy efficient light distribution, should be chosen.
- Control gear (ballasts) required for lamp functioning should be energy efficient, for example high frequency electronic ballasts are up to 20 per cent more efficient than the norm.

The on/off controlled switching of lighting systems needs careful consideration for optimum performance. Four types of control are available.

Timed control

- Used to switch lights off automatically according to a specified schedule; with lights switched on manually.
- Lights near windows should be separately controlled; this can produce savings in spaces regularly used by more than two people.

Occupancy linked control

- Sensors (ultrasonic, infra-red, microwave or acoustic) are used to detect presence of occupants.
- Switching on is for a set period, lights switched off if presence no longer detected.
- This type is particularly appropriate for spaces with low occupancy levels.

Daylight linked control

- Can be used in conjunction with timed and occupancy linked systems.
- Photocells are installed to detect when natural light is sufficient at which point artificial lighting is switched off.
- Recent developments include use of dimming control to avoid abrupt change as lights are switched off.

Localised switching

- Allows partial illumination of large areas when not fully occupied.
- Gives individual control to occupants.
- Some form of override switching off required when building becomes unoccupied.

To conclude, of all the factors under the designer's control, lighting is probably the most powerful influence on mood and demeanour. It makes direct contact with the emotions. As such its disposition, quality and means of control are critical factors in determining the well-being of the occupants of a building. Leaving aside the moral arguments, this can have a direct effect on the bottom line.

Cautionary notes

Chapter Sixteen

Having outlined techniques for optimising natural resources in the operation of offices, it is necessary to temper enthusiasm with a cautionary note. The Chartered Institute of Building Services Engineers commissioned a number of post-occupancy studies of buildings designed to achieve a high level of environmental sophistication. These 'Probe' studies brought to light a number of problems which caused some buildings to perform well below their design prediction. These are some of the outcomes of the study.

Why do things go wrong?

There is evidence that many recent offices designed to be energy efficient are not performing as well as expected, sometimes by a margin of 25 per cent. A factor which is often overlooked is that energy is comparatively cheap and accounts for only 1–2 per cent of total occupancy costs including salaries. This means that there is not the incentive to incur extra expenditure to modify systems to meet the original performance specification.

It must be said, however, that this is in the context of relatively low energy prices. However, the picture changes when energy costs are related to profits where they can range from 10 to 20 per cent of the total. Where an environmentally effective building really does score is in the sphere of staff well-being. For example, a joint examination by the US Department of Energy and the Rocky Mountain Institute of a number of refurbished offices found that renovations involving lighting and ventilation led to significant increases in productivity. A mere 1 per cent increase in productivity paid for a typical company's annual energy bill.

In a specific example, the US report states that when Lockheed commissioned a new 60 000 m² office complex, their architect persuaded them to invest in an extra 4 per cent to benefit from energy efficient design. The result was that absenteeism dropped 15 per cent as against their previous headquarters. Energy savings were worth $500 000 per year.

Not all the fault lies with clients. Many professionals are reluctant to negotiate new design territory for fear of falling victim to untried technology or because they will not make the effort to learn new construction techniques. All construction professionals operate in the shadow of 'professional indemnity' which tends to make them overcautious and not ask questions after completion.

Whilst design professionals are urged to work as a team, this is often difficult in practice. Operating against integrated design procedures is fee competition which sometimes reduces returns for design work to less than cost. In a cut-throat world, designers across all disciplines are more often competitors than collaborators. A consequence of this is that services designers are often brought into the project at a late stage. Furthermore, a fee structure which is based on contract or subcontract cost operates as a disincentive to services engineers. They are less likely to embrace low energy design which involves excluding engineering hardware, the costs of which would enhance their fees.

High profile/low profile

In the drive to reduce energy consumption, attention has tended to focus on insulation standards and heating/cooling installations. Now that Building Regulations are driving up insulation standards, other factors become more energy significant such as duct sizes and fan motors. In many, if not most, cases, fan motors are substantially oversized leading to significant excess energy costs. Leaving computers switched on unnecessarily not only wastes energy directly, it also adds to the cooling load of the building. Lights are another source of concern which will be considered in more detail later.

In many instances, substantial improvements to energy efficiency can be achieved by paying sufficient attention to the low profile details of design (Bordass, W., PROBE studies).

The 'high-tech demand'

Some designers are seduced by the imagery of advanced technology and install hardware that greatly exceeds the real demands of the building and its occupants. Avoiding the technological fix and installing only essential technology that is efficient, not overcomplex, easy to use and maintain, should be the aim of designers. Overcomplex systems which require elaborate maintenance tend to deteriorate fairly rapidly because service managers are not up to the demands of the technology. In extreme cases the system is abandoned altogether.

One problem facing clients is the relative scarcity of information which is accessible to the non-specialist. Even the professionals have problems in this respect though here there is useful guidance in the document 'Energy Use in Offices' 2003' published under the Energy Efficiency Best Practice Programme (now called 'Action Energy').

Operational difficulties

It is unfortunately the case that guidance/instruction manuals are often poorly written and inadequate in terms of information. There is a universal problem with instruction manuals because they are written by experts on the system in question, who find it impossible to empathise with the uninitiated installer and operator. They cannot conceive the breadth of the knowledge gap. This problem seems to be especially acute in terms of services technology.

Another problem which is all too common is that installers are expected to be able to comply with almost impossibly short completion dates. Commissioning is hurried to avoid activating penalty clauses in the contract. It may be less of a financial risk to commission the system properly after practical completion. If the system goes into operation at a substandard level of efficiency due to time constraints, service managers and office staff are at a disadvantage from the start. This is a recipe for high energy consumption and less than perfect comfort conditions.

Building related illness

Over recent years there has been awareness of the phenomenon 'sick building syndrome', more accurately termed 'building-induced sickness'. Factors like off-gassing from plastics in furnishings and fittings or the frequency of fluorescent lights have been implicated. Poorly designed heating and ventilation systems have also been identified as culprits, aside from the most spectacular problem of Legionnaires disease. There have been numerous horror stories of badly maintained systems providing a comfortable habitat for all manner of unmentionable life forms as well as closed systems recycling bacteria and viruses resulting in high levels of absenteeism.

Recent studies have suggested that sick building syndrome is also related to job satisfaction. Job satisfaction is more easily achieved in a pleasant comfortable environment in which the occupants are permitted some degree of control over their surroundings. When energy efficient design sets a good baseline of environmental conditions, the extra effort necessary to fine tune comfort to an individual's personal preferences quickly pays off.

Inherent inefficiencies

A system designed to be energy efficient can be totally undermined if the whole system has to be operated to meet a small demand. For example, in small-scale buildings, it is not unusual to find an entire heating plant being run in summer to supply hot tap water. Unreasonable overcapacity is another problem. An elaborate and expensive chiller may be installed to meet the cooling demand of a few days in the year or to supply cool air to a small number of prestigious rooms. The scale of such inefficiencies may go unnoticed because of the absence of proper monitoring systems. System efficiency can drop dramatically without the management being aware of the problem. Often a catastrophic failure is the first indication that something is wrong.

Sophisticated controls and electronic management systems combined with zonal submetering will ensure that faults are pinpointed and system inefficiencies identified. The relatively small capital costs involved in such equipment will quickly be paid back. The operation of such systems must be supplemented by adequate supervisory and analytical input from knowledgeable staff.

Common architectural problems

- Adverse effects of too much glass being underestimated. Maximisation of daylight can produce problems for VDU operators.
- Inappropriate window design lacking refinement and ease of control.
- Poor controls and user interfaces.
- Fitting-out which may contradict original design intentions, leading to poor performance.
- Tendency to highlight the positive and play down the negative. Downside risks not given the same weight as upside visions.

Common engineering problems

- Adoption of inappropriate standards regarding climate control, lighting and distribution of services.
- Optimised engineering solutions which may not be robust and flexible.
- A blind faith in technology tends to underrate the human factor and fails to focus down to the finely tuned needs of occupiers.
- Mechanical ventilation inappropriately designed in terms of rate of ventilation, efficiency, operating hours and zoning. Special problems occur with night ventilation.

Avoiding air conditioning – the issues

- Whilst the avoidance of air conditioning, and thus reduction of plant, leads to a lower cost per m^2 it may be that there are fewer 'usable' m^2 across the site as a whole due to problems of the distribution of cooling and ventilation.
- Lower energy consumption is probable when air conditioning is not installed, but not always easy to quantify.

- Lower running costs for the building when avoiding air conditioning may be at the expense of staff satisfaction. The alternative of a balanced natural/mechanical system requires sophisticated design techniques which may pose too much of a challenge to system designers.
- Natural ventilation is claimed to be more adaptable but it is not always appreciated how this adaptability can be achieved.
- Naturally ventilated buildings are claimed to offer greater occupant satisfaction. This can create variable climate conditions at any given time, and the level of occupant satisfaction is difficult to measure on a constant basis.
- The drive towards green design has sometimes led to the use of untried and inadequately researched alternatives to air conditioning.
- Designers can place too much faith in arrows showing expected air flow when natural ventilation is used – a rigorous approach to patterns of expected air movement is necessary.
- Natural ventilation is less controllable.
- There is less plant to maintain without air conditioning, but what there is may be more complex because of modes of operation.

Common failures leading to energy waste

- Designers tend to err on the side of caution. There is less risk in overdesigning than underdesigning. Accordingly systems are often overpowered and therefore wasteful.
- Often the most convenient operating strategy is for switches to default to *on* whereas *manual on* and *automatic off* is the more energy efficient provided safety is not compromised.
- Small demands like domestic hot water can require whole systems to be in operation as stated earlier.
- Inadequate monitoring systems can fail to identify progressive failure.
- Intrinsic faults in the system may remain hidden but may nevertheless adversely affect energy use without any detectable effect on service.

The human factor

- People are more tolerant of conditions in a naturally run building than in sealed air conditioned boxes, for example the acceptable range of temperature is wider and perceptible air movement more acceptable. The reasons are that people like to feel in control, hence the need to avoid excessive automatic control and also that they make unconscious adjustments for longer in environments that are congenial.
- Occupants generally do not have the patience to keep fine tuning their building environment and will tend to do what is most convenient. Robust, clearly articulated systems are the answer.

- As a general rule people find it easier to switch systems on than off, hence, again, *manual on, automatic off* should be the norm. At the same time, the inertia factor tends to increase when people are in groups. There is a reluctance to be conspicuous with its potential for risking criticism.
- Sudden changes are disrupting therefore automatic climate modifications should occur imperceptibly where this is possible.
- Awareness of the outside world is an important component of contentment. Most of the time external views are perceived at a nonconscious level, but psychological studies indicate that the mind can make a very full response to the visual milieu without reference to consciousness.

Summary of recommendations

- The temptation to opt for complex and 'heavy' engineering should be resisted in favour of 'gentle engineering' in which loads on the HVAC (heating, ventilating and air conditioning) system are kept to a minimum by appropriate, climate sensitive, building design.
- The passive potential of buildings should be fully exploited with care taken to ensure that building form, controls, ventilation, blinds, windows etc. are all supportive of natural systems.
- Mixed mode ventilation and cooling systems with different services zoned according to use patterns and need are often the most suitable strategy. Where natural and mechanical systems are designed to work in a symbiotic relationship it is necessary to ensure that, in changeover conditions, the system does not default into concurrent operation of the mechanical and natural systems.
- Monitoring is essential to determine running costs and to identify critical failure paths before they lead to catastrophic failure.

Conclusions

A number of factors are now tending to direct designers away from fully automated systems. These are:

- Preferred conditions in offices are now complex and unpredictable, making it impossible to design for average needs. So often averaging out was another term for a 'lowest common denominator' solution. Even so, designers and modellers are still reluctant to abandon their faith in fully automated controls. Too often there is still no clear analysis of what controls can really achieve and how proficient people will be at operating and servicing them.
- Overcomplex systems can generate unpredicted consequences and even episodes of total failure. In such instances it is often perceived as easier to decommission the system than rectify it.

- Changes in office routine and design have revealed that opting for maximum daylight can produce irritating consequences, such as glare on VDU screens. Furthermore, maximum daylight designs rely on the reliability and user friendliness of blinds and this reliance has often been misplaced.
- To repeat: the objective should be to design straightforward, robust systems which are well within the abilities of both service and office managers to understand and users to operate. This will deflect occupants from resorting to easy, energy wasteful options.

The aim of the design team should be to achieve maximum energy conservation, consistent with operational realism. This is the recipe for sustainable design.

Chapter Seventeen

Life-cycle assessment and recycling

Waste disposal

'The Earth is infinitely bountiful', so say the eco-sceptics. The reality is that society cannot continue to consume natural assets at the current rate. For example, the ecological footprint is the area of land (and sea) taken up to meet the needs of individuals or societies. A citizen of the US uses 34 acres; in the UK the average per capita is 14 acres; Pakistan, 1.6 acres. Worldwide the average is 4.5 acres due mainly to consumption in the industrialised nations. In ecological terms this means that the Earth is already living beyond its means. In 1962 it took 0.7 years for the annual biological harvest to regenerate. Currently it takes 1.25 years which means the natural capital account is going increasingly 'into the red' (Mathis Wackernagel at a conference 'Redefining Progress', February 2003 reported in *The Guardian*, 20 February 2003). This provides the context for considering the problems of waste.

The waste being generated by the increasing consumerist ethos of the industrialised nations imposes four penalties:

- depletion of natural resources;
- energy involved in disposal;
- increasing pressure on land for waste disposal;
- pollution arising from landfill disposal.

There is a temptation to think that when waste is thrown away, that's the end of it. Far from it. From being our problem it becomes someone else's. At the same time we may be placing a valuable recyclable resource beyond use. As the natural capital of the Earth is being steadily eroded this is increasingly an ethical as well as an economic problem. Land is Earth's most valuable commodity which is being increasingly diminished by building development and landfill sites.

The market economy encourages ever more vigorous consumerism which, in turn, increases the rate of obsolescence. Packaging and style upgrades exploit the human drive to be seen to be in the height of fashion. The irony is that our most expensive artefact after a house is the car which is designed for increasingly longer life. More and more cars are being claimed to have passed the million mile mark. So, constant style changes and technological tinkering rather than functional efficiency are needed to keep the market buoyant. Nations measure their success by the level of per capita GDP and the extent of annual economic growth. These dictate a nation's standing in relation to other countries, not least within highly influential bodies like the International Monetary Fund and World Bank.

The consequence of this is that there is growing concern about how to dispose of the escalating quantities of waste. The solution starts in the home. Local councils are under growing pressure to collect waste in segregated bins to facilitate recycling. This should be a major issue in local elections. At the same time householders can do a great deal to help the process along by:

- reusing items wherever possible, notably plastic bags and containers;
- composting organic kitchen waste and most garden waste (some plants are not suitable for composting). Some councils offer composting bins at a discount;
- separating waste at source and, where there are not segregated collection facilities, delivering to appropriate waste bins.

There may be an added incentive to reduce the amounts of household waste. Plans are being considered to levy a charge for each bin collection from a home.

Recycling

We are slowly moving to a position where there will be no such thing as waste, merely transformation. This is what recycling is mainly about.

It is in the sphere of building that recycling has considerable potential, and this applies to renovation as well as new build. There are at least three aspects to this:

- reused items for the same or an alternative purpose;
- refurbished materials;
- reconstituted materials.

Reuse

Building demolition provides an endless source of items which can be reused with almost no adaptation. Architectural salvage has become a significant industry. A first point of reference could be the Architectural Salvage Index operated by Hutton + Rostron (www.handr.co.uk/salvage_home.html; e-mail debi@handr.co.uk). This index was started in 1977 to recycle building materials and architectural features from buildings that are being demolished or renovated. The Index covers:

- building materials: bricks, slates, tiles, stone and timber;
- internal features: panelling, flooring, fireplaces, stairs, windows, doors and central heating items;
- external features: a range of garden features and furniture;
- complete structures: barns, conservatories and pergolas.

There is also N1 Architectural Salvage at www.salvoweb.com/dealers/ n1architectural for architectural features and www.salvoweb.com/ dealers/v-and-v/index.html for reclaimed bricks, flagstones and other heavy items.

The construction industry is the sector which carries the most guilt in this respect with its voracious appetite for raw materials and its resistance to cutting waste. This has led to mounting pressure to employ recycled materials. An example of good practice is the case of Dartford Hospital. It was estimated that 20 per cent of plasterboard comprises waste off-cuts. By agreement with the manufacturers all off-cuts were kept in separate containers taking care to keep them clean and then returned to the manufacturers to be recycled into new plasterboard.

The first requirement in minimising waste is to segregate materials – timber, metals, plasterboard, aggregates, hard plastics – to be recycled on site where possible. If this is not feasible local markets may well find a use for them.

Refurbished materials

As the pace of economic change accelerates, relatively recent buildings are being demolished to make way for more intensive and lucrative site development. This means that many items are being dismantled long before they should be retired offering good opportunities for refurbishment. Radiators, pumps etc. are obvious candidates, as illustrated by the Earth Centre case study below.

Reconstituted materials

In refurbishment schemes it is likely that there will be some element requiring the use of concrete. This is normally an energy intensive material due to the mining of aggregate and the production of cement. Normal concrete uses about 323 kg/m^3 of cement. This figure can be reduced to 100 kg/m^3 by the introduction of ground granulated blast furnace slag (GGBS) to provide additional bulk. This can reduce the cement content by 70 per cent in mass concrete for bases etc. The only drawback is that the curing time is increased from the normal 28 days to 56 days. In many situations this may not be a problem, though not in the case of multi-storey buildings.

The upgrading of the railways has resulted in a good supply of timber railway sleepers – an excellent source of recycled timber that can be put to a range of uses, particularly in gardens.

Waste glass has found a new incarnation as decorative tiles and blocks. Crushed and mixed with resin, it is available in a wide variety of colours and textures. In translucent form it can be backlit as illuminated flooring or walling. It is an ideal cladding material. (See Crystal Paving Ltd of Ecclesfield Sheffield, web address: http://crystalpaving.co.uk, e-mail info@crystalpaving.co.uk, Tel. 0870 770 6189.)

The mountains of waste slate in North Wales are slowly being ground into powder form to be transformed into resin-based building materials which can receive a high polish. As wall tiles they have the appearance of polished granite at a fraction of the cost.

Life-cycle assessment

Pressure is mounting to derive standards for environmental performance over the lifetime of a building by targeting the environmental impact of its component materials. In parallel with this there is also growing awareness of the value of calculating the economic cost of a building from inception to demolition.

In 1998 the Building Research Establishment (BRE) developed a scoring system for environmental impacts known as Ecopoints. It is based on Howard, N., Edwards, S. and Anderson, J. (1999) *Methodology for Environmental Profiles of Construction Materials, Components and Buildings, BRE*. The system deals with the extraction, processing, manufacture, transport, building-in-use and disposal stages of a product's life-cycle.

These various environmental impacts are then assessed against 13 categories including climate change, atmospheric pollution, water pollution and raw materials extraction. Clearly some of the categories have a greater overall impact than others, like climate change. There is therefore a system of weighting which reflects these differences. To avoid the charge of subjectivity the BRE consulted with a wide range of construction professionals and environmentalists before fixing on a system of weightings.

The outcome is a system of Ecopoints and the higher the score the greater the environmental impact. The benchmark is the environmental impact caused over a year by the average UK citizen which is set at 100. Details of this system may be found on at www.bre.co.uk/envest.

Whole life costing

This focuses on the financial profile of a building and its market cost. It covers some of the same ground as life-cycle costing but excludes the production process. The important point is that it marks a move from pure capital costing to integrating capital and revenue costs into an over-all whole life cost. This is a paradigm shift of considerable significance and may well operate in favour of much more environmentally advanced buildings by acknowledging that additional capital expenditure may be heavily outweighed by revenue gains as the price of energy continues to rise. Whole life costing information may be found on www.wlcf.org.uk.

Eco-materials

Concrete

As possibly the most extensively used building material, concrete attracts criticism from environmentalists on account of its carbon inten-sive production techniques and its use of a once-only natural resource, limestone. Cement is formed by heating clay and lime in a rotary kiln to a temperature of about 1450°C which produces some 3000 kg per tonne of carbon dioxide (CO_2). In addition the heating process pro-duces a chemical reaction through the conversion of calcium carbonate into calcium oxide which releases about 2200 kg of CO_2. Add to this the carbon miles in transportation, the impacts caused by mining etc. and concrete gains few points on the sustainability scale.

The development of the technology of geopolymers offers the prospect of a more eco-friendly concrete. Geopolymerisation is a geosynthesis which is a reaction that chemically bonds minerals to form molecules that are structurally comparable to the molecules which pro-vide the strength to rocks. In the opinion of Jean Davidovits of the French Geopolymer Institute at St Quentin these 'geopolymeric' con-cretes would reduce CO_2 emissions associated with conventional con-crete by 80–90 per cent. This is said to be due to the avoidance of calcination from calcium carbonate and the lower kiln temperature of 750°C. The market availability of this material is said to be at least five years away (see www.geopolymer.org).

Saving energy is one thing; buildings as carbon sinks is another, yet this is the destiny of buildings according to John Harrison, a technolo-gist from Hobart, Tasmania. He has produced a magnesium carbonate-based 'eco-cement'. In the first place it only uses half the energy for process heating required by calcium carbonate (Portland) cement. The roasting process produces CO_2 but most of this is reabsorbed by a process of carbonation as the cement hardens. Using eco-cement for such items as concrete blocks means that nearly all the material will eventually carbonate resulting in an absorption rate of 0.4 tonnes of CO_2 for every tonne of concrete. The ultimate eco-credential of this material is the rate of carbon sequestration. According to Harrison 'The opportunities to use carbonation processes to sequester carbon from the air are just huge. It can take conventional cements centuries or even millennia to absorb as much as eco-cements can absorb in months'

('Green Foundations', *New Scientist*, 13 July 2002, p. 40). This means that an eco-concrete tower block can perform the same function as growing trees as it steadily fixes carbon. Harrison estimates that a shift to eco-cement could ultimately cut CO_2 emissions by over 1 billion tonnes since it could replace 80 per cent of uses currently served by Portland cement.

There is one further attribute to this material. Being less alkaline than Portland cement it can incorporate up to four times more waste in the mix than conventional cement to provide bulk without losing strength. This could include organic waste which would otherwise be burnt or added to landfill, sawdust, plastics, rubber and fly ash.

Eco-cement is not unique in its pollution absorbing properties. Mitsubishi is producing paving slabs coated with titanium dioxide which remove most pollutants from the air. In Japan 50 towns are already using these photocatalytic cements and in Hong Kong it is estimated that they remove up to 90 per cent of the nitrogen oxides or NOx gases that create smog. Magnesium-based concrete coated with titanium dioxide could be the basis for eco-cities of the future.

External finishes

A similar principle has been incorporated into a paint that is now available. Called 'Ecopaint' it is designed to reduce levels of NOx in the atmosphere. The paint contains nanoparticles of titanium dioxide and calcium carbonate. These particles absorb ultra-violet radiation and they use this energy convert NOx into nitric acid which is either washed away by rain or neutralised by the calcium carbonate particles. The manufacturers (Millennium Chemicals of Grimsby, UK) claim that a coating of the paint will continue to be effective for five years in a heavily polluted city.

Paints

Paints have three constituents: pigment for colour, a binding substance to hold the particles of pigment together and a solvent to enable the mixture to flow freely. It is the solvents which are the main problem since they are designed to evaporate. Most of the solvents used come into the category of volatile organic compounds (VOCs) and are aggressive pollutants. It has been calculated that over 500 000 tonnes of solvent are released into the atmosphere globally each year (Harland, E. (1999) *Eco-Renovation*, Chelsea Green Publishing Company, Vermont, USA, revised edition). Another statistic is that organic solvents are responsible for 20 per cent of the hydrocarbon pollution in the atmosphere and second only to motor vehicles (Berge, B. (2000) *Ecology of Building Materials*, Architectural Press, Oxford).

It is the solvents which derive from the petrochemical industry that are the most toxic and are implicated in the phenomenon of off-gasing. This may continue for a considerable time with sometimes serious health consequences. (A comprehensive list of surface treatments and their solvents is to be found in Berge, ibid., p. 405 and also Edwards, L. and Lawless, J. (2003) *The Natural Paint Book*, Rodale Press, available from the AECB book service: www.aecb.net.) There are alternatives such as those containing natural resin emulsions. They appear much the same as conventional petrochemical emulsions, are as easy to apply, are solvent free, do not have the pervasive smell of chemically based paints and are also biodegradable.

Humidity

The choice of paints and varnishes can have an impact on the level of humidity within a building. Temperature is the key factor in determining how much moisture the air can hold. At 20°C air can hold 14.8 g/m^3; at 0°C it can only hold 3.8 g/m^3. On average a living room contains 5–10 g/m^3. Fluctuations in temperature will alter the carrying capacity of the air and may result in condensation. It is important that the materials of the walls can absorb much of this moisture which means the use of hygroscopic materials, that is, materials that can take up moisture. Such materials act as a stabilising agent, keeping the humidity level reasonably constant. In other words, hygroscopic materials have a damping effect on moisture fluctuations just as thermal mass regulates temperature (Berge, ibid., pp. 251–253).

It is recommended that internal walls should be finished in hygroscopic emulsion paint over plaster. This ensures that excess moisture can be absorbed by the plaster and masonry wall, releasing it when the internal humidity level creates imbalance. A further benefit is that water vapour carries some gas contaminants like nitrogen oxide and formaldehydes. When the water vapour enters the hygroscopic materials these chemicals may be deposited and broken down giving these materials a degree of air cleansing capacity. However, the transfer of moisture will not happen if wall surfaces have impermeable finishes like oil-based paints or varnishes, plastic wallpaper or even wallpaper fixed with plastic-based pastes. Internal walls need to breathe, otherwise condensation is virtually inevitable.

Materials and embodied energy

In addition to the energy used during the occupied life of a building there is also a significant energy factor in terms of the materials used in its construction. It falls into five divisions:

- the extraction from the earth of raw materials;
- the processing of the raw material into finished products;

- the transportation to the supplier and then to the site;
- the construction process;
- the demolition and recycling of materials.

Assuming an average life for an office building in the UK of 15–20 years, about 7 per cent of total energy consumption is embodied in materials. However, if buildings were to be made more adaptable, and thereby more accommodating to numerous changes of work pattern, their lifetime would be extended, thus reducing the overall percentage attributable to embodied energy. In the UK, for example, the present replacement rate of housing means that life expectancy of a home is around 2000 years, making the embodied energy an insignificant element. On the other hand, as buildings become more energy efficient, so the reverse is true and ultimately the embodied energy may become the prime factor.

The problem with embodied energy is that it is difficult to quantify with any confidence. For example, with the first two stages, extraction and processing, the energy used in the processes may be withheld for commercial reasons. The matter will only be resolved when disclosure becomes a legal requirement.

The situation is further complicated when some of that energy is from renewable sources, as in the case of aluminium processed in Canada from hydroelectric power, or bricks in Nottinghamshire fired by landfill methane.

There are strong environmental reasons to use timber in construction, since it is a renewable resource with the added benefit of fixing CO_2 during growth. However, in the UK most softwood is imported, adding a significant transport component. Energy inputs into metals such as copper and aluminium can vary according to whether the source is from ore or recycled material.

At this stage in the development of disclosure about embodied energy, the most direct impact can be made on 'carbon miles', sourcing materials as near as possible to the construction site.

A case study will illustrate a whole building approach to recycled materials.

Low energy Conference Centre, Earth Centre, Doncaster

This is a building built to the highest super-insulation standards which is no less than we would expect from its architect, Bill Dunster. It has natural wind-driven ventilation with heat recovery from exhaust air transferred to incoming air. Solar collectors on the roof direct warm water to a calorifier in an underground insulated 400 m³ tank. Heat is stored over the summer to be circulated throughout the winter, with a wood burning stove for backup heat. A wind generator mounted in the boiler flue helps to meet the electricity demand (Figure 17.1).

The Conference Centre walls are of gabion construction, that is, loose stones contained with a galvanised steel mesh. In this case the filling comprises crushed concrete from a nearby demolished colliery.

Figure 17.1
Conference Centre, Earth Centre, under construction and completed

The timber supports for the main structure are rejuvenated pylons, probably telegraph poles, discovered in a lorry park. Most of the timber is either recycled or has received a certificate from the Forestry Stewardship Council. Only the Gluelam beams are from new timber in order to meet the manufacturer's performance guarantee.

It is impossible to avoid using cement, despite its very high embodied energy. Where possible GGBS concrete has been used in foundations etc. (p. 204).

Even the wet heating system uses radiators recovered from demolished buildings and the steel for the conical roof to the conference space is recycled I beams. The entrance steps are redundant railway sleepers (a growth industry). A useful website is www.salvo.co.uk.

There are problems associated with recycled materials. For example, subcontractors may be reluctant to work with them because of hidden hazards like nails in timber which can wreck valuable tools. In the Earth Centre example the contractor was able to underwrite extra costs arising from work on recycled materials. A main contractor may also experience difficulty in guaranteeing time and quality on a design and build fixed price contract. Sadly in 2005 the Earth Centre closed.

Recycling strategy checklist

- First a client should be encouraged to sanction the use of recycled materials. This is an important precondition of a project. Reference to best practice case studies is useful in this respect.
- Design practices need to adapt to accommodate the recycling culture. At the same time designers should maximise the opportunities for materials to be recycled after demolition. Buildings which can be dismantled rather than demolished are much better in this respect.
- In determining costs, considerations about embodied energy and resource depletion should be factored in. At the same time there should be considerable overall savings as against new materials which should have an impact on the whole life cost assessment.
- Contractors should be persuaded to be co-operative about the use of recycled materials and willing to accept a degree of liability on behalf of subcontractors. In the case of the Conference Centre, Earth Centre, the main contractor was an enthusiastic advocate of the strategy.
- All site waste should be sorted and recycled where possible. This can save the costs of transport and landfill fees.
- On the supply site, retailers of recycled materials should provide a measure of quality assurance if not a full guarantee.

All these items should contribute to a favourable life-cycle assessment score.

Chapter Eighteen

State of the art case studies

The National Assembly for Wales

Richard Rogers Partnership

Following devolution, the Principality of Wales was granted greater autonomy resulting in the need for an assembly building for which the Richard Rogers Partnership was appointed architects with environmental engineer BDSP. It is a classic example of architect and engineer working in concert from the earliest stage of the project. The design brief was for a building which reflected the democratic nature of government whilst also being a landmark example of low energy design. It also has to last 100 years. Given this lifespan, embodied energy will only be a tiny fraction of the energy in use over the life of the building, so the primary aim was to drive down operational energy demand. The engineers are confident that the building will use no more than 50 per cent of the energy of a building conforming Regulations in this location.

The roofed public spaces offer a phased progression in terms of environmental control from a minimum at the entrance overlooking Cardiff Bay to the highly controlled debating chamber at the heart of the complex. Airflow over and around the building has been modelled using computational fluid dynamics (CFD). Ventilation air enters at low level since there is little low level pollution, and rises through the debating and reception chambers through the stack effect. The rotating roof cowls ensure that the grilles for exhaust air are always in the lee of the wind which is predominantly from the south west. The curved member on the top of the cowl has an aerofoil profile creating negative pressure on the underside thus assisting the extraction of exhaust air (Figure 18.1).

The results of extensive modelling of solar penetration and daylight at different times of day and at all seasons of the year have been factored into the design. When completed it should prove to be one of the most accessible and user-friendly parliamentary buildings of any state or principality in Europe.

Figure 18.1
National Assembly for Wales
(photograph Eamonn O'Mahony)

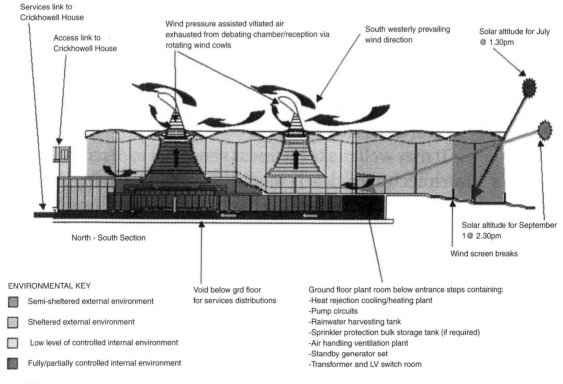

Services link to
Crickhowell House

Access link to
Crickhowell House

Wind pressure assisted vitiated air
exhausted from debating chamber/reception via
rotating wind cowls

South westerly prevailing
wind direction

Solar altitude for July
@ 1.30pm

North - South Section

Solar altitude for September
1 @ 2.30pm

Wind screen breaks

ENVIRONMENTAL KEY

Semi-sheltered external environment

Sheltered external environment

Low level of controlled internal environment

Fully/partially controlled internal environment

Void below grd floor
for services distributions

Ground floor plant room below entrance steps containing:
-Heat rejection cooling/heating plant
-Pump circuits
-Rainwater harvesting tank
-Sprinkler protection bulk storage tank (if required)
-Air handling ventilation plant
-Standby generator set
-Transformer and LV switch room

Figure 18.2
Welsh Assembly natural light and ventilation diagrams

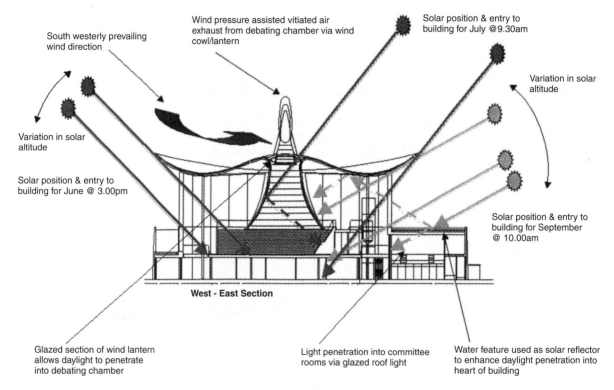

South westerly prevailing
wind direction

Wind pressure assisted vitiated air
exhaust from debating chamber via wind
cowl/lantern

Solar position & entry to
building for July @9.30am

Variation in solar
altitude

Variation in solar
altitude

Solar position & entry to
building for June @ 3.00pm

Solar position & entry to
building for September
@ 10.00am

West - East Section

Glazed section of wind lantern
allows daylight to penetrate
into debating chamber

Light penetration into committee
rooms via glazed roof light

Water feature used as solar reflector
to enhance daylight penetration into
heart of building

Figure 18.3
Welsh Assembly detail of natural light
and ventilation

Zuckermann Institute for Connective Environmental Research (ZICER)

RMJM Architects

The University of East Anglia has a reputation for commissioning environmentally advanced buildings. The Elizabeth Fry building set the standard for low energy university buildings (see Smith and Pitts, ibid.). As part of the School of Environmental Sciences, the ZICER building has set even higher standards of bioclimatic performance with the Elizabeth Fry building acting as the benchmark. Designed by RMJM Architects and Whitbybird for the building physics, this building was conceived to make a powerful statement about sustainable design. It was designed to represent an improvement over Elizabeth Fry in several respects, including:

- better construction standards with a higher standard of air tightness;
- higher standard of insulation;
- higher standard windows;
- lower energy fans with better controls and lower pressure ductwork;
- heat and cool energy from a central university CHP system;
- better mixing of extract air for heat recovery (Figure 18.4).

Figure 18.4
ZICER building south elevation with facade and roof PVs

The 3000 m² building was opened in 2003 and is principally a research facility with a mixture of cellular and open plan spaces on the ground, first and second floors. The top floor houses a large seminar and exhibition space in which natural light is moderated by wall and roof PV panels (Figure 18.5).

The basement houses a Virtual Reality Theatre which is the centrepiece of the Social Science for the Environment, Virtual Reality and Experimental Laboratories. This facility provides opportunities for research into environmental decision making within real and hypothetical landscapes.

Overall, it is expected to realise a total energy use of 77 kWh/m²/year despite the fact that it houses at least 150 computer terminals. It should achieve this record breaking performance by a combination of energy efficient construction and electricity production from PV cells in facade and roof. The building is linked to the main teaching block by a glazed bridge from an atrium at its eastern end.

ZICER has an impressive array of sustainability credentials.

First, the design had to achieve a high level of air tightness, with a target permeable rate of 3.0 m³/h/m² at a pressure of 50 pascals (Pa). In practice it performs even better than this.

Second, the elements of the building have U-values substantially better than are required by the current Building Regulations, for example:

walls	0.10 W/m²K
floors	0.16 W/m²K
roof	0.13 W/m²K
windows	1.0 W/m²K triple glazed

Figure 18.5
ZICER building Seminar Room with facade and roof PVs and thermal mass suspended ceiling panels

Third, thermal modelling of the building indicated the use of natural ventilation on the south elevation with fresh air entering at low level, rising through thermal buoyancy to pass behind the PV facade of the seminar space to remove heat from solar gain and the action of the PVs. Exhaust air is expelled at high level on the north elevation. Thermal mass at ceiling level on the top floor helps to ensure that no additional cooling is required. A TermoDeck ventilation system comprising hollow core concrete slabs supplies air to the floors via vertical ducts. The air is released to rooms through louvers controlled by the building management system. This is still undergoing fine tuning. The high thermal mass of the floor slabs flattens the peaks and troughs of temperature. Users are also provided with opening windows.

Fourth, the top floor features 402.5 m² of double glazed laminated monocrystalline PVs for the roof and polycrystalline PVs for the facade with a rated output of 33 kWp. The PVs are grid connected to offset the electricity consumption of the building (Figure 18.5).

Fifth is the fact that artificial lighting using low energy luminaries and controls is mostly subject to movement sensors which can be overridden by local switching when required.

Finally, attention has been paid to the environmental sensitivity of materials used in construction. Recycled aggregate and timber from certified sustainable sources have been used. Most of the concrete, steel, aluminium and insulation are capable of being recycled.

The finishing touch is provided by over 70 covered cycle spaces coupled with locker spaces and shower facilities. A large waste storage space at lower ground level allows waste to be sorted into appropriate recycling containers.

SOCIAL HOUSING

Beaufort Court, Lillie Road, Fulham, London, 2003

Feilden Clegg Bradley Architects

This is a high density development which epitomises the government's policy on affordable housing, embracing shared ownership and key worker rental provision. The accommodation ranges from one bedroom flats to family apartments. Its social credentials are particularly signalled by the fact that it contains an element sponsored by the Rough Sleepers Initiative.

Two things make this scheme stand out.

First, it is a low energy building constructed well in excess of Building Regulations and fulfils the aims of sustainable development. The aim has been to surpass best practice for energy efficiency and provide affordable warmth for all its inhabitants.

Its energy efficiency is achieved by:

- high levels of thermal insulation and draught sealing;
- assisted passive stack ventilation with humidity controlled dampers to the kitchens and bathrooms;
- the atria that serve the six-storey block have south facing glazing and are naturally ventilated at night to moderate summer temperatures;
- low energy, high efficiency lighting throughout;
- units designed to maximise natural lighting;
- trees introduced to the site, improving air quality and providing some insulation from the noise of adjacent roads
- the roofs of two low blocks covered with sedum which provides a habitat for wildlife and reduces the runoff from rainwater.

Second, the method of construction involves three aspects of off-site fabrication:

- a prefabricated steel load-bearing system with large-scale cold-rolled panels;
- large-scale hot-rolled elements;
- three-dimensional modular construction.

Figure 18.6
Lillie Road flats; courtyard view
(photograph by Mandy Reynolds)

It is the first social housing project in the UK to incorporate these three off-site fabrication techniques in one scheme. The Commission for Architecture and the Built Environment described the project as 'one of the more sustainable schemes to be built anywhere in England because it sharply addresses energy efficiency and life maintenance cost, combined with a range of generously proportioned, well laid out, affordable accommodation' (Building for Life Gold Standard) (Figure 18.6).

Beddington Zero Energy Development (BedZED)

Bill Dunster Architects

BedZED is not just another low energy housing scheme, it is a prescription for a social revolution; a prototype of how we should live in the twenty-first century if we are to enjoy a sustainable future (Figure 18.7).

Figure 18.7
BedZED west elevation

The design was led by Bill Dunster Architects who are one of the UK's top evangelists for ecologically sustainable architecture with the services and energy strategy developed by Arup Associates.

The Innovative Peabody Trust commissioned this development as an ultra-low energy mixed use scheme for the London Borough of Sutton. It consists of 82 homes with 271 habitable rooms, 2500 m² of space for offices, workspaces, studios, shops and community facilities including a nursery, organic shop and health centre, all constructed on the site of a former sewage works – the ultimate brownfield site. The housing comprises a mix of one- and two-bedroom flats, maisonettes and town houses.

Peabody was able to countenance the additional costs of the environmental provisions on the basis of the income from the offices as well as the homes. Though the Trust is extremely sympathetic to the aims of the scheme, it had to stack up in financial terms.

In every respect this is an integrated and environmentally advanced project. It is a high density development along the line recommended by the Rogers Urban Task Force.

It realises an overall density of 50 dwellings per hectare plus 120 workspaces per hectare. At such a density almost 3 million homes could be provided on brownfield sites with the additional benefit of workspaces for the occupants, radically cutting down on the demand for travel. This density includes the provision of 4000 m² of green space including sports facilities. Excluding the sports ground and placing cars beneath the 'village square' the density could be raised to 105 homes and 200 workspaces per hectare.

Some dwellings have ground level gardens whilst the roofs of the north facing workspaces serve as gardens for the adjacent homes (Figure 18.8).

The energy efficiency of the construction matches anything in the UK or mainland Europe. External walls consist of concrete block inner leaf, 300 mm of Rockwool insulation and an outer skin of brick adding up to a U-value of 0.11 W/m²K (Figure 18.9).

Roofs also contain 300 mm of insulation, in this case Styrofoam with a U-value of 0.10. Floors contain 300 mm of expanded polystyrene also having a U-value of 0.10. Windows are triple glazed with Low-E glass and argon filled. They are framed in timber and have a U-value of 1.20. These standards of insulation are a considerable improvement over those required by Part L of the 2002 Building Regulations in the UK. Masonry external and internal walls and concrete floors provide substantial thermal mass sustaining warmth in winter and preventing overheating in summer. In traditional construction up to 40 per cent of warmth is lost through air leakage. In the case of BedZED great attention has been paid to maximising air tightness which is designed to achieve two air changes per hour at 50 pascals (2ac50P).

One of its primary aims was to make the most of recycled materials and the main success in this respect was to obtain high grade steel from a demolished building as well as timber. The majority of all the materials were sourced within a 35 mile radius.

Materials containing volatile organic compounds (VOCs) have been avoided as part of the strategy to use low allergy materials.

Figure 18.8
North elevation with workspaces at ground level and roof gardens serving dwellings opposite

Figure 18.9
Masonry wall construction

Ventilation becomes an important issue as better levels of air tightness are achieved. In this case the design team opted for passive natural ventilation with heat recovery driven by roof cowls. A vane mounted on the cowls ensures that they rotate so that incoming air always faces upwind with exhaust air downwind. The heat recovery element captures up to 70 per cent of the heat from the exhaust air.

The energy efficiency drive does not end there. South facing elevations capitalise on solar gain with windows and their frames accounting for nearly 100 per cent of the wall area. Sunspaces embracing two floors on the south elevation add to the quality of the accommodation (Figures 18.10 and 18.11).

According to the 1998 version of SAP ratings BedZED achieves 150. Until the 2002 revision of the Regulations dwellings were required to achieve around SAP 75. It is predicted that space heating costs will be reduced by 90 per cent against a SAP 75 building. Overall energy demand should be reduced by 60 per cent.

BedZED aims to reduce domestic water consumption by 33 per cent. This is to be achieved by the use of water-saving toilets, dishwashers and washing machines. Toilets normally use 9 litres per flush; regulations now stipulate a 7.5 litre maximum. Here 3.5 litre dual flush toilets are provided producing an estimated saving of 55 000 litres per household per year. Taps are fitted with flow restrictors; showers that rely on gravity replace baths in single bedroom flats. As the scheme uses metered water it is expected that these measures will save a household £48 per year. On average, 18 per cent of a household's water

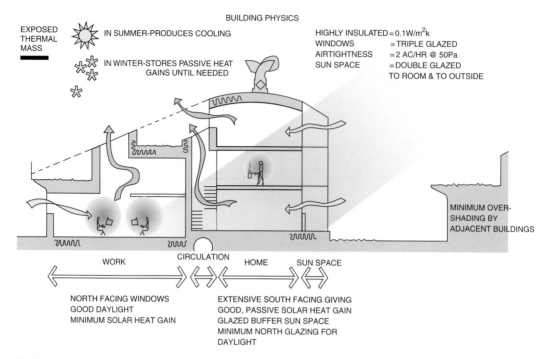

EXPOSED
THERMAL
MASS

IN SUMMER-PRODUCES COOLING

IN WINTER-STORES PASSIVE HEAT
GAINS UNTIL NEEDED

BUILDING PHYSICS

HIGHLY INSULATED = 0.1W/m²k
WINDOWS   = TRIPLE GLAZED
AIRTIGHTNESS = 2 AC/HR @ 50Pa
SUN SPACE   = DOUBLE GLAZED
                TO ROOM & TO OUTSIDE

MINIMUM OVER-
SHADING BY
ADJACENT BUILDINGS

WORK   CIRCULATION   HOME   SUN SPACE

NORTH FACING WINDOWS
GOOD DAYLIGHT
MINIMUM SOLAR HEAT GAIN

EXTENSIVE SOUTH FACING GIVING
GOOD, PASSIVE SOLAR HEAT GAIN
GLAZED BUFFER SUN SPACE
MINIMUM NORTH GLAZING FOR
DAYLIGHT

Figure 18.10
Section showing the passive features
(courtesy of ARUP and BRE)

Figure 18.11
South elevation with PVs integrated
into the glazing

requirements will be met by rainwater stored in large tanks integrated into the foundations.

Foulwater is treated in a sewage treatment plant housed in a greenhouse. It is a biologically based system which uses nutrients in sewage sludge as food for plants. The output from the plant is of a standard equivalent to rainwater and therefore can supplement the stored rainwater to be used to flush toilets.

Household waste normally destined for landfill will be reduced by 80 per cent compared with the average home.

The energy package

The principal energy source for the development is a combined heat and power unit which generates 130 kW of electric power. This is sufficient for the power needs of the scheme. The plant also meets its space heating and domestic hot water requirements via a district heating system served by insulated pipes. The CHP plant is reckoned to be of adequate output due to the high standard of insulation and air tightness and the fact that the peaks and troughs of seasonal and diurnal temperature are flattened by the high thermal mass.

A combustion engine generates the heat and power producing 350 000 kWh of electricity per year. It is fuelled by a mixture of hydrogen, carbon monoxide and methane produced by the on-site gasification of wood chips which are the waste product from nearby managed woodlands. The waste would otherwise go to landfill. The plant requires 1100 tonnes per year which translates to two lorry loads per week. In the future rapid rotation willow coppicing from the adjacent ecology park will supplement the supply of woodland waste. Across London 51 000 tonnes of tree surgery waste is available for gasification. It is worth restating that this is virtually a carbon neutral route to energy since carbon taken up in growth is returned to the atmosphere. Excess electricity is sold to the grid whilst any shortfall in demand is met by the grid's green tariff electricity. It is predicted that the scheme will be a net exporter to the grid (see Chapter 8) (Figure 18.12).

There is a further chapter to the energy story. Figure 18.11 illustrates the inclusion of PVs in the south glazed elevations of the scheme. They are also sited on southerly facing roofs. Their purpose is to provide a battery charging facility for electric vehicles. How the decision was made to dedicate the PVs to this role is worth recording.

Originally the idea was to use PVs to provide for the electricity needs of the buildings. Evacuated tube solar collectors would provide the heating. It turned out that this arrangement would involve a 70 year payback timescale. If the electricity were to be used to displace the use of fossil fuels in vehicles, taking into account their high taxation burden, the payback time would be about 13 years. So, it was calculated that 777 m^2 of high efficiency monocrystalline PVs would provide a peak output of 109 kW, sufficient for the energy needs of 40 light

BIO-FUELLED CHP

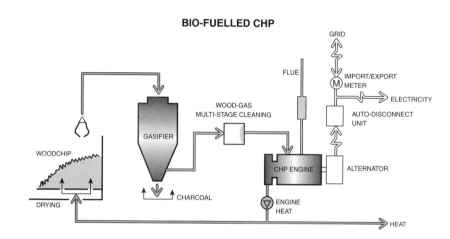

Figure 18.12
Wood chip gasification plant within
the development (courtesy of ARUP
and BRE)

electric vehicles covering 8500 km per year. It has to be remembered
that, in a project like BedZED, the energy used by a conventional
car could greatly exceed that used in the dwelling. As a yardstick, a
family car travelling 12 000 miles (19 000 km) per year produces almost
as much carbon dioxide (CO_2) as a family of four living in a typical
modern home.

The aim is that the 40 vehicles would provide a pool of cars to be
hired by the hour by residents and commercial tenants. Other car pool
schemes have indicated that hiring a pool car to cover up to 13 000 km
a year could save around £1500 in motoring costs. And that is without
factoring in the potential avoided cost of pollution. With congestion
charges due to be levied on vehicles using streets in other major cities
besides London, the exemption of electric vehicles will provide an even
greater incentive to adopt this technology.

The co-developers Peabody and Bioregional agreed as part of
the terms of the planning consent to enter into a Green Travel Plan
which meant a commitment to minimise the residents' environmental
impact from travel. On-site work and recreational facilities together
with the electric vehicle pool of 'Zedcars' would more than satisfy that
commitment.

A diagram produced by Arup summarises the ecological inventory
of the project (Figure 18.13).

This development has come about because the right people were
able to come together in the right place at the right time. The idea came
from Bioregional Development Group, an environmental organisation
based in Sutton who secured Peabody as the developer. Peabody is one
of the most enlightened housing associations in Britain. Bill Dunster was
engaged on the strength of Hope House which he designed as an ecologically sound living/working environment and which served as a
prototype for BedZED. Chris Twinn of Ove Arup and Partners worked

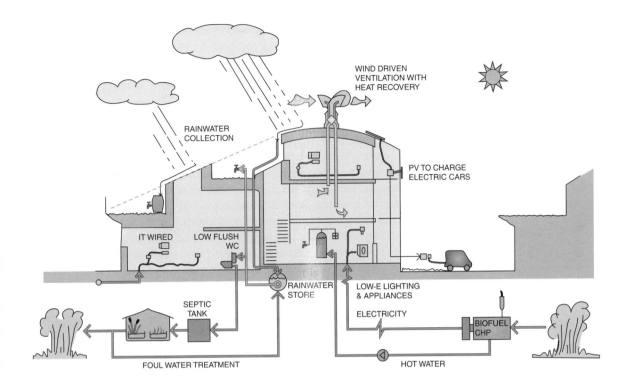

RAINWATER
COLLECTION

WIND DRIVEN
VENTILATION WITH
HEAT RECOVERY

PV TO CHARGE
ELECTRIC CARS

IT WIRED

LOW FLUSH
WC

RAINWATER
STORE

LOW-E LIGHTING
& APPLIANCES

ELECTRICITY

SEPTIC
TANK

BIOFUEL
CHP

FOUL WATER TREATMENT

HOT WATER

Figure 18.13
The ecological inventory of BedZED
(courtesy of ARUP and BRE)

with Bill Dunster when the latter was with Michael Hopkins and Partners so he was a natural choice as adviser on the physics and services of BedZED. The project happened due to a fortuitous conjunction of people committed to the principles of sustainable development. In future, developments of this nature must not rely on the chance collision of the brightest stars in the environmental firmament.

For a more detailed description of this project, refer to 'General Information Report 89', BedZED – Beddington Zero Energy Development, Sutton, published by BRECSU at BRE e-mail address: brecsuenq@bre.co.uk

Beaufort court renewable energy centre zero emissions building

Studio E Architects

Where possible the reuse of existing buildings is the best way to meet the sustainability agenda. An excellent example of this strategy is the headquarters of an energy company near London. The description of the development by David Lloyd Jones of Studio E Architects is quoted at length as being the most appropriate explanation of the design strategy.

Solar design aspects of the renewable energy centre and interim findings

David Lloyd Jones, Studio E Architects

The Renewable Energy Centre at Kings Langley in the UK is the new headquarters and visitors' centre for Renewable Energy Systems Ltd, a company whose business is developing wind farms on a global basis. The original buildings on the site housed chickens to provide eggs for the nearby Ovaltine malt drink plant. These buildings, derelict for 10 years, have now been converted and extended to provide for the office and visitors' centre accommodation. A sustainable approach was taken, particularly in respect to energy supply and use. The design was based on the comprehensive application of passive and active solar measures and is believed to be the first commercial net zero carbon dioxide emissions building in the UK. The project was completed in December 2003 and the energy systems, weather and internal comfort are being monitored over a 2 year period. An EC Framework 5 grant contributed to the cost of a hybrid PV thermal array, a seasonal heat store, the space heating and the associated mechanical and electrical systems (Figure 18.14).

Design principles

The Renewable Energy Centre is the first commercially developed building to be carbon neutral and entirely self-sufficient in energy. Indeed the various integrated renewable energy systems will, over any year, generate a surplus. This will be fed into the electricity grid for the use of the community.

No attempt was made to replicate the arts and crafts style of the original buildings in the new building works. The editions and replacements are expressed in a clean, modern, albeit sympathetic, idiom reflecting the contemporary concerns of Renewable Energy Systems and the leading edge energy technologies deployed over the site and concealed within the buildings.

The project brief was the conversion and extension of the former Ovaltine egg farm to provide 2665 m^2 of headquarters office accommodation for RES. This was to be carried out using, so far as economically practical, a range of renewable energy measures and employing 'best practice' sustainable strategies. RES was assisted in this objective by the contribution from the EC Framework 5 Programme. This funding was conditional on the adoption of a radically innovative approach to resolving sustainable issues and the involvement of a pan-European design and development team. On the basis of this innovative content, RES requested that additional facilities for visitors and parties

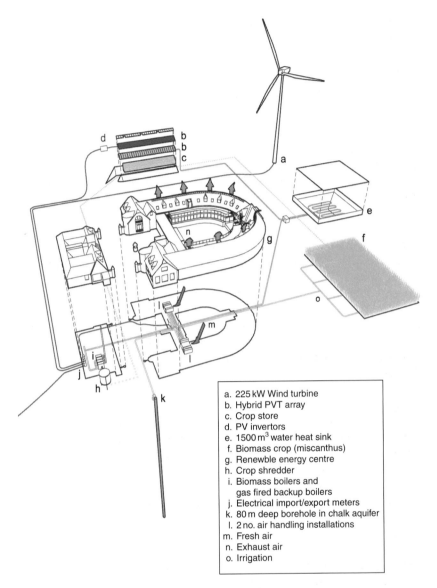

a. 225 kW Wind turbine
b. Hybrid PVT array
c. Crop store
d. PV invertors
e. 1500 m³ water heat sink
f. Biomass crop (miscanthus)
g. Renewble energy centre
h. Crop shredder
i. Biomass boilers and
   gas fired backup boilers
j. Electrical import/export meters
k. 80 m deep borehole in chalk aquifer
l. 2 no. air handling installations
m. Fresh air
n. Exhaust air
o. Irrigation

Figure 18.14
Energy strategy

who might wish to see and learn about the building and its energy systems.

Accordingly, the design principles upon which the development is based were to:

- provide a fully operational head office which meets the commercial needs and conditions of the property market;
- provide exhibition, conference and facilities for the use of RES and visitors to the building;

227

- deliver a building that minimises energy consumption and the use of scarce resources and that contributes positively to local economic and community needs;
- deliver a building whose energy consumption is provided entirely from on-site renewable energy sources;
- integrate seamlessly the social, technical and aesthetic aspects of the project.

The new buildings

In order to provide for the new uses, the existing buildings had to be radically altered and extended. However, the local planning authority required that the views of the outside of the building must remain largely unchanged. Both the 'coach house' and 'horseshoe' buildings had to be converted for modern office use with, in addition, exhibition, catering, conference, meeting, and main plant spaces.

The conversion of the coach house was relatively straightforward: the building fabric was upgraded to meet contemporary office use and the courtyard was enclosed by inserting a new steel structure. The conversion of the horseshoe was more complex. The construction between the two towers, except for the timber roof structure, was entirely demolished, the ground floor was lowered, the upper level floor and the roof reinforced, and the outer external wall rebuilt. The ground floor was extended into the courtyard by 5 m and a new single-storey link, incorporating the main entrance, was placed between, and connecting, the two wings of the horseshoe. Turf was planted on the roof of the new office space.

A third entirely new building was introduced close to the northern perimeter of the site. So as not to intrude in the landscape, this building was partly sunk into the ground and the excavated earth banked up against the north wall. This building provides storage for the harvested biomass crop. Its roof comprises the hybrid photovoltaic/thermal array.

The site layout

The triangular site comprises 7.5 ha of farmland located in the metropolitan green belt. The boundary of the site is formed, to the south, by the M25 orbital motorway; to the west, by the mainline London to Glasgow railway; and, to the north east, by a private road. The egg farm is set out on an axis, which, if extended northwards, aligns with the Ovaltine factory – the destination of all the eggs laid on the old farm. The layout of the various elements comprising the development is shown on the site plan. Its location adjacent to one of Europe's busiest motorways brings sustainability in action closer to the millions of people using the road.

The energy strategy

It is intended that all energy used at the Renewable Energy Centre be provided by renewable sources located on the site. The project demonstrates the integration of passive solar techniques with a range of inter-related renewable energy systems. The energy provision derives from:

- optimising the use of natural ventilation, daylight, high insulation, low air infiltration, solar control, materials that derive from the minimum use of energy in their manufacture and transport (low embodied energy materials), recycled materials, the minimisation of resource depletion, low use of water, car sharing and the encouragement of the use of public transport;
- a hybrid photovoltaic/thermal (PVT) array providing both electricity and hot water installed as the roof to a biomass crop store, the heat of which is passed to:
    - a seasonal heat store, comprising a 1100 m² body of water concealed beneath the ground, used to assist heating of the buildings in winter (Figure 18.15);
    - a biomass crop (miscanthus or 'elephant grass') cultivated on the surrounding land, harvested annually, dried and stored in the earth-sheltered space beneath the PVT array;
- future biomass plant which shreds the miscanthus and burns it to provide heating for the building (and, possibly, in a forthcoming adaptation, combined heat and power (CHP));
- ground water cooling pumped from an 80 m deep bore hole to cool the buildings in summer (and then passed out of the building to irrigate the biomass crop);
- a 225 kW wind turbine supplying, with the PVT installation, all the electrical power required by the building and a significant surplus fed into the national grid.

Clean and green
Bringing back to life a derelict building rather than building new is a considerable benefit in terms of land utilisation, use of resources and improving the amenity of the area. The construction work was undertaken on the basis of minimising waste and using materials and components with low embodied energy from readily available resources.

In order to minimise the need for energy, a judicious combination of active systems (mechanical ventilation, artificial cooling, heating and lighting, building management systems) and passive systems (solar heating, natural ventilation and lighting, solar shading, a well-insulated building envelope incorporating thermal mass) was developed.

The buildings are exposed to considerable external noise from passing trains to the west and the motorway to the south. To cut out the disturbance from noise inside the buildings, the outward facing facades had to be sealed. This, together with the relatively high levels of heat generated by modern office use, requires the building to be artificially cooled in summer months. The cooling source is water drawn from aquifers located in the chalk below the building. This strategy avoids the heavy energy consumption and potential polluting effects of refrigeration

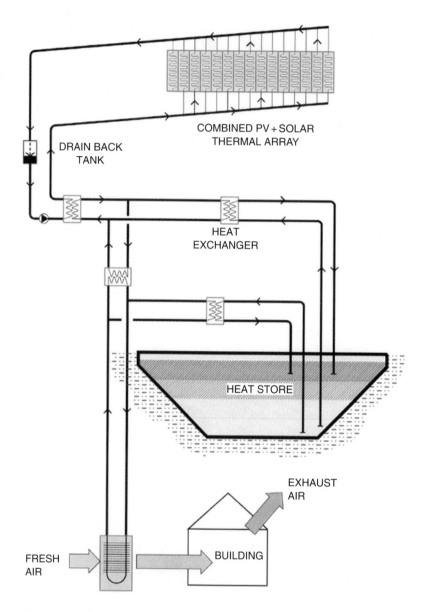

COMBINED PV + SOLAR
THERMAL ARRAY

DRAIN BACK
TANK

HEAT
EXCHANGER

HEAT STORE

EXHAUST
AIR

FRESH
AIR

BUILDING

Figure 18.15
PVT/heat store/space heating

plant normally used for air conditioning. The cool water is used to drop
the temperature of air being fed into the building and/or is circulated
through convectors within the office space, cooling the air within it.

Heat is supplied from the biomass boiler (or gas boiler until such
time the biomass plant is installed) and from the PVT array, either direct
or via the seasonal ground heat store. Hot water from these sources is
used in a similar way as the chilled water for cooling. Electricity is generated from the PVT array and the wind turbine.

Windows can be opened in facades and roofs facing away, or sheltered from, the motorway and the railway, to ventilate the building in

temperate conditions. Exposed windows are shaded from the sun by fixed glass or aluminium screens and by deciduous tree planting, thereby reducing unwanted solar gains and the need for cooling. The building is well insulated and sealed.

Predicted energy use and energy supply is shown in the table below. The current monitoring programme will show whether these predictions are borne out in reality.

Estimated energy balance for the site:

	Electrical	Space heating
Building annual loads (2500 m² building gross area)	115 MWh	85 MWh
PV/T direct contribution	3.2 MWh*	15 MWh
Heat collected into storage		24 MWh
Pumping load/heat lost from storage	−4.5 MWh	−12 MWh
Wind turbine	250 MWh	
Miscanthus: peak expected production (60 odt/year)		160 MWh
Net contribution	248.7 MWh	187 MWh
Potential electrical export	133.7 MWh	
Potential surplus miscanthus for heat export		102 MWh

* With 48 m² of PV.

A building management system (BMS) controls and optimises all the energy systems, including opening and closing the roof lights. It also records all monitored results from the various energy systems before passing the results to a site in Denmark for uploading onto the website.

RES actively encourages staff to use public transport, bicycles and car sharing for travel between home and office.

About 5 ha of the 7.5 ha site are given over to miscanthus cultivation. In addition there is a car park and a 5 aside football pitch. The remainder of the land is planted with indigenous species of trees, shrubs and grasses. Wildlife is encouraged by the re-creation of natural habitats.

The renewable energy sources

Wind Turbine

The 225 kW wind turbine has a hub height of 36 m and a rotor diameter of 29 m and is a Vestas V29 model previously in operation in the Netherlands. The turbine is connected to the buildings' electrical distribution network and to the national grid. It is expected to generate 250 MWh annually, which is greater than the anticipated building consumption, and excess power (equivalent to the needs of around 40 homes) will be exported to the grid.

Biomass

The buildings' heating needs will primarily be met by a biomass boiler fuelled by the energy crop: miscanthus or 'elephant grass', 5 hectares of which have been planted on the site. The crop is harvested annually in the late winter with conventional harvesting equipment and stored as bales until needed. The bales are shredded before being fed into the biomass boiler. The field is expected to yield 60 oven-dried-tonnes per year with a calorific value of 17 GJ/tonne. The 100 kW biomass boiler is provided by Talbott's heating. It is 80 to 85 per cent efficient and can modulate down to 25 per cent of full load. The shredded bales are fed into the boiler by a mechanical screw auger. Biomass is carbon neutral as the CO_2 emitted during combustion is balanced by the CO_2 absorbed by the crop, which is coppiced on short rotation. The emissions from the boiler comply with the Clean Air Act. The boiler is expected to be installed and operating in 2004–2005.

Ground water cooling

Ground water is used to cool the buildings during the summer. Water is extracted from the local aquifer at 12°C via a 75 m deep borehole. First, it is used to cool and dehumidify the incoming air to the buildings in the air handling units. The water is then circulated at 15°C through chilled beams (finned tubes) at high level in the offices. Finally, the water is used to irrigate the energy crop.

PVT array

The 170 m² solar array comprises 54 m² of hybrid PV/thermal (PVT) panels and 116 m² of solar thermal panels. The PVT panels consist of a photovoltaic module, which converts light into electricity, and a copper

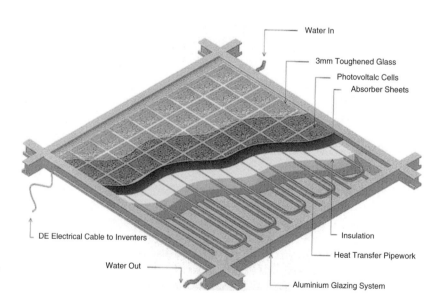

Figure 18.16
PV/thermal panels (Courtesy of Studio E Architects)

heat exchanger on the back to capture the remaining solar energy. The panels have been developed by ECN in the Netherlands, incorporating Shell Solar PV elements and Zen Solar thermal elements. They produce electricity and hot water (Figure 18.16). The solar thermal panels are identical to the PVT panels, but without the photovoltaic element.

Seasonal underground heat store

The underground heat store is an 1100 m^3 body of water that stores the heat generated by the PVT and solar thermal panels for use in the buildings during the colder months. The top of the store is insulated

Figure 18.17
General views of Beaufort Court

View from Southwest

PVT array

Heat stone prior to lid being installed

Figure 18.18
Forecourt, Beaufort Court

with a floating lid of 500 mm expanded polystyrene. It is hinged around the perimeter to allow for the expansion and contraction of the water and the design also incorporates a suspension system to support the roof should the water level reduce. The sloping sides are uninsulated. As long as the ground around the store is kept dry, it will act as an insulator and additional thermal mass, increasing the capacity of the store. The high specific heat capacity of water (4.2 kJ/kg°C) makes it a good choice for storing heat.

During the summer there will be little or no demand for heat in the building, so the heat generated by the PVT array will be stored in the heat store. In the autumn some of the solar heat generated will be used directly in the buildings and the excess will be added to the heat store. The temperature of the water in the store will gradually rise over the summer and early autumn. During the winter the solar heat generated will be less than the buildings' heat load, and heat will be extracted from the heat store to heat the incoming air to the building. The temperature of the water in the store will drop as the heat is extracted. Some heat will also be lost to the surroundings. This is estimated to be about 50 per cent of the total heat put into the store over the summer. The relatively low-grade heat from the store can be used to preheat the incoming air to the building, as the outside air will be at a lower temperature than the water.

Integrated district environmental design

Chapter Nineteen

Demographic changes are creating a demand for new communities in developed countries. For example, in the UK there is a projected need for nearly 4 million new homes, mostly in the Southeast of England. One suggestion by the planner Peter Hall is that there could be three new cities around London which he calls City of Kent, City of Anglia and City of Mercia. These will focus on existing towns and cities: Ashford, Cambridge, Peterborough, Wellingborough and Rugby. They would comprise clusters of new communities which would create the ideal opportunity to realise the goal of integrated environmental design at the district level.

One project that has gone some way down this route is in Switzerland at Plan-les-Ouates, a solar city near Geneva.

The driving force behind the scheme was the proposal for legislation to reduce the use of non-renewable energy by means of a carbon tax, energy efficiency subsidies and the greater use of renewable energy sources. In anticipation of these measures this community constructed a major housing development consisting of nine apartment blocks which took the exploitation of solar radiation to the limit of current technology.

First, two thirds of the roofs are covered by black coated stainless steel solar collectors. These are about 30 per cent less efficient than the most advanced glazed solar panels but they are significantly cheaper and can rapidly be installed to form an integral part of the roof system.

Second, the solar panels supply hot water to two storage tanks per block, each of 50 000 litres. They supply domestic hot water in summer and supplement space heating during spring and autumn.

Third, the project employs a double flow ventilation system which provides all apartments with one to two air changes per hour with full heat recovery. The extract air is pumped into the car park thus avoiding the need for additional ventilation.

The fourth attribute of the scheme is the 'earth source preheater'. This comprises a 6 km grid of pipes under the car park. In winter fresh air entering the ventilation system in the apartments first passes through the grid warming the air by up to 10°C due to the fact that the earth temperature never falls below 10°C. In summer the system is reversed to provide space cooling. The project was completed in 1996.

In Austria, the European Commission is sponsoring the Linz Solar City. The first phase of building will consist of 600 social housing units built to strict energy conservation standards and designed by some of Europe's leading architects. Linz City Council envisages that this will ultimately be a new town accommodating 30 000 people. The purpose of the project is to demonstrate that solar housing can be viable in high density urban situations. The performance of the houses will be monitored by a new method of measuring carbon dioxide output devised by energy expert Norbert Kaiser.

Ecological City of Tomorrow, Malmo, Sweden

A European Commission demonstration project is almost completed in Malmo, comprising a whole new district consisting of housing, shops, offices and other services. It aims to be a zero net energy scheme, with its 11 GWh/year energy demand making no net contribution to carbon dioxide (CO_2) emissions. It is being built on a reclaimed industrial site by the Ribersborg beach and close to the historic centre of Malmo. The project is the first phase of a 10 year programme to make the city of Malmo a model of sustainable regeneration. It formed the centrepiece of an exhibition 'Bo01' held in June 2001 (Figure 19.1) under the direction of Professor Klas Tham.

The objectives of the scheme are to:

- meet 100 per cent of energy needs from renewable sources by providing innovative energy generation plant and distribution systems;
- integrate appropriate technologies like solar, wind, heat pumps and aquifer storage to produce cost-effective clean heat and electricity;
- engage in holistic design procedures involving architects, services designers and builders from inception to completion;
- establish synergy between Malmo's existing electricity and district heating system and the local system.

The district will include 800 homes in a mixture of detached, terraced and apartment dwellings. A canal, harbour, promenade, parks and covered walkways are incorporated into the development.

Energy strategy

A 2 MW wind turbine and 120 m^2 of PV cells connected to the grid will account for the area's electricity demand. They will also power a heat pump which will extract heat from underground aquifers and the sea to meet about 83 per cent of district heating requirements. The same aquifer system will store cold water to provide cooling in summer. About 15 per cent of the remaining heat demand will be met by

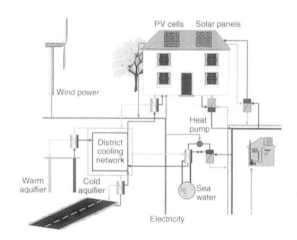

Figure 19.1
Model of the 'City of Tomorrow' and the integrated energy system

2000 m² solar collectors. Biogas produced from local waste will meet the remaining 2 per cent of heat requirement. The aim is to keep energy consumption in buildings below 105 kWh/m² per year. At this rate it should be possible for the inhabitants to maintain the comfort standards to which they have become accustomed. It is worth noting that the Swedes tend to regard 22°C as a minimum level for comfort compared with 18–20°C in the UK. Occupants will have the opportunity to adjust and monitor their energy consumption with the help of IT. All households will be connected to a broadband network equipping them for advanced communication functions such as voice activated systems as well as monitoring management systems.

A biogas digester treats organic waste from the district converting it to fertiliser and producing biogas for heating and vehicle fuel. There is also a plant which extracts energy and nutrients from the sludge from a sewage works.

A 'vacuum refuse chute' extracts organic waste from household refuse. Disposal hatches attached to each property lead to holding tanks from which the waste makes its way to two docking stations at the edge of the site. From there it goes to the biogas digester. All residents receive up-to-date information about waste separation and disposal. The target is to reduce unsorted waste by 80 per cent.

By connecting the renewable generators to Malmo's existing distribution system, the project is assured of security of supply of electricity. Over the year there should be a balance between the district's electricity production and consumption, hence the zero net energy label.

All the buildings are designed to the highest energy efficiency standards, keeping space heating demand to a minimum. The design of buildings and energy systems is integrated under a single management strategy with the whole process being subject to stringent quality control.

Information technology is used not only to regulate the different elements of the energy system but also to inform residents about their energy consumption and allow them a degree of control over their energy management and comfort. Completed at the end of 2001 it forms an appropriate gateway to Sweden situated as it is at the end of the spectacular Oresund bridge and tunnel complex linking the country with Denmark.

Transport is a key factor in any sustainability policy. It is planned to embark on a programme of vehicles powered by environmentally friendly fuels. The public transport system will be adapted accordingly and the pool of cars within the development will include electric and gas powered vehicles. The management vehicles will be electrically powered. There will be charging points for electric vehicles and a station providing natural gas for vehicles.

Towards the less unsustainable city

The ultimate challenge will be to transform existing towns and cities so that they become less of an 'ecological black hole'. The city is an epicentre of consumption, but also capable of being the highest visible manifestation of civilisation – 'civis' the city. Cities have powerful symbolic resonance which means that there are considerable constraints on change. Over the next 50 years, barring catastrophes like sea level rise, the basic form and infrastructure of European cities will not change all that much. Even after the 1940s blitz which destroyed the heart of many great cities like Liverpool, the reconstruction process in most cases followed the routes of the original infrastructure. As much as anything this was because of services routes and the complexities of land ownership.

Individual buildings will be replaced or radically upgraded and the economics of the process will depend on uncertainties like the value of land and the price of energy. As suggested at the beginning energy prices as likely to rise steeply as demand increasingly outstrips supply. But the most important priority is for towns and cities to make drastic reductions in their demand for fossil-based energy and in this respect there is a borough in the UK heading in the right direction.

Woking: a pace-setting local authority

Woking is south east of London close to the M25 motorway with a population of over 89 000. It can claim to have one of the most environmentally progressive local administrations in the UK which has committed the authority to eight key themes under the headings:

- energy services;
- planning and regulation;
- waste;
- transport;
- procurement;
- education and promotion;
- management of natural habitats;
- adapting to climate change.

Energy services

It is in this sphere that the local council has been particularly far sighted by recognising that energy has both immediate social and long-term global implications. On the one hand it seeks to eliminate fuel poverty and, on the other, drastically reduce CO_2 emissions. They have subscribed to the Royal Commission on Environmental Pollution's targets of a 60 per cent reduction in emissions by 2050 and an 80 per cent by 2100.

In order to implement its energy strategy a council-owned company was formed called Thameswey Limited to act as an Energy and Environmental Services Company. The company has entered into an agreement with the borough to act as its contractor to provide combined heat and power to the borough. In 1999 Thameswey Energy Limited was formed in partnership with a Danish energy service company (ESCO) International ApS. Its purpose is to build, finance and operate CHP stations of up to 5 MW capacity throughout the town and offer energy services to institutional, business and residential customers.

The first project was a CHP station supplying heat and chilled water services by private pipes and electricity by private grid to the principal energy users in the town centre including the council offices. It was officially commissioned in 2001 (Figure 19.2).

The most innovative enterprise by Thameswey Energy is the Woking Park project. The park complex includes a 200 kWe fuel cell, together with plans to include an 836 kWe CHP reciprocating gas powered engine, two 75 kWe CHP engines and 9.11 pkW PV installation. These together with heat fired absorption cooling and a thermal store add up to a CHP capacity of 1.195 MWe.

The fuel cell is of the phosphoric acid type which uses hydrogen reformed from natural gas. It supports the heating and power needs of the pool in the park and leisure centre, with surplus heat in summer used to generate absorption cooling and dehumidification. There is also provision to direct surplus electricity to sheltered housing accommodation (Figure 19.3).

The extensive use of photovoltaics also features in the borough's strategy. Brockhill, an 'extra care' sheltered housing scheme, was the first in the UK to use a combination of CHP and PVs to serve its energy needs. In all 117 sheltered housing tenants receive PV electricity, including Prior's Croft. This development is also served by a small CHP unit producing 22 kWe and 50 kW of heat backed up by a 6 × 50 kW boiler (Figure 19.4).

In order to sidestep the problems of supplying small amounts of PV electricity to the grid at an uneconomic rate, the council has created a mini-distribution system of private wires enabling it to sell PV and CHP electricity direct to customers. The CHP stations achieve 80–90 per cent

Figure 19.2
Combined heat, cooling and power grid, Woking town centre

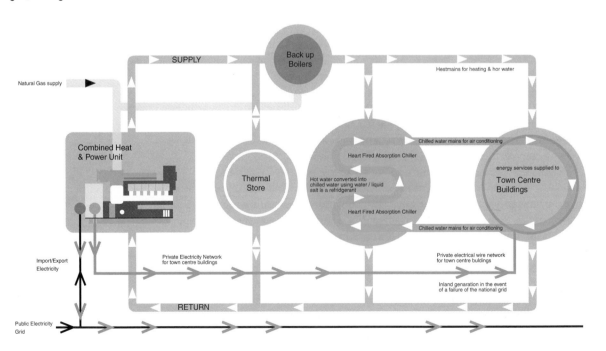

Figure 19.3
Phosphoric acid 200 KWe fuel cell,
Woking Park

efficiency compared with coal fired power stations at 25–35 per cent. This is because of the utilisation of heat from the engine and compact grids with minimum distribution losses.

Planning and regulation

The main concerns are:

- land use;
- location;
- layout;
- landscape;
- sustainable construction.

The concept of 'environmental footprint' is a prime consideration in land use policy. This is particularly concerned with the CO_2 emissions that are generated by the current use of the land. The aim is that, when land use is changed, the new use should represent an 80 per cent reduction in CO_2 emissions.

As regards location, the council operates a measure called Public Transport Accessibility Level Rating (PTAL), ranging from 1 to 7 with 7 being the most proximate to public transport. New development proposals are assessed according to where they feature on the scale. Most new development in the borough scores near the top of the scale.

Planning policy promotes housing layouts which maximise passive solar design and a preference for terrace housing and flats which minimise heat loss through external walls. It is estimated that such measures reduce energy use by 20 per cent.

Figure 19.4
Prior's Croft PVs and inverters to
convert DC power from the PVs to AC
electricity

In terms of landscaping the planting of trees and shrubs is encouraged with benefits that include a reduction in the heat island effect, solar shading in summer and protection from wind.

Energy use in buildings is targeted by encouraging insulation standards above those required by the Building Regulations, installing community heating, building integrated renewable energy systems and requiring water conservation measures to be adopted. The council has the most energy efficient public housing stock in the UK with an average NHER rating of 8. The target for all the stock is NHER 9 or SAP 74 with the aim of limiting energy costs to 10–15 per cent of income of those dependent on a state pension. This should eliminate fuel poverty in this sector.

In the private sector the council had topped up government grants to provide full insulation measures to 3026 homes up to 2002. It aims to solve the fuel poverty problem in this sector, especially in rented accommodation, by 2010–11.

Waste

The council has adopted plans for a borough-wide zero waste strategy ultimately to reduce the need for landfill disposal to 10 per cent of current use. It operates a two-bin domestic waste system with a division into dry goods and organic waste. The anaerobic digestion of organic waste provides gas for CHP engines and compost. Thermal gasification of other waste provides the hydrogen for the fuel cell. Diverting waste from landfill could equate to a CO_2 reduction of 100 000 tonnes. Recycling also plays a major part in its waste strategy, especially in terms of the reuse of materials in construction. The council operates an energy recycling fund which benefits from saving due to energy and water efficiency measures and the recycling/reuse of materials. Sums from the fund are ploughed back into energy efficiency projects.

Transport

Council promotional campaigns seek to raise awareness of the benefits of alternative fuel vehicles at the same time encouraging local filling stations to provide liquid petroleum gas (LPG), compressed natural gas (CNG), liquid natural gas (LNG) and hydrogen. The council also intends to ensure that its own vehicles will be low carbon technology (i.e. less than 100 g/km of CO_2 equivalent) by 2010–11 when such vehicles should be in volume production.

Procurement

Where possible the council obtains materials from local sources reducing carbon miles. It ensures that timber is obtained from sustainably managed forests. It encourages its contractors also to adopt sustainable procurement policies.

The conclusion to be drawn from these case studies is that sustainable design is a holistic activity and demands an integrated approach. Reducing the demand for energy and generating clean energy are two sides of the same coin. Examples have been cited where buildings and transport are organically linked with building integrated renewables providing power for electric cars. BedZED, Malmo and Woking are signposts to new and more sustainable and agreeable patterns of life.

An American perspective

Chapter Twenty

In environmental terms the United States is a paradox. On the Federal level it opposes the Kyoto Accord and refuses to acknowledge the spectre of the fossil fuel trap. On the other hand many states have impressive environmental policies, especially on the west coast. One of the great pioneers of the environment movement is Amory Lovens who founded the Rocky Mountain Institute in Colorado in the 1980s. This was a ground-breaking organisation epitomised by its ultra-low energy buildings. The spin-off has been organisations such a 'Earthship Biotecture'. This promotes a way of building that aims to realise the ultimate aspirations of sustainable architecture with its concept of 'earthships'.

In several respects the USA is a special case. First, compared with western Europe it has much greater extremes of climate which presents a formidable challenge to environmental designers and perhaps calls for greater tolerance on the part of environmental devotees in Europe. Buildings which have to cope with a seasonal temperature range of over 60°C demand rather exceptional treatment, even to having a dispensation as regards air conditioning.

Second, it enjoys cheap energy which distorts the cost effectiveness of renewable energy and energy efficiency design measures. On the other hand, stand-alone energy generation is attractive where continuity of supply cannot be guaranteed.

Not surprisingly, one of the driving forces behind environmental design is the 'bottom line'. A study conducted by Ian McHard of the University of Pennsylvania concluded that a 1 per cent increase in productivity is equivalent to eliminating the whole energy bill. The research found that companies which were exploiting natural light coupled with better lighting design and better thermal comfort significantly raised worker productivity.

This was demonstrated some years ago by the Lockheed Corporation with its $50 million engineering production centre accommodating 2600 workers. It has high ceilings (15 feet) and light shelves enabling natural light to penetrate to the core of the building. At the heart of a building is an atrium except that they call it a 'lightrium' to get round the Defense Department's ban on atria! The building used only half the energy of buildings designed to the strictest codes in the country. As a result the energy measures paid for themselves in four years. However, the most striking benefit was that absenteeism fell by 15 per cent. This enabled the firm to win a contract, the profits of which paid for the whole building.

Another salutary tale comes from the Wal-Mart enterprise. It has a prodigious appetite for space, amounting to one new store per working day at about 100 000 square feet each time. In one store they were persuaded to daylight half of the sales area. After only two months it found that sales were significantly higher in the daylit half, leading them to make a considerable investment in research into daylighting.

In Bozeman, Montana, the state university is investing in a project for a naturally lit, passively ventilated and passively cooled laboratory. It is calculated that the Montana State Green Laboratory Complex will need heating for only six days in the year which will be supplied by radiant coils. It has to be remembered that Montana experiences extremes of cold. Like many other states, Montana has what is called an 'extraction economy' which means that it not only consumes its natural capital assets at a great rate, it also produces considerable waste.

For a start the purpose in this project is to source all materials from within a 300 mile radius, which, for a country the size of the USA, is ambitious. Also, there is an emphasis on recycling the materials after demolition. As regards the construction, a high strength, lightweight concrete has been developed using fly-ash aggregate, similar to the Conference Centre at Earth Centre in the UK. But perhaps the most interesting innovation is the gluelam beams made from salvaged timber. The novelty lies in the adhesive which is made from bacteria and called Adheron. Its secret lies in the fact that it can be decomposed. At the end of a product's life it can be placed in an autoclave and an enzymatic key introduced. This unlocks the bond and the timber is available to be reused.

One of the most energy efficient buildings in the USA is the Zion National Park Visitor Center, Springdale, Utah, by architect James Crockett (Figure 20.1). It uses 80 per cent less energy than a 'code compliant' building and cost less to build than a conventional equivalent. This is due in part to the omission of heavy services. The building is naturally lit with substantial eaves shading the south facing windows from summer sun. When there is inadequate daylight the BEMS compensates with energy efficient fluorescent and high intensity discharge lamps.

The building is also naturally ventilated. Cooling towers supplement cross ventilation (Figure 20.2). They contain pads that soak up pumped water providing evaporative cooling. The cool dense air exits through large openings at the base of the tower.

The National Park is in a remote area of southern Utah where the electricity grid is somewhat unreliable. Roof mounted PVs linked to battery storage provide the uninterrupted supply required by the National Park Service. The PVs meet 30 per cent of the electricity demand and

Figure 20.1
Zion National Park Visitor Center
showing cooling towers and
Trombe wall

Figure 20.2
Zion National Park Visitor Center, cooling towers

excess electricity is exported to the grid on the basis of net metering. This system of metering could transform the rate of uptake of PVs in the UK.

The design features a Trombe wall enabling a masonry wall behind to store heat. In winter the temperature in the cavity can reach 38°C (100°F) which is gradually radiated into the building.

Glenwood Park, Atlanta, Georgia

Figure 20.3
Glenwood Park neighbourhood as proposed

Due to be completed in 2006, Glenwood Park (Figure 20.3) aims to be 'a model of environmentally conscious urbanism' according to its developer Charles Brewer. The site is two miles east of downtown Atlanta and the developers have managed to 'civilise' a state highway, converting it to the development's main street with traffic calming

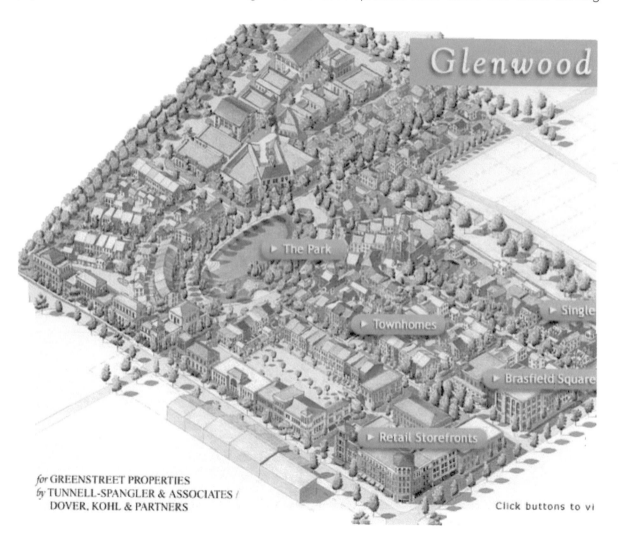

for GREENSTREET PROPERTIES
by TUNNELL-SPANGLER & ASSOCIATES /
DOVER, KOHL & PARTNERS

measures and lined with trees and shops. The object is to be pedestrian friendly; 'to create a sociable, walkable community where there's less need for driving' (Brewer). Dedicated cycle lanes will further reduce the need for car travel. There will be direct access to the local rail services which adds up to an estimated reduction in car travel of 1.6 million miles compared with average regional driving patterns which is the equivalent of removing 100 cars from the roads.

The township will feature up to 70 000 ft^2 of shops and offices serving residents and nearby communities. An existing brick building will be upgraded to supply 22 000 ft^2 of office condominiums over covered parking. It will have a mix of individual houses, 'townhouses', apartments, stores and parks interspersed with 1000 trees to moderate the heat island effect. Housebuilders will be required to meet the high energy efficient design standards of the EarthCraft House programme which includes not only levels of energy conservation but also water conservation and methods to reduce soil erosion.

The residential component of the township will comprise 60 single family houses, up to 130 townhouses and 200 apartments.

The site is a typical brownfield location which involved demolishing and recycling 40 000 yd^3 of site concrete as well as recycling 700 000 lb of granite blocks for use in the parks. An innovative stormwater system will reduce runoff by nearly 70 per cent. The landscaping will be irrigated by ground water rather than the mains supply. The street layout will echo traditional European towns with narrower widths and tighter corners than is the norm in US neighbourhoods.

An important aspect of the project is that it will be totally funded by Brewer's development company Green Street Properties, formed for this project. This means that there will not have to be compromises on standards to satisfy lending institutions. Over the past 3 years the company has invested $8 million in buying the 28 acre site, remediation and creating the infrastructure of roads and sewers.

In the context of the norms of American urbanism Glenwood Park is a considerable step in the right direction (www.glenwoodpark.com).

A signpost to the future is being offered by the state of California. Its Environmental Protection Agency is proposing that one million homes will be equipped with PVs over the next 10 years in line with a pledge by the state governor. State subsidies would ensure that householders would make a net gain from exporting to the grid. The EPA considers that the incentives will be sufficient to get PVs on 40 per cent of new homes by 2010 and 50 per cent by 2013. It is estimated that the solar installations would be equivalent to the output from 36 gas fired 75 MW power plants, avoiding 50 m tonnes of carbon dioxide emissions. The ultimate aim is that 1.2 million new and existing homes will be producing solar electricity by 2017.

It is a paradox that, whilst the Federal government seems to be dragging its feet on climate change issues, individual states are leading players on a world stage in converting to renewable energy.

Chapter Twenty One

Emergent technologies and future prospects

No other century has begun with such an awareness of the potential for change and of the uncertainties that underlie that perception. The best we can do is identify the developing technologies and socio-economic trends that are clearly discernible and extrapolate from them. There are some predictions we can make with reasonable confidence and consider the implications for architects and related professions.

There is little doubt that global warming will trigger changes that will fundamentally change the practice of architecture. Already the prediction that global warming will lead to greater intensity and frequency of storms is being realised. It is inevitable that, as heat is built up within the biosphere, this results in the release of energy which powers more extreme climate activity. We have noted examples of the predicted rate of return of the 1 in 100 year storm as currently defined. Newhaven headed the list with a return rate of 1 in 3 years by 2030. The immediate consequence for architects is that design wind loads should be amended to cope with this progressive change and the fact that buffeting will increase in intensity.

Another probability is that extreme heat episodes with occur more frequently. This needs to be considered when incorporating passive solar design and the design of atria and conservatories. At present natural ventilation and the omission of air conditioning is justified on the grounds that cooling is only required for a short period in a year. This may change and mechanical ventilation incorporating some form of cooling will become a necessity such as aquifer or ground source cooling.

At the same time there is a possibility that winters will become more severe due to the weakening or rerouting of the Gulf Stream. Much greater extremes of temperature will have major design implications, both for the stability of materials and the levels of insulation. As fossil fuel prices rise, this will increase the appeal of building integrated renewables plus active solar heating and seasonal heat storage.

The possibility of colder winters adds urgency to the need to tackle the problem of the unacceptable numbers of unfit homes in the UK as outlined in Chapter 10.

Rainfall patterns will change. In the south it is anticipated there will be much less rainfall and frequent drought conditions. This will increase the pressure for water conservation and the harvesting and purification of both rainwater and grey water for use other than for human consumption. The design of substructures and foundations will need to take account of progressive drying out of clay subsoils. In the north rainfall amounts will rise, increasing the risk of flash floods as rivers rise and the surrounding land is saturated. It is unlikely that the Environment Agency will have the resources to provide protection against the prospect of an increasing threat. For example, devastating floods hit Boscastle in Devon in 2004 with 75 mm (3 inches) of rainfall in 15 minutes.

It is inevitable that sea levels will rise. Already there are compelling reasons not to develop below the 5 metre contour at or near the coasts. The predictions of rising levels are becoming more alarmist, with the doomsday scenario of a 110 metre rise if Antarctica melts (Sir David King, Chapter 2). The least we can expect is a rise of 1 metre over the next century due mainly to thermal expansion. The more immediate threat lies in storm surges since a small rise in sea level greatly amplifies the impact of a storm surge. Add to this the fact that the predicted intense low pressure systems can cause the sea level to rise locally by over half a metre, and you have the recipe for serious sea incursion.

This will have an impact not only on where we build but the way we design buildings. In areas which will increasingly be threatened by flooding, one answer could be that new homes should have the living accommodation at least 2 metres above ground level, with garages, workshop, leisure activities below.

Energy for the future

If demand continues to rise at the present rate it is expected that most of the world's fossil fuel resources will run out around the middle of this century. There are still those who put their faith in the commercial application of nuclear fusion perhaps relying on the fact that an energy vacuum will radically alter the definition of 'commercial'. However, this goal still seems as elusive as ever. On a global scale there is no real optimism about the capacity of current renewable technology to meet the energy needs of the next century especially the exploding economies of the Far East. At the same time there is considerable anxiety about allowing the proliferation of nuclear technology.

More than ever before there is hope that someone will find the 'Rosetta Stone' that will redefine physics and lead to limitless cheap, clean energy. For example, on the threshold between science fiction and reality is the greatest potential energy source of all, namely the exploitation of antimatter. Physicists from Germany, Italy and Switzerland have managed to combine single antiprotons and positrons to create antiatoms of antihydrogen. Antimatter is destroyed when it comes into contact with normal matter, releasing massive amounts of energy (*New Scientist*, 'Antiworld flashes into view', 6 January 1996). It's a case of 'watch this space, but don't stand too close'.

The predicted rise in oil consumption considered in Chapter 2 is nothing compared with the anticipated demand for electricity. One of the leading think-tanks in this sphere is the Electric Power Research Institute (EPRI) at Palo Alto in California. Its chief executive Kurt Yeager points out that 2 billion people are without electricity. By 2050 this will have risen to 5 billion unless there are fundamental changes in the way we produce and distribute electricity. This in part will be driven by the digital revolution; as computers get faster they will require reliability of power in the order of 99.9999999 per cent. At present the reliability is 99.9 per cent which amounts to stoppages of a few minutes at a time but adding up to about 8 hours a year. This is fatal for microprocessors which are upset by millisecond disturbances. As Yeager puts it, we will need power delivery systems with switching operations that reach the speed of light.

The challenge which the EPRI presents is to provide a minimum of 1000 kWh of electricity per year to everyone in the world by 2050, about the same as the US in the 1920s, remembering that by then the estimated global population will be 9–10 billion. This would be the equivalent of tripling the world's generating capacity which translates to building a 1000 MW power station every two days.

The revolution which will make this vision possible is the shift from mega power plants and creaking national grids to much smaller dispersed grids. Large overland grids are inefficient and expensive to maintain. They are subject to frequent failure and even at the best of times incur up to 10 per cent line losses. In the UK it is claimed the grid is well over its 30 year replacement date.

Above all, the answer is to devote massive resources to the development of renewable energy technologies to harness a mere 1/15 000th of the energy of the sun. Solar energy promises unlimited free meals.

The Royal Commission on Environmental Pollution sees:

> a shift from very large, all-electricity plant towards smaller and more numerous combined heat and power plants. The electricity distribution system will have to undergo major changes to cope with this development and with the expansion of smaller scale, intermittent renewable energy sources. The transition towards a low-emission energy system would be greatly helped by the development of new means of storing energy on a large scale.
>
> 22nd Report, *Energy, the Changing Climate*,
> p. 169, Stationery Office, 2000

This ties in with the Washington Worldwatch Institute which states that 'An electricity grid with many small generators is inherently more stable than a grid serviced by only a few large plants.' It will of course be the perfect way to exploit renewable energy. So-called intelligent grids which can receive as well as distribute electricity at every node are already emerging. Another Yeager suggestion is that we create DC microgrids which, he says, will, 'eliminate much of the imperfections in the sine wave that creates the upsets for microprocessors – those millisecond or nanosecond disturbances' (*Electrical Review*, 10 October 2000, p. 27). Most significant of all is his prediction that in the future most of our electricity will come from millions of micro-turbines, solar panels and hydrogen powered fuel cells. He is one of many who believe that the fuel cell is the power source of the future.

As indicated earlier a fuel cell is a reactor which combines hydrogen and oxygen to produce electricity, heat and water. In effect it is a continuously regenerating battery in which the chemical equivalent of combustion takes place to release energy.

The route to electricity from sewage is normally via the digestion process which produces biogas which, in turn, powers conventional generators. Now there is on the horizon a system of producing electricity directly from a microbial fuel cell (MFC). Researchers at Pennsylvania State University have a developed a device which serves dual roles of generating electricity and, at the same time, performing the function of a sewage treatment plant. The bacteria in normal sewage treatment use enzymes to oxidise organic material and in the process release electrons. The MFC is a cylinder with a central cathode rod surrounded by a proton exchange membrane (PEM). A cluster of graphite anode rods surrounds the cathode. Bacteria become attached to the anodes causing the organic waste to be broken down into electrons and protons. A charge separation occurs with protons allowed to pass through the PEM to the cathode but not the electrons. These are diverted to power an external circuit. The circuit is completed to allow the protons and electrons to recombine at the cathode to produce pure water (Figure 21.1).

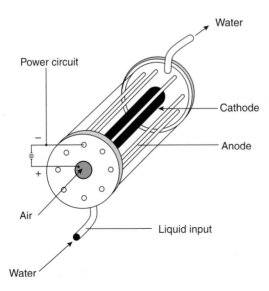

Figure 21.1
Microbial fuel cell (derived from *New Scientist*)

This is the first MFC designed specifically to process human waste. As the first prototype, there is considerable further research and development to be undertaken and it may take another 20 years for it to achieve the scale of output which would make it commercially viable (*New Scientist*, 13 March 2004, p. 21).

The holy grail of energy is the fuel cell that creates power with absolutely no polluting emissions. That will happen when the electrolytic process to split water into oxygen and hydrogen is driven by zero carbon renewable energy systems. But, if you are already producing carbon-free electricity why incur an efficiency drop by creating hydrogen? The obvious answer is that it is the way of ensuring continuity of supply. Most renewable systems are intermittent and hydrogen supplies the so-called flywheel effect smoothing out the peaks and troughs. It is also transportable so has universal application.

Producing hydrogen by the electrolyser method is fairly energy intensive and not carbon free unless it involves carbon neutral generation systems. A less carbon intensive alternative being developed is the hydrogen generator fuel cell (HGFC). Its fuel is a mixture of ethanol and water. Ethanol (alcohol) is produced by the breakdown and fermentation of crop waste or fuel crops. The ethanol and water are mixed with air and then heated to 140°C causing the mix to vaporise. The gas then passes over a catalyst (rhodium and cerium oxide) which increases the temperature to 700°C and breaks down the ethanol into hydrogen, carbon monoxide and carbon dioxide. Some of this heat is used to heat up the incoming mixture. The gases pass to a cooling chamber reducing the temperature to 400°C. They then pass across a second catalyst (platinum and cerium oxide) which causes the carbon monoxide to react with the hot water producing carbon dioxide and hydrogen in a 50–50 split. The carbon dioxide (CO_2) balances that absorbed by the biological waste during growth.

This system could be scaled up to supplying grid-scale fuel cells by using a combination of agricultural waste and dedicated rapid rotation energy crops. The initial heating process could be assisted by evacuated tube solar thermal collectors (Figure 21.2).

Next generation solar cells

From the point of view of buildings, the most obvious renewable electricity source is the solar cell. High unit cost is the barrier which is preventing production achieving economies of scale. But here again things could be about to change. The solar cells of the future are likely to use thin film technology, for example titanium-oxide coated nanocrystals with ruthenium dye which mimic photosynthesis and which are now being developed in Switzerland. They absorb light strongly in the red and green parts of the visible spectrum. They should prove to be a fraction of the cost of silicon-based cells.

The next step in the progression is to create cells which absorb light in the infra-red part of the spectrum. These would be coated with

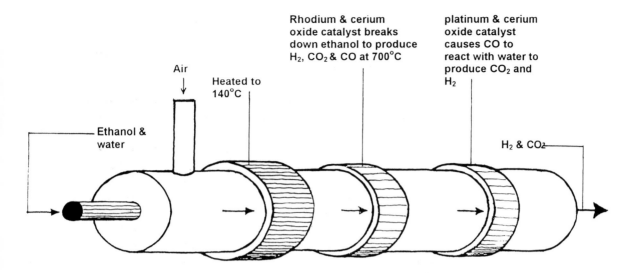

Rhodium & cerium oxide catalyst breaks down ethanol to produce H_2, CO_2 & CO at 700°C

platinum & cerium oxide catalyst causes CO to react with water to produce CO_2 and H_2

Air

Heated to 140°C

Ethanol & water

H_2 & CO_2

Figure 21.2

Compact fuel cell hydrogen generator (courtesy of *New Scientist*)

a dye that is transparent yet still absorbs enough in the invisible part of the spectrum to provide electricity. Michael Gratzel of the University of Lausanne estimates that a 10 per cent conversion rate should be possible (*New Scientist*, 23 January 1999, p. 40). So, being transparent, they will have an application for windows as well as roofs.

Creating the solar cell which will use an organic solid to replace the liquid electrolyte of conventional cells is Gratzel's latest objective. Others are looking at capturing energy using biological rather than electrochemical cells. This is literally mimicking natural photosynthesis; in current terms, 'biomimicry'.

A chance discovery in a laboratory could be the key to the ultimate breakthrough in solar cell technology. It resulted from etching silicon with a powerful laser hundreds of billions of times brighter than the sun. The result was a jet black structure of microscopic spikes which absorbs 97 per cent of visible light. What really surprised the researchers was that it absorbs 97 per cent of infra-red part of the spectrum and even extends into the microwave end of the spectrum. Normal grey silicon is transparent to infra-red light. Not only does this create a whole new field of opportunity for communications it could also herald the birth of much more efficient solar cells. A normal silicon cell will absorb only about half the light that falls on it. At 97 per cent absorption rate the black silicon photovoltaic cell could represent a quantum leap in efficiency and therefore cost effectiveness (*New Scientist*, 13 January 2001, pp. 34–37).

In 2004 it was reported that a team in the Los Alamos National Laboratory in New Mexico had found a method of considerably increasing the efficiency of crystalline solar cells. Normally a single photon knocks one electron out of the crystal structure creating a current. However, when a high energy photon hits a nanocrystal semiconductor the extra energy liberates two or even three electrons. A solar cell which employs this technology could convert 60 per cent of solar energy into electricity. The theoretical limit of conventional solar cells is 44 per cent (*Physical Review Letters*, vol. 92, pp. 186, 601 and reported in *New Scientist*, 15 May 2004, p. 16).

Artificial photosynthesis

The dream of researchers in energy is to replicate the process of photosynthesis to produce hydrogen. Photosynthesis is 'the most successful solar converting mechanism on Earth' (*New Scientist*, 1 May 2004). In this process sunlight splits water into its constituents of oxygen, hydrogen ions and electrons.

Up to now the way plants perform this miracle has been a mystery. However, a team at Imperial College, London, may have made the crucial breakthrough, having identified a plant's photosynthetic machinery where water splitting occurs. This is called the 'catalytic core' and it provides the platform for research into artificial photosynthesis called 'artificial chloroplasts'.

The difference between natural and artificial photosynthesis is that the latter is designed only to produce hydrogen. Within the next decade it may be that scientists will have replicated nature's most ingenious process, opening up the prospect of producing hydrogen on an industrial scale, paving the way for unlimited quantities of sustainable energy (see *New Scientist*, 'Flower Power', 1 May 2004, pp. 28–31).

Solar cell technology will achieve its ultimate breakthrough when it is coupled to an effective electricity storage system.

A team led by Professor A. Paul Alivisatos of the University of California, Berkeley has made cheap plastic solar cells flexible enough to paint onto any surface. The task now is to raise the efficiency to ~10 per cent. This is yet another application of nanotechnology. (www.Azonano.com).

Energy storage

At Baltimore University there is a project to produce an all-plastic battery. Already operational cells have been produced that have polymers as both anode and cathode with a special solid plastic gel as the electrolyte. The prime target is cars, but where cars go buildings cannot be far behind (*Autocar*, 28 May 1997).

The quantum leap in storage technology should emerge by around 2020 with the development of high temperature superconductors. According to the director of the Interdisciplinary Research Centre at Cambridge University, there is the prospect of storing massive amounts of electricity in a ring of superconducting cables. Electricity will run around the cables with no power loss until it is needed either for the grid or a stand-alone use. These superconducting reservoirs will be ideal for storing power from intermittent renewable sources and will change the whole economic status of, for example, tidal energy (*New Scientist*, 26 April 1997, p. 19). At present the highest temperature at which superconductivity has been achieved is minus 70°C which represents a considerable advance towards the goal of room temperature superconductivity.

These are all systems which store chemical or kinetic energy to be converted into electricity.

Hydrogen storage

The most promising safe storage technology so far has recently emerged from Japan and Hong Kong. It is nanofibre carbon. This consists of cylinders 0.4 nanometres (0.4 billionths of a metre) in diameter which is just right size to accommodate a hydrogen atom. A nanofibre pack has the capacity to store up to 70 per cent of hydrogen by weight compared to 2–4 per cent in a metal hydride. It is claimed that a cartridge in a hydrogen car could fuel it for 5000 kilometres. For buildings the storage potential is enormous.

Flywheel technology

The problem with flywheels is that the G-forces can cause a catastrophic explosion. Space technology is the driving force behind the development of superfast flywheels that can store a considerable quantity of kinetic energy to be converted into electricity. The future seems to point to materials like composites of carbon fibre and epoxy resin. However, early in the 1990s research in Japan was developing a 3 m flywheel made from stainless steel levitating between powerful magnetic fields generated by superconducting ceramics. The flywheel is set in motion by electromagnetic conduction. Energy can be drawn off by permanent magnets in the disc inducing electric current in a coil. There is no friction only air resistance and if the system operates in a near vacuum then it would be capable of storing 10 000 watt hours of energy. Over a 24 hour period the loss of energy would be negligible. The outcome of this research remains to be seen. Others are concentrating on small flywheels floating on magnetic bearings and capable of reaching 600 000 rpm with an energy density of 250 Wh/kg. More conventional flywheels will prove an economic way of enabling solar energy to cover the diurnal cycle. Ultimately interseasonal storage may not be out of the question.

The inevitable conclusion is that fuel cell, solar cell and storage technologies could all be on the verge of commercial viability. Fuel cells and titanium oxide solar cells are within a few years of presenting a serious challenge to conventional energy systems. They are being spurred on by the pressing need to bring down carbon dioxide (CO_2) emissions, and by anxieties about the security of supply of fossil fuels. The end of the world of fossil fuels is at hand and beyond it is the much brighter prospect of the post-hydrocarbon society.

This has enormous implications for the design of buildings now. Large structures like sports stadia are particularly good candidates for embedded systems which provide heat and power. No more power failures during football matches. The really big incentive is cost. A large stadium has intermittent use but also huge energy costs. It also has a massive roof area which could house acres of solar cells dedicated to producing hydrogen easily sufficient to meet the surge of demand for events by day or night. There would be a backup system of natural gas to provide hydrogen in the unlikely event that solar panels failed to perform adequately. It might require a leap of faith to make the new Wembley independent of the grid but that could be the shape of things to come.

This all bolsters the case for incorporating renewable generation systems into buildings at the earliest stage of design. Within the next 5 to 10 years there should be a quantum improvement in the efficiency of solar cells coupled with a substantial reduction in unit cost. Roofs and whole elevations will be able to accommodate solar cells, particularly when cells have been produced commercially which are transparent.

Advances in lighting

Another technical step change will occur in the sphere of lighting. Already the days of the compact fluorescent light are numbered. It will be made redundant by developments in light emitting 'photonic' materials. Solid state light emitting diodes (LEDs) are based on the quantum principle that an atom's electrons emit energy when they jump from a high energy level to a lower one. By adjusting the 'band gap' between the two levels, light of different colours can be emitted. LEDs are a by-product of semi-conductor technology and produce light at much lower watts per lumen than conventional systems. They also have a size advantage. For example, an LED of less than one square centimetre would emit as much light as a 60 watt bulb using only 3 watts. Whereas an incandescent lamp achieves an efficiency of 10–20 lumens per watt, LEDs are predicted to realise 300 lumens per watt. They are almost unbreakable and have a life expectancy of 100 000 hours. It is estimated that, if existing light sources in the US were converted to LEDs, there would be no need for new power stations for 20 years, assuming the present annual rate of increase of consumption of 2.7 per cent. As lighting accounts for most electricity used in most offices, LEDs will offer significant savings in annual costs. However, a note of caution. According to *Scientific American* 'White LEDs are possible, but affordable ones powerful enough to illuminate a room remain at least a decade away' (February 2001). Nevertheless, what all this amounts to is that wholly electricity autonomous buildings should be an economic reality around a decade from now, avoiding the necessity of being connected to the grid.

The photonic revolution

The battle between traditional electronics is being fought on two fronts:

- information transmission;
- information processing, in other words, computers.

We are already into the era when information is transmitted by pulses of light rather than through a copper wire. Particles of light – photons – can carry many thousands of times more information than wires. Optical fibres work by trapping light within a solid rod of glass which is surrounded by a cladding material with different optical properties, that is, a lower refractive index, than the core. The difference in refractive index causes light to be bounced off the outer casing with little loss of intensity over a considerable distance. Because of this, rates of transmission of information will increase at an exponential rate. The limiting factor is the speed of light.

Optical fibres can carry up to 25 trillion bits per second. Quite soon the whole world will be linked to an optical fibre superhighway based on photonic materials. One consequence is that teleworking will become much more prevalent, enabling commercial enterprises to scale down their centralised operations. High capacity communication systems based on a multimedia supercorridor accommodating audio, computer and visual communication will have a major impact on work patterns. Already teleconferencing is reducing the need for costly gatherings of executives as companies spread their operations globally. This will offer much greater freedom to employees as regards their place of abode.

It is probable this will lead to a considerable reduction in the need for high concentrations of office accommodation. Towns and cities will compete on the basis of amenity and quality of life since people will have much greater freedom as to where to live. This will be further driven by developments in transport.

The second theatre of war was information processing. At present optical fibres require electronic devices to convert information into optical pulses and, at the receiving end, to decode the information. The goal of current research is to create the photonic integrated circuit, that is, one that is free of electronic mediation. This will herald the next IT revolution when, as Philip Ball puts it:

> The photonic integrated circuit which processes light on a chip ... will see computers change *qualitatively*. Not only will they be faster, but entirely new kinds of computer architecture

should become possible. In other words, we will discover new ways to make machines think.'

(Made to Measure, Princeton, 1997 p. 58)

Computers are major consumers of energy not only in use but also because of the heat they generate which often must be disposed of mechanically. The all-photonic computer will be much faster, use a fraction of the energy of an electronic computer and generate virtually no heat. This will make a significant impact on the energy demand of the standard office. It will also have implications for design of the building fabric and the services. Couple this with the introduction of LEDs and it is certainly conceivable that commercial buildings will more than meet their energy demands by means of the next generation of photovoltaic cells. The autonomous office is nigh.

Smart materials

Materials science is entering a whole new realm. As Philip Ball puts it: 'Smart materials represent the epitome of the new paradigm of materials science whereby structural materials are being superseded by functional ones'. Smart materials carry out their tasks as a result of their intrinsic properties. In many situations they will replace mechanical operations. We will see 'smart devices in which the materials themselves do the job of levers, gears and even electronic circuitry'. There is even the prospect of 'A house built of bricks that change their thermal insulating properties depending on the outside temperature so as to maximise energy efficiency' (op. cit., p. 104).

Smart materials are already on the market, like thermochromic or electrochromic glass. At present electrochromic glass is a sandwich construction with a gel which changes its light emission properties in response to an electric current. The current is required to change its state not to maintain that state. Pilkington is developing a solid state version of this glass which should make both cheaper and available in much larger sizes. This will dispense with the need for mechanical blinds and solar shades and will give individuals much greater control over their immediate environment. Such materials come into the general category of *passive* smart materials. The really exciting advances are in *active* smart materials. An active system is controlled not only be external forces but also by some internal signal. In smart systems an active response usually involves a feedback loop that enables the system to 'tune' its response and thus adapt to a changing environment rather than be passively driven by external forces. An example is a vibrating–damping smart system. Mechanical movement triggers a feedback loop into providing movement that stabilises the system. As the frequency or amplitude of the vibrations changes so the feedback loop modifies the reaction to compensate.

One useful class of smart materials are 'shape memory alloys' (SMAS) alternatively called 'solid state phase transformations'. These are materials which, after deformation, return completely to their former shape. They function by virtue of the fact that the crystal structures of SMAS change when heated. An application already being exploited are thermostats where bimetal strips are replaced by alloys. They can be incorporated into mechanisms for operating ventilation louvres or ventilation/heating diffusers.

In general smart systems can be divided into sensors and actuators. Sensors are detection devices to respond to changes in the environment and warn accordingly. Actuators make things happen; they are control devices that close or open an electrical circuit or act as a valve in a pipe.

For example, they may perform a dual role extracting heat from low grade sources like ground water or geothermal reservoirs and serve as mechanical pumps to deliver the warmed water to the heating system of a building. No moving parts; no possibility of mechanical breakdown and all at low cost; it seems 'such stuff as dreams are made of'.

In principle SMAS can be used for any application which requires heat to be converted into mechanical action.

Smart fluids

By introducing a strong electrical field, certain fluids can change to a near solid state. They are called 'electrorheological fluids' (rheology is the study of the viscosity and flow capacity of fluids). They can be made intelligent by coupling them to sensor devices which detect sudden movement. They have the potential to replace a range of mechanical devices such as vehicle clutches, springs and dampening devices to eliminate mechanical vibrations.

Another class of smart fluid is activated by being exposed to a magnetic field. Linked to sensors they would be ideal for buildings in earthquake zones. Buildings would be constructed off concrete rafts which in turn would be supported by an array of magnetorheological dampers. At the onset of vibrations these would instantly change from solid to fluid and soak up the movement of the earth. In Tokyo and Osaka several recent buildings already exploit vibration damping and variable stiffness devices to counteract seismic movement.

There is yet another dimension to the characteristics of smart materials – materials that learn, that get smarter as they get older. They have an inbuilt degree of intelligence and are capable of optimising their performance in response to feedback information.

What we will see in the near future are smart structures equipped with an array of fibre optic 'nerves' that will indicate what a structure is 'feeling' at any given moment and give instant information of any impending catastrophic failure. If the end of the last century was characterised by the rise of high technology with ever more complex electronic wizardry packed into ever smaller spaces, the future, according to materials scientists, 'may hold an increasing simplicity, as materials replace machines' (Ball, op. cit., p. 142). We will learn to be adaptive rather than assertive. This surely is what environmental responsibility is all about.

Socio-economic factors

The focus of the book began at the global scale and gradually sharpened down to the detailed design of buildings. It seems appropriate to end by again speculating more widely about socio-economic issues which will affect all who operate within the construction industry.

Despite government exhortations to convert to public transport, motorists are showing no sign of responding. At present the average distance travelled by car per day is 28 miles. By 2025 it is expected that this will rise to 60 miles. Despite the rail chaos of late 2000 and early 2001, it is still the view that superfast trains will be in service within the next decade which will create the conditions for a more dispersed, hypermobile society. This, in turn, will create a demand for new kinds of development, given added impetus by the demographic changes that have created the need for 4 million new homes, mostly in southern England. It seems inevitable that there will be a new crop of new towns but designed to a high density. It is likely and desirable that the Rogers Task Force (recommendations will be influential in the design of the next generation of new towns *Towards an Urban Renaissance*, June 1999).

The meteoric growth of 'turbo-capitalism' with its single-minded purpose of optimising market opportunities is likely to lead to a sharp decline in public funded services. This will have an impact on procurement as the public sector building realm declines. It might also have a negative effect on quality as price alone is the deciding factor. Many would agree that:

> The cold economic rationality of capitalism, in which every institution is subordinated to the calculus of profit and loss, does not answer the question posed by every human being – that there is more to life than the pursuit of economic efficiency. We are social as well as economic beings.
>
> *The Observer*, 2 January 2000

One outcome of the development of IT is that the economic and business certainties of the twentieth century are disintegrating. As electronic commerce grows, governments will find it ever harder to raise taxes. Each day trillions of dollars move around the global money market as corporations locate their transactions in low tax jurisdictions. Add to this the fact that people are increasingly obtaining goods and services via the Internet from places with the lowest taxes and it is clear that national governments will have diminishing power to raise revenue, with obvious consequences for the social services.

One scenario is that the growing gap between the poor and the affluent will continue to widen. The dividing line will become sharply defined as between those with IT and communication skills who can keep up with the pace of change and those who increasingly fall behind in this new Darwinian environment. As Ian Angell (head of the Department of Information Systems, London School of Economics) puts it:

> People with computer skills are likely to end up winners. Those without are likely to emerge as losers. The power of the nation state will weaken. Communities that invest substantially in communication technologies will thrive. Those who don't, or those whose citizens are isolated from the new ways to communicate, will suffer. Change is inevitable. The Information Age will be kindest to those who adapt.
>
> *New Scientist*, 4 March 2000, pp. 44–45

This progressive bi-polarisation will produce social tensions with decreasing social cohesion and an increase in crime. This will be a countervailing trend to the ideals within the Rogers Urban Task Force for a more mixed and integrated society. Instead, according to Professor John Adams of University College, London, we are likely to see the well-off retreating into gated and guarded communities (*The Social Implications of Hypermobility*, 1999). If this prediction is realised, security will become a major design determinant in all types of building. A rising crime rate will lead to anxieties which increase the attraction of buying the necessities of life though the Internet with obvious consequences for high street and even neighbourhood shops.

Within the current economic climate, to spend money now to limit catastrophic climate change in 50 years' time is not an efficient way to deploy capital. The reality is that we should not only now be imposing severe constraints on the use of fossil fuels, we should also be accumulating a contingency fund to deal with the future effects of global warming that are inevitable due to the momentum generated by past emissions of greenhouse gases. Many circumstances are conspiring to ensure that, if we do not revolutionise the way we produce and distribute energy, the prospect of runaway global warming becomes a virtual certainty and that's not an inviting prospect for our children and grandchildren.

On the positive side, there are huge economic opportunities to be grasped in the development and manufacture of products related to the sphere of sustainability. The UK has the expertise but will not be a key player if it continues to be fixated on short-term profits and allows capital costs to outweigh the benefits of medium-to long-term revenue gains. Other nations subsidise technologies, pump-priming them so that they quickly achieve economy of scale.

Of this there can be no doubt: the next decades will witness the accelerating pace of change. For the early part of the century it is likely that wealth will increase. Later in the century, huge uncertainties emerge, mainly associated with the social and political consequences of climate change, the growing tensions arising from competition for access to water and fertile land exacerbated by the widening gap between rich and poor. Designers within construction have it in their power to help with the solution rather than add to the problem.

Key indicators for sustainable design

- Minimising the use of fossil-based energy in terms of the energy embodied in the materials, transport and construction process and the energy used during the lifetime of the building.
- Making best use of recycled materials and renewable materials from a verifiable source.
- Avoiding all ozone depleting chemicals in terms of manufacture and system operation including HCFCs.
- Where possible using alternatives to materials containing volatile organic compounds.
- Designing to make maximum use of natural light whilst also being aware of its limitations.
- Exploiting the potential for natural ventilation in the context of an overall climate control strategy which minimises energy use and maximises comfort.
- Making best use of passive solar energy whilst employing heating/cooling systems which are fine-tuned to the needs of the occupants with air conditioning used only in exceptional circumstances.
- Ensuring that building management systems are user-friendly and not overcomplex.
- Identifying opportunities to generate on-site renewable electricity (embedded systems).
- Identifying the potential for exploiting the constant ground temperature for evening out the peaks and troughs of summer and winter temperature.
- Minimising the use of water; harvesting rainwater and grey water and purifying for use other than human consumption.
- Minimising rainwater runoff by limiting the extent of hard external landscape.
- Creating an external environmental which is both a visual amenity and also offers environmental benefits such as summer shading from deciduous trees and evaporative cooling from water features.
- Whilst taking account of these key indicators, ensuring that designs meet the highest standards of technical proficiency in combination with aesthetic excellence.

Environmental checklist for development

- Is it proposed that there will be consultation with the local community at the design stage?
- Has every attempt been made either to develop on a brownfield site or reuse an existing building?
- Will the proposed development achieve the highest standards in terms of energy efficiency and the conservation of natural resources?
- Will consideration be given to the production of on-site electricity from renewable sources?
- Has the opportunity to use recycled materials been explored?
- Is the proposed development capable of being adapted to other uses in the future?
- Will it achieve optimum standards of comfort for its inhabitants?
- Does the proposal achieve an appropriate density for its location?
- Has the potential for a mixed development on the site been realised?
- Does the proposal involve significant investment in landscaping?
- Does the proposed development make a significant contribution to the economic and social well-being of the community?
- Does the proposed development have access to a range of public transport options?
- Will the proposed development make a significant addition to the amenity of the wider area and does it pose any threat to the amenity of its immediate neighbours?
- Will the development be in harmony with the wider built environment?
- Is it proposed that the design process will, from the start, be a collaborative enterprise involving all the design professions?
- Have steps been taken to ensure that the development will not adversely affect the micro-climate, for example by downdraughts or funnelling of wind?
- Will the proposed development contain areas of public access or create new pedestrian routes?

These recommendations and checklists are intended to give a flavour of the challenges which face all who are associated with the design and production of buildings over the next decades. They should be viewed in a positive light since they offer an unprecedented range of development and design opportunities.

An outline sustainability syllabus for designers

The change to environmentally advanced design needs to be driven by a conviction that it is necessary.

Natural resources and pollution

Global natural assets, fixed and finite, e.g. minerals and fossil hydrocarbons. Predicted problems associated with resource depletion coupled with estimated population growth (11 billion by 2050).

'Soft' assets: soil, oceans, forests, troposphere.

Processes: photosynthesis, hydrological cycle and carbon cycle, soil formation and waste assimilation.

Problems associated with pollution, e.g. acid rain and low level ozone. Soil erosion and oxidation. Soil exhaustion through intensive use of agrochemicals. Salination as a consequence of hydroelectric schemes and runoff. Continued deforestation in tropical and temperate rain forests.

Contaminated land and remediation strategies.

Nuclear waste disposal and decommissioning of nuclear power stations.

Climate change

The mechanism of the greenhouse. The carbon cycle and current imbalance. Evidence of past fluctuations and link between global temperature and CO_2 in the atmosphere.

The evidence

Rise in sea level over the past 150 years; rise in surface global temperature and temperature records in the last decade; increasing intensity and frequency of storms and floods; severe heat episodes; migration to temperate zones of subtropical diseases; melting of polar ice and glaciers.

Present position compared with pre-industrial in terms of temperature and level of atmospheric CO_2.

Scientific evidence for attributing most of the change to human activity (UN IPCC report 2001).

Predictions

IPCC predictions regarding level of atmospheric CO_2 by 2050 assuming 'business as usual' (at least double pre-industrial level) and consequent temperature rise.

Increase in temperature = greater energy in the system = greater turbulence. Steeper pressure gradients and deeper troughs = more intense and more frequent storms.

Potential changes in ocean currents, e.g. threat to the Gulf Stream from melting Greenland ice.

Rising sea levels through expansion and melt ice threatening island states, maritime cities and coastal agricultural belts. Migration of plants, crops, animals and diseases. Problems arising from the rate of climate change exceeding adaptation capacity of forests.

The outlook for conventional energy. International comparisons of per capita annual CO_2 emissions (UN statistics). Future prospects for availability of fossil fuels based on latest estimates of reserves. Nuclear outlook including scenarios in Royal Commission on Pollution Energy Report.

Projections of energy consumption: US, Europe, China, India, SE Asia. Concept of carbon trading and international agreements: Rio, Kyoto, The Hague.

The case for a shift from neo-classical economic theory which regards the Earth's assets as free to eco-economics which factors in the environmental and social costs of human actions, e.g. including the external costs in fixing fossil fuel prices. The 'externalities' include the contribution to global warming, effects on health, damage to crops and wildlife of low level pollution.

Ozone depletion

Caused by CFCs and HCFCs creating aerosols in the upper atmosphere which erode the ozone shield which protects against ultra-violet radiation. This causes skin cancer and damages the immune system plus damage to crops.

Renewable technologies

Marine systems

Hydroelectric generation; small-scale hydro; 'run-of-river' systems; tidal energy – barrage systems and the tidal fence, underwater turbines, impoundment systems; wave power, coastal and offshore oscillating water column; the 'Tapchan' system.

Other renewable technologies

The solar chimney; thermal concentrator; wind power; photovoltaics; power from biomass and waste; direct combustion from rapid rotation crops; biogas; liquid fuels, rapeseed diesel; geothermal energy; hydrogen; nuclear.

Construction systems: masonry, frame, innovative techniques.

Low energy housing

Passive solar design; Trombe walls.

Active solar thermal systems: flat plat solar collector; double sided collector.

Windows and glazing

Types of energy efficient glazing with U-values.

Net U-values including solar gain.

Heat reflecting and heat absorbing glazing.

Photochromic, thermochromic and electrochromic glass.

Developments in glass technology, e.g. solid state electrochromic glass.

Insulation

Types of insulation material and thermal performance: natural organic, inorganic, synthetic organic.

Thermal conductivity of various insulation materials.

Construction techniques

High and superinsulation standards and specimen built examples.

Transparent insulation materials, aerogels.

Technical risks of insulation, thermal bridges.

Domestic energy

Photovoltaics (PVs) and the principle of PV generation.

Types of PV cell and energy output.

Remote and integrated systems.

Thermal mass and the 'flywheel' effect.

Heating.

Embodied energy in materials.

Advanced and ultra-low energy housing – examples

Hockerton self-sufficient housing project, Nottinghamshire.

Beddington zero-energy development (BedZED).

'House of the Future' Museum of Welsh Life.

Timber construction

The environmental benefits of timber in construction.

Means of ensuring that timber originates from a sustainable source. Examples: 'House of the Future', Museum of Welsh Life.

New centre at Weald and Downland Open Air Museum; Singleton near Chichester.

Multi-storey experimental timber house by the Building Research Establishment, Cardington.

Sibelius Concert Hall, Lahti, Finland.

Wintergardens, Sheffield.

Summary

Checklist for the energy efficient design of dwellings.

Housing – the existing stock

Assessment methods for energy efficiency: SAP, NHER, BEPI and CO_2 measure.

Buildings in use account for 47 per cent of total UK CO_2 emissions with an additional 5 per cent for those under construction.

When transport attributable to buildings is added, this rises to <75 per cent. Of this total, 29 per cent comes from housing. 98.5 per cent of the total comes from older building stock.

State of the housing stock from English House Condition Survey 2001. Breakdown of SAP ratings across the stock.

Standards for domestic warmth defined as 'adequate' and 'minimum'. Incidence of fuel poverty as defined by DETR and health problems directly attributable to poor housing. Energy use across appliances.

Retrofit examples, e.g. Penwith, Cornwall, and Peabody Trust.

Offices and institutional buildings

Six performance indicators from Movement for Innovation (M4I).

Environmental considerations in the design of offices; passive solar design.

Construction technologies: climate facades, floors and ceilings.

Ventilation

- Natural ventilation
- Unassisted natural ventilation
- Gravity ventilation and 'stack effect'
- Mechanically assisted ventilation
- Displacement ventilation
- Cooling strategies' evaporative cooling
- The ecological tower, examples: Commerzbank and Swiss Re
- Ventilation and air movement, summary of recommendations
- Air conditioning as distinct from mechanically assisted ventilation, heating and cooling.

Energy options

- Carbon intensity of different fuels
- Energy distribution in a combined heat and power (CHP) system
- The fuel cell; basic operation of the fuel cell
- Storage techniques – electricity
- Storage techniques – warmth and cooling
- PV applications; building management systems (BMS)
- Energy storage: underground thermal storage, phase change materials, dense storage medium
- Electricity storage to overcome intermittence of supply by renewables:
  - Latest battery technology, pump storage
  - Creation of hydrogen by reformation of methane etc. and by dedicated PV/electrolyser

        – Hydrogen storage by pressurised tanks, metal hydrides
        – Regenerative fuel cell storage and 'Regenesys' technology
- Building management systems and Building Energy Management Systems.

Tools for environmental design
Lighting – designing for daylight

Factors influencing levels of daylight.

Design considerations – danger of excessive contrast, heat gain, glare.

The atrium; light shelves; prismatic glazing; light pipes; holographic glazing; solar shading.

Lighting controls and the human factor

Post-occupancy analysis and differences between expectation and reality; photoelectric control and the human behaviour; dimming control and occupancy sensing; switches; system management, problems relating to occupants and managers; air conditioned offices.

Conditions for successful design, e.g. timed controls, occupancy linked control, daylight linked control, localised switching.

Environmental design and common problems

The 'Probe' studies and the lessons from post-occupancy analysis. High profile–low profile; the 'high-tech' demand; operational difficulties; building related illness/sick building syndrome; inherent inefficiencies; common architectural problems; common engineering problems; common failures leading to energy waste; the human factor.

Summary of recommendations
Life-cycle assessment and recycling

BRE Ecopoints system for construction materials and components. Whole life costing.

Precautions regarding recycled materials, e.g. risks regarding timber and quality control.

Recycling strategy checklist.

Further reference to embodied energy.

Recycling case study, e.g. low energy Conference Centre, Earth Centre, Doncaster (Bill Dunster).

Integrated district environmental design

Beyond the individual building; emergent technologies for combined heat and power systems for groups of houses or commercial/institutional buildings driven by micro-turbines.

Examples: Plan-les-Ouates solar city near Geneva; Linz Solar City, Austria. Case study: Ecological City of Tomorrow, Malmo, Sweden.

Emergent technologies and future prospects

Recap of the likely consequences of global warming as they affect buildings; energy for the future; shift from mega power plants to many smaller dispersed generators using a range of renewable technologies; impact of economic PVs for embedded installation; next generation solar cells; electricity storage, polymer batteries, high temperature superconductivity; energy storage: hydrogen storage and the potential of nanofibre carbon; flywheel technology; advances in lighting – LEDs; the photonic revolution; smart materials; smart fluids; socio-economic factors; implications of expansion of IT and the impact of optical fibre technology.

Index

INDEX